THE EVIDENCE FOR GOD

If God exists, where can we find adequate evidence for God's existence? In this book, Paul K. Moser offers a new perspective on the evidence for God that centers on a morally robust version of theism that is cognitively resilient. The resulting evidence for God is not speculative, abstract, or casual. Rather, it is morally and existentially challenging to humans, as they themselves responsively and willingly become evidence of God's reality in receiving and reflecting God's moral character for others. Moser calls this "personifying evidence of God," because it requires the evidence to be personified in an intentional agent – such as a human – and thereby to be inherent evidence of an intentional agent. Contrasting this approach with skepticism, scientific naturalism, fideism, and natural theology, Moser also grapples with the potential problems of divine hiddenness, religious diversity, and vast evil.

Paul K. Moser is professor and chair of the philosophy department at Loyola University Chicago. Editor of *Jesus and Philosophy* and the journal *American Philosophical Quarterly*, he is author of *The Elusive God: Reorienting Religious Epistemology*, *Philosophy After Objectivity*, and *Knowledge and Evidence*, as well as co-editor of *Divine Hiddenness* and *The Rationality of Theism*.

The Evidence for God

Religious Knowledge Reexamined

PAUL K. MOSER
Loyola University Chicago

CAMBRIDGE
UNIVERSITY PRESS

CAMBRIDGE UNIVERSITY PRESS
Cambridge, New York, Melbourne, Madrid, Cape Town, Singapore,
São Paulo, Delhi, Dubai, Tokyo

Cambridge University Press
32 Avenue of the Americas, New York, NY 10013-2473, USA

www.cambridge.org
Information on this title: www.cambridge.org/9780521736282

First published 2010

Printed in the United States of America

A catalog record for this publication is available from the British Library.

Library of Congress Cataloging in Publication data
Moser, Paul K., 1957–
The evidence for God : religious knowledge reexamined / Paul K. Moser.
p.   cm.
Includes bibliographical references and index.
ISBN 978-0-521-51656-3 (hardback)
1. God – Proof.   2. God (Christianity)   3. Knowledge, Theory of (Religion)   I. Title.
BT103.M67   2009
211′.3–dc22   2009037197

ISBN   978-0-521-51656-3 Hardback
ISBN   978-0-521-73628-2 Paperback

For Anna and Laura

Among the mature we do speak wisdom, but not the wisdom of this age.

1 Corinthians 2:6

Contents

Preface

The question of whether God exists is enduringly with us, whether we like it or not; so, we might as well deal with it straight up. This book approaches the question of whether God exists from a new perspective, in which humans themselves are put under moral question, before God's authority, in raising the question of whether God exists. The result is a new perspective on the evidence for God, including a morally robust version of theism that is cognitively resilient, even against skepticism.

The resulting evidence for God is not speculative, abstract, or casual but is, instead, morally and existentially challenging to humans. This evidence becomes salient to inquirers as they themselves responsively and willingly become evidence of God's reality in receiving and reflecting God's moral character for others. The book calls this *personifying evidence of God*, because it requires the evidence to be personified in an intentional agent, such as a purposive human, and thereby to be evidence inherently of an intentional agent. The book contrasts its approach with skepticism, scientific naturalism, fideism, and natural theology, and it faces directly the potential problems for theism raised by divine hiddenness, religious diversity, and vast evil. In the end, a morally challenging version of theism emerges as cognitively tenable.

The book draws from revised parts of some of my recent essays in the philosophy of religion: "Farewell to

Philosophical Naturalism" (with David Yandell), in William Lane Craig and J. P. Moreland, eds., *Naturalism: A Critical Analysis* (London: Routledge, 2000); "Religious Exclusivism," in Chad Meister, ed., *The Oxford Handbook of Religious Diversity* (New York: Oxford University Press, 2010); "Sin and Salvation," in Charles Taliaferro and Chad Meister, eds., *The Cambridge Companion to Christian Philosophical Theology* (Cambridge: Cambridge University Press, 2010); and "Faith in God," in Michael Austin and Doug Geivett, eds., *Christian Virtue* (Grand Rapids, MI: Eerdmans, 2010).

Many people have been helpful with comments, suggestions, questions, and discussions, including Linda Moser, Tom Carson, Arnold vander Nat, David Yandell, Chad Meister, Gregory Wolcott (who gave special help with the index), Mark McCreary, Bryan Kibbe, Meghan Sullivan, Keith Yandell, Paul Knitter, Paul Copan, William Abraham, Jason Baehr, John Bishop, Jay Wood, Tedla Gebreyesus, Paul Mueller, Tom Wren, J.D. Trout, Andrew Cutrofello, Alvin Plantinga, Randy Newman, and the students in my philosophy graduate seminars at Loyola University Chicago. I thank them for their kind and significant help. I also thank the audiences at various presentations of some of the book's material, including at Loyola University Chicago, Princeton Seminary, Baylor University, Loyola Marymount University, Wheaton College, Bethel College (Indiana), and some recent meetings of the Evangelical Philosophical Society in Chicago and Providence. In addition, I thank Samuel Attoh, the Associate Provost for Research at Loyola University Chicago, for important assistance. Finally, Andy Beck, Beatrice Rehl, and James Dunn have been very helpful at Cambridge University Press, and Ken Karpinski at Aptara and Linda H. Smith have been very helpful in the production process.

Paul K. Moser
Chicago, Illinois

Introduction

"Many questions are answered wrongly, not because the evidence is contradictory or inadequate, but because the mind through its fundamental dispositions and presuppositions is out of focus with the only kind of evidence which is really available."

– H.H. Farmer 1927, p. 5.

The question of whether God exists is at least as old as the hills, and the human race, too, but old age in this case has not yielded undisputed wisdom or even broad clarity. In fact, although obviously of first importance, the question of whether God exists has suffered from a certain widespread human bias regarding the manner in which we should approach it. The bias obscures how human inquirers themselves are arguably put under question, before God's authority, in raising the question of whether God exists. This book uncovers this bias, challenges it, and offers an alternative, more defensible approach to the question of whether God exists. The result is a new perspective on the evidence for God.

Upon asking aright the question of whether God exists, the book contends, we find a morally robust version of theism that is cognitively resilient. We also then find that the evidence for God is not speculative, abstract, or casual, after all, but is, instead, morally and existentially challenging to us humans. This evidence thus extends beyond the

1

argumentative domain of philosophers and theologians, and engages people from all walks of life at the levels of who they are and who they should be. The evidence in question, we shall see, has a distinctive character: *this evidence becomes salient to inquirers as they, themselves, responsively and willingly become evidence of God's reality,* in willingly receiving and reflecting God's powerful moral character – specifically divine, unselfish love for others, even one's enemies. We shall call this *personifying evidence of God,* because it requires the evidence to be personified in an intentional agent, such as a purposive human, and thereby to be evidence inherently of an intentional agent. Such evidence, in keeping with its divine source, is inherently for the sake of others and, ideally, it is realized *intentionally* by humans for others. Philosophers, among many others, have neglected to look in this quarter for evidence of God, but this book offers the needed correction and thereby gives new foundations to belief in God.

Personifying human evidence of God, although widely neglected, would fit well with the reality of a God who aims not simply to inform humans but primarily to draw them noncoercively into taking on, or personifying, God's perfect moral character, in fellowship with God. Part of this divine aim would be to have humans become bearers of God's moral character in a way that brings God's distinctive, if elusive, presence near to others. This book presents the case for such morally challenging personifying evidence of God. In doing so, it attends to the role of human resistance to such evidence in obscuring the reality of not only this evidence but also God himself.

1. A WILDERNESS PARABLE

A reality-based parable will give us needed focus, and save us from undue abstractness, in our inquiry about God's existence. During summertime hiking, we have become lost in the expansive wilderness area of Hells Canyon between western Idaho and northeastern Oregon. North America's deepest river gorge, Hells Canyon drops about 8,000 feet below Idaho's Seven Devils Mountains, and is carved by the wild Snake River. The Canyon is ten miles wide, and is happily free of cars, trucks, and even roads – and therefore McDonald's drive-throughs. It is notorious for being inaccessible by any easy means. Unfortunately, we have ended up deep in this river gorge, without a helpful exit map or any other worthwhile plan of departure.

We are now confronted with many difficulties, including the following: seemingly endless miles of seemingly directionless foot trails, dangerous western rattlesnakes, roaming mountain lions (a.k.a. cougars), howling coyotes, unpredictable temperatures, meager supplies, dying cell phone batteries, increasing hunger, and no satellite navigation system. However, we happen upon a dilapidated, abandoned shack hailing from the short-lived gold miners of the 1860s. The shack contains, not a double-quad-core computer with broadband internet access, but instead some rusty pots and pans and a barely functional amateur (ham) radio left behind recently by distracted employees of the US Forest Service. The radio's battery still works but probably not for long. As a result, our predicament in Hells Canyon seems bleak indeed, but perhaps is not without some hope. How, then, might we survive?

Obviously, we need a way out of Hells Canyon, sooner rather than later. In particular, we need instructions and even an *instructor* to help us to get out, given that we lack the resources, including a trustworthy plan, to make our way out on our own. We need a personal agent who is an intentional instructor, beyond mere instructions, because we need someone who (a) will intentionally and reliably identify our particular location now relative to a path that leads to our rescue, and (b) will supply further resources we will need along the path to our safety, including corrections, reminders, and perhaps even encouraging words to sustain us. As a result, we should not assume that our problem is

simply cognitive; in our journey to safety, we shall need
some ongoing aid beyond known information.

A particularly noteworthy need concerns our deepest
motives and related attitudes. If we are to be guided trustworthily but noncoercively along the path to safety, we will
need to be ready and willing to be so guided. As a result,
we may need some motivational and attitudinal transformation, and even moral transformation. We shall be particularly aware of this kind of need in subsequent discussion,
once we turn directly to knowledge of God's reality. Even
so, we need at least someone who can identify a trustworthy
path from where we are now to eventual safety, in contrast
with all of the dead ends facing us in the vast wilderness. A
mere map or set of instructions will fail us, if only because
we do not know our actual location on the map or in the
instructions, and, in any case, we shall need ongoing intentional and corrective guidance along the path to safety. In
short, the path we need calls for a path *finder* and a path *sustainer* for us. The first step for us is sincerely to acknowledge
our need in our predicament.

Can we knowingly make contact with an intentional rescuer who will locate us and then help us to reach safety?
If so, as we shall see, we would do well to ask what purposes *the rescuer has* in helping us to reach safety. Perhaps
the rescuer's purposes are more profound and morally better than ours. The ham radio, at any rate, seems to be our
only medium of hope, although it definitely has seen better
days. Still, might it put us in touch with someone who will
intentionally help us out of our lost state? If we fail in this
connection, we will perish, given our breathtakingly austere wilderness surroundings. Our predicament in the river
gorge is life or death, rescue or destruction. Our either–or
situation is urgent and obvious; as a result, we should own
it, and deal with it.

Is there life beyond Hells Canyon? Particularly, is there
life *accessible by us* beyond Hells Canyon? The latter question
now amounts to this: is there an intentional rescuer available

to us beyond Hells Canyon? Or, in other words, are we all up a river gorge without a rescuer? Being nothing if not orderly thinkers, we call an emergency strategy meeting to sort out our main options for handling the dire predicament before us.

Option 1: Despairing

We can just give up now in abject despair, yielding to hopelessness and its resulting destruction of us all. Our being lost will then become final, and our hope will disappear altogether as we ourselves disappear. On this option, we will yield to Hells Canyon as our wilderness grave, and give up on finding a way out to safety. Our conviction will be just this: "we can't get there from here." We then will not bother even to pursue the question of whether there is an intentional rescuer available to us beyond Hells Canyon. On this option, we are practical *atheists* about a rescuer, and we succumb to the downward pull of fatal despair. Still, we will have to face the question of whether, given our available evidence, our despairing is premature and at least initially ill-advised. We cannot responsibly ignore this life-or-death question.

Option 2: Passively Waiting

We can just sit back in the dilapidated miners' shack and wait, largely in doubt, for any possible (if supposedly improbable) rescuer to find us. Our casual waiting must make do without a television and a computer, of course, but we might play tic-tac-toe or some other trivial pencil-and-paper game while we remain practically skeptical about the intervention of a rescuer. On this option, we are practical *agnostics* about a rescuer, and we might even take some pride in our disciplined refraining from actively seeking a rescuer. Our pride might be accompanied by a self-indulgent demand that we be spoon-fed by any rescuer, without our taking an active and cooperative cognitive or practical role in our rescue. In any case, we will have to face the question of whether our available evidence, in conjunction with our best interest, supports our passively waiting. We might find that passively waiting would be irresponsible of us.

Option 3: Leaping

We can throw caution to the wilderness wind, and leap onto a foot path, even in the absence of evidence in favor of success (that is, eventual safety) in taking that path. We might conveniently pick a familiar path, one that is well-trodden, widely approved of, and historically dignified in the eyes of our peer group or doxastic community. Indeed, our taking this path could amount to an embraced "form of life" or a virtual social institution among our lost peers, including those who have jumped onto it before us. Of course, we would not presume to recommend this path as supported by conclusive evidence or even significant evidence of its success, but we do not therefore shrink back. Instead, we gladly leap onto this path, in keeping with the familiar practices of our wilderness forebears and contemporaries. On this option, we are practical *fideists* about a rescuer, because we proceed as if conclusive evidence is not available or even needed in support of either a rescuer or our adopted plan for being found by a rescuer. Eventually, we will have to face the natural question of whether our leaping amounts to anything more than wishful thinking on our part. A definite problem, in any case, is that many of the available paths lead to dead ends (where *we*, too, are dead) rather than to safety. As a result, we should not take this option blithely.

Option 4: Discerning Evidence

We can tighten our belts, given our impending food shortage, and take a hard look at our available evidence for a way out of our dangerous wilderness predicament. This option seeks an alternative to (1) despairing, (2) passively waiting, and (3) leaping, at least as an initial strategy. It takes two significantly different forms.

A. PURPOSE-NEUTRAL DISCERNING OF EVIDENCE. What appears to be an old directional map leading from somewhere to somewhere else emerges from a pile of clutter near the ham radio. The origin and destination points on the map are far from obvious, but they seem not to involve a McDonald's restaurant or even a Starbuck's. *Purpose-neutral* discerning or characterizing of the apparent map would be free of identifying any purposes, or intentions, involving the map. It would identify, however, various *non*purposive features of the map, including geometric properties (such as shapes), constituent parts (such as opposing corners), and sensory features (such as textures). The natural sciences, unlike the social sciences and the humanities, typically settle for purpose-neutral discerning of available evidence. Such discerning can be very helpful as far as it goes, but it seems not to be exhaustive in all cases. It seems not always to offer full coverage of the actual evidence we have, particularly in connection with functional social artifacts, such as radios, telephones, computers, and MP3 players. In any case, we will need to ask how this very restrictive approach comports with our actual available evidence of the world around us and within us. We would suffer harm, of course, by omitting crucial evidence of a rescuer.

B. TELIC DISCERNING OF EVIDENCE. We sometimes can discern available evidence in terms of relevant *purposes* indicated in the evidence. For instance, regarding our apparent directional map, we can try to discern the cartographer's purpose in sketching the map as it actually is rather than as it would be as a result of a different purpose. Such discerning would be "telic" (from the Greek word, *telos*, for "purpose") in virtue of seeking a goal or (in Aristotelian language) a "final cause" in the relevant evidence. Accordingly, we might explore the map in terms of a directional purpose: that is, the cartographer's aim to direct readers from Point A (say, the miners' shack in Hells Canyon) to Point B (say, Baker City, OR, on the Old Oregon Trail). We therefore can imagine that the main purpose of the cartographer and her map is to lead lost people to safety.

It may be difficult for us sometimes to confirm the reality of a purpose indicated by evidence, but in telic discerning we would be attentive to this prospect, and we would be willing to explore any evidence for the purpose in question. In doing so, we would move beyond the immediate concerns of the natural sciences, but this would not necessarily be a cognitive deficiency at all. In fact, our available evidence could call for our attending to purposive considerations for the sake of *accurate* comprehensive treatment of our evidence. The propriety of telic discerning therefore cannot be excluded as a matter of logical or cognitive principle. It remains as a logically and cognitively live option, and this will surprise no one who is not in the grips of a supposed monopoly by the natural sciences.

Telic discerning of evidence takes two main forms: *direct* and *indirect*. Direct telic discerning identifies certain evidence as inherently and directly purposive and thus immediately indicative of a personal agent. In contrast, indirect telic discerning identifies certain evidence as extrinsically and indirectly purposive and thus inferentially indicative of a personal agent. Much of so-called "natural theology" offers (whether accurately or inaccurately) indirect telic discerning of certain evidence, characteristically by inference to the divine reality of (a) a purposive designer of nature, (b) an intentional first cause of observed contingent events, (c) a personal ground of moral values, or (d) a purposive basis of reflective consciousness. Questions of accuracy aside, such natural theology seeks rationally to identify divine reality indirectly, inferentially, and discursively, and thus uses distinctive premises to infer a conclusion in a natural–theological argument of one form or another. It does not offer, however, evidence as inherently purposive in the way that direct telic discerning does.

The direct form of telic discerning finds purposive reality indicated directly in some evidence. For instance, it identifies intentional communication in some evidence without an intermediary, particularly such communication as an invitation, a call, a command, or a challenge. If human conscience could be a means of such communication, at least under some circumstances, then direct telic discerning could look in conscience for noninferential evidence of intentional communication, even from God. We shall consider this prospect in Chapter 4, in connection with a position called *volitional theism*. It promises to underwrite some important theological knowledge without the unduly abstract and suspect baggage that burdens much natural theology.

We can use the presence of the ham radio in the miners' shack to illustrate the distinction between purpose-neutral discerning and telic discerning. Hoping against hope that a needed rescuer is accessible, we turn on the radio and scan some easily located regional frequencies. Surprisingly, we vaguely detect an apparent voice that evidently is calling to us while breaking up in crackling static. Purpose-neutral discerning would attend to various physical features of this intriguing radio transmission: its volume, its temporal length, its auditory sharpness, and so on. Such features, of course, are important and even physically measurable, but they do not include what a person *intends to communicate* in a radio transmission. They are, after all, purpose-neutral, and therefore do not include or entail purposes.

Telic discerning, in contrast with purpose-neutral discerning, would consider any evidence of an *intended* communication via the ham radio. As a result, it would attend to the radio in the light of what (primarily) it was intended to convey: intentional communication among purposive agents. Indeed, the very notion of a ham radio (functionally characterized) involves the idea of such purposive communication. Accordingly, if we dispense with the notion of purpose (as even possibly represented in evidence), we put the very notion of a ham radio at risk. Typical goal-oriented explanation in the social sciences, in the humanities, and in nonacademic contexts will then disappear as well. As a result, our cognitive and practical lives will suffer drastically, in being limited to nonpurposive explanations, say from the natural sciences. This lesson applies likewise to our predicament in Hells Canyon. Our inanimate surroundings, although beautiful and highly structured in many ways (and ugly and seemingly chaotic in other ways), will not by themselves guide us to safety, given that we need intentional guidance. The corresponding purpose-neutral discerning of our evidence will evidently share that inadequacy.

Telic discerning inquires about the reality of purposes or intentions, and therefore exceeds not only inquiry about inanimate physical objects, circumstances, processes, or events, but also inquiry about abstract entities, such as properties, sets, or propositions. Telic discerning includes inquiry about goal-directed, intentional actions, and not just inanimate things or happenings. Clearly, we cannot plausibly assume at the start of inquiry that reality is devoid of purposes and intentional actions. Nothing in logic or in the notion of reality or even in science precludes the reality of either purposes or intentional actions. Of course, one might fervently embrace an austere ontology that, in keeping with an extreme, eliminative version of materialism, excludes the reality of purposes, but any such ontology would be logically optional, and not logically required. In addition, any such ontology would invite assessment of its accuracy on the basis of the actual evidence available to us. In the absence of such assessment, it would risk becoming a dogmatic ideology that seems as cognitively arbitrary as any other such ideology.

The evidence available to us in everyday human-to-human interactions certainly appears to support the reality of purposes and of resulting intentional actions. Frequently, it seems, humans set goals, identify means to achieve those goals, and then enact their preferred means to their goals, sometimes predictably achieving their goals. They even do this, apparently, in a socially coordinated way at times, whereby they share goals and means to those goals and thus act cooperatively to arrive at the same destination. Accordingly, some people, including careful philosophers, sometimes show up at a common meeting at the same time and place – no small accomplishment in the larger, causally elaborate scheme of things.

In cases of everyday social coordination, acknowledgment of human purposes explains an important part of what we experience, and it does so in a way that conforms to our available evidence. Accordingly, the social sciences, including social psychology and sociology, flourish in their acknowledging human purposes that can be socially shared and coordinated. We, in fact, have no equally accurate alternative explanation of much human behavior and experience; accordingly, our overall evidence appears positively to favor intentional or purposive explanation in many cases. As a result, we may reasonably proceed with such explanation when accurate treatment of our overall evidence calls for it. This will take us beyond explanation in the natural sciences but will yield cognitive gain nonetheless.

Returning to our Hells Canyon predicament, we should attend carefully to the surprising voice-like transmission from the ham radio. Exactly *how* are we to do this? That is the big question. Some people in our lost group might insist on purpose-neutral discerning, but that perspective would foreclose a significant prospect: namely, that we can identify in our evidence a rescuer who intends to communicate with us in order to lead us to safety. That is now a life-or-death prospect for us, and we therefore should avoid foreclosing it, unless, of course, we must yield to compelling evidence in favor of foreclosing it. As a result, we resolve to allow for telic discerning, at least in principle, given that intentional considerations very well may be present in our radio evidence.

In our bleak situation, we know what *we* want – namely, to be rescued from the wilderness gorge. Another question, however, seems relevant: what *should* we expect of a rescuer? This suggests another question: what would *the rescuer* (if there is one) want from us? Perhaps the rescuer in question would want us fully to appropriate the rescue and thereby to be fully freed by it, and not just to believe that the rescue is available or to go along half-heartedly. The rescuer, as suggested previously, might also be interested in our *moral* well-being, beyond our fleeting pleasures, and might even take the initiative in the rescue process and include some needed moral challenges for us. In that case, our wilderness gorge would be used by the rescuer as the school ground for our intended moral transformation. Perhaps, in addition, the rescuer in question would want us to "shut up" and to listen for the needed guidance and expectations, for our own genuine good. To the same end, the rescuer might send a capable representative into the gorge to identify with us and to aid our transformation and rescue. In any case, we shall carefully explore such widely neglected matters in subsequent chapters.

This book extends the wilderness parable to introduce what is arguably the common human predicament in our planetary wilderness canyon, where we all face the prospect of ultimate physical death and social breakdown. From the perspective of our species overall, our food and water supplies are threateningly low, with little hope of being adequately replenished. On many fronts, our relationships with one another are unravelling, and have resulted in selfish factions and fights. The factions and fights often involve race, religion, nationality, or economic class, but they sometimes cut across familiar divides. Selfishness transcends common categories, always, of course, for the sake of selfishness. We have become willing even to sacrifice the minimal well-being of others for our own selfish ends. As a result, economic injustices abound among us, wherever a sizeable group resides. Accordingly, genuine community has broken down on various fronts, and, in the absence of a rescuer, we shall all soon perish, whether rich or poor.

Our planetary wilderness canyon continues to suffer various grave troubles, as do we, as our lives clearly show. Evidently, successful scanning for a rescuer is our only hope. Will we connect with a rescuer? Will we survive? Will our rescue come in stages rather than all at once, and will it call for our moral transformation? Will only some of us survive? Some of us, in any case, give up hope, and turn to convenient diversions from our unfortunate predicament. (The list of such diversions seems endless.) Others lack the energy for diversions, and end up as the despairing lost ones among us. Any daily newspaper will confirm our difficult predicament, with depressing war stories, troubling cases of personal and corporate greed, striking revelations of political and religious corruption, and very sad obituaries as the disappointing culmination of human troubles.

Our well-founded access to the reality of a perfectly loving God arguably would be analogous to our access to an actual wilderness rescuer via frequencies on a ham radio. In particular, we would need somehow to "tune in" to (or to "appropriate") the reality, and the corresponding available evidence, of God. After all, God would be an invisible personal Spirit who has definite character traits and purposes that are perfectly authoritative and loving and thus morally superior to ours. We would need, accordingly, to point ourselves, rather like a radio antenna, in the right direction to receive, at least clearly, any divine intervention aimed at noncoercively transforming and rescuing us. The right direction, relative to a perfectly loving God, would not automatically match the self-chosen directions of our own lives, and we should not expect God to adopt our selfish ways. Being perfectly loving, God would have a character and related purposes significantly different from our own, given our selfish and other imperfect ways. God's direction therefore would differ notably from our own self-chosen directions, even if we suffer from grave delusions of being acceptable to God on our own imperfect terms.

As people lost in the wilderness canyon, we should not expect ourselves to have any control or authority over which radio frequency a potential rescuer uses. If we stubbornly insist on such authority, we may completely overlook the frequency actually occupied by a potential rescuer. We therefore should ask this simple question: *who* is entitled to choose the potential rescuer's frequency for communication – the lost people or the potential rescuer? In addition, are we willing to be rescued, or found, on the terms of the rescuer rather than on our favored terms? Once we ask such questions, we should see that the lost people have no decisive authority of their own to demand exactly how the potential rescuer is revealed or proceeds. Their expectations of the potential rescuer, at least for practical purposes, should conform to the character and purposes of the potential rescuer, and not vice versa. Likewise, we should not expect a perfectly loving God to appear on our convenient terms (say, on the nightly news) if this would be at odds with God's perfectly loving character and purposes. For good reason, including for our own good, God might not want to be heard in the popular news media or in the money-driven broadcasts of many televangelists. A media-packaged, domesticated God would arguably be an imposter at best, given the unmatched demands of worthiness of worship.

Our crucial initial question becomes not so much whether God exists as what the *character and purposes* of a perfectly authoritative and loving God would be, if God exists. In addition, we should explicitly ask the following question, in keeping with our previous observations: what *kind* of evidence and knowledge of God's reality would a perfectly loving God offer to humans, particularly humans needing transformation toward God's moral character? The most direct answer is that God would offer the kind of evidence and knowledge that represents and advances God's kind of unselfish love among humans. The crucial next question is whether we are sincerely willing to conform to God's terms for our rescue, by way of evidence, knowledge, and expectations. Are we willing to be rescued on God's terms, even if those terms call for our moral transformation toward God's character of perfect, unselfish love? In other words, are we ourselves willing to become, in volitional interaction with God, evidence of God's reality, thereby reflecting God's reality for others? The latter question reorients inquiry about God's existence by bringing it into line with self-reflective existential questions about who we are and who we should be, in the presence of God's reality. It includes the key notion of our becoming personifying evidence of God, in order to highlight the cooperative role humans have in appropriating evidence of God's reality. (Chapter 4 returns to this notion.)

We will use the wilderness parable to examine, without needless abstraction, the main approaches to knowledge of God's existence. Those approaches are analogous to the options noted previously. More specifically, they are: *nontheistic naturalism*, including atheistic and agnostic naturalism (combining either Option 1: Despairing or Option 2: Passively Waiting, with Option 4a: Purpose-Neutral Discerning of Evidence), *fideism* (analogous to Option 3: Leaping), *natural theology* (combining Option 4b: Telic Discerning of Evidence, with its indirect variation), and *volitional theism* (combining Option 4b: Telic Discerning of Evidence, with its direct variation).

Let's think of *conclusive* evidence as the kind of evidence needed for satisfaction of the justification condition for knowledge. At least for all actual cognitive and practical purposes, nontheistic naturalism gives up on (the reality of) conclusive evidence of God's existence, and offers a naturalistic limit on reasonable explanation and belief that excludes irreducible purposes or intentions. Fideism disowns any *requirement* of conclusive evidence of God's existence but tries, nonetheless, to sustain belief that God exists, sometimes on moral grounds or on grounds of social propriety in one's social context. Natural theology, in contrast, holds out for conclusive evidence of God's existence but makes its case on the basis of inferential evidence and corresponding arguments available to natural cognitive sources. Without depending on any argument of natural theology, volitional theism acknowledges evidence of purposive divine intervention in the world, but does not characterize (all) such evidence in terms of inferential evidence or arguments. It acknowledges, more specifically, that a perfectly loving God would seek noncoercively to transform the wills of wayward humans, and thereby to have humans themselves become personifying evidence of God's reality, in willingly receiving and reflecting God's powerful moral character for others and thus bringing God's presence near to others. Additional positions and variations are possible, of course, but they are beyond our direct concern. (On the fine points regarding conclusive evidence and knowledge in general, see Moser 1989.)

In asking about God's existence, we should clarify at the start the general kind of matter we are considering. Otherwise, we could end up hunting the snark, and therefore may find nothing at all.

2. BEYOND TASTE

We must ask, sooner or later, how a question about God's existence relates to actual reality, particularly regarding whether reality includes God. Clearly, reality surpasses human opinions at least in the natural sciences, and, as a result, we sometimes have scientific discoveries that do not reduce to human opinions or inventions. For instance, our best science in molecular chemistry reveals molecular processes that preceded the existence of humans and therefore cannot be reduced to human opinions or inventions. The existence of atoms in covalent bonds, in particular, did not wait for the inventive powers or even the messy emergence of human beings, however important we humans may be in other respects. Instead, our best chemistry discovers such antecedently existing molecular realities and seeks to explain them with illuminating chemical theories. Any current textbook on molecular chemistry supplies the fascinating evidence, with the help of abundant charts, graphs, and illustrations.

Does reality in theology surpass human opinions and inventions, as it does in chemistry and the other natural sciences? More directly, is there anything *independent* of us humans in the domain of theology to be discovered rather than merely invented by us? In particular, is there a human-independent divine rescuer? Theological *realists* answer yes, whereas theological *antirealists* answer no. Theological *agnostics* collectively shrug their shoulders, and settle for disavowing any genuine knowledge, pro or con, regarding existence in the theological domain. Such agnostics therefore are known by the fruits of their familiar refrain: "we don't know." Let's postpone now the beguiling higher-order question whether they *know* that they lack knowledge in this area. That question would take us far afield in epistemology, and we would then have trouble finding our way back to the wilderness predicament.

Some theological antirealists, going beyond agnosticism, recruit support for their antirealism from the widespread human disagreement about matters theological. It may seem that for any two people brought together, we find at least two or three opposing theological positions. Of course, the reality of the situation is not quite so fractured, but it is nonetheless fractured deeply and widely, if not irredeemably. The natural sciences appear to sing happily, even proudly, in unison by comparison with the cacophony of theology. Notoriously, philosophy is likewise fractured deeply and widely, but we need not belabor this obvious point for current purposes. We are not pursuing the sociology of theology or philosophy, because we are concerned with a larger rescue operation.

Although the natural sciences have enjoyed more agreement (and more federal grant money) than the field of theology, we need to be cautious about the actual take-home lessons of this undeniable difference. Widespread human disagreement about a topic, such as the topic of God's existence, does not entail or otherwise support antirealism about that topic. Clearly, there can be a determinate fact of the matter in an area, including theology, despite widespread human disagreement regarding that area. For instance, the considerable disagreement among educated humans regarding (the causes and effects of) global climate change in recent decades does not entail that there is no fact of the matter regarding (the causes and effects of) such climate change. After all, there is a fact of the matter, and it merits human pursuit, given our vulnerable environmental predicament. Climate change, in any case, is not at the mercy of human opinion, and much of reality undeniably follows suit.

A fact of the matter, although stubbornly real, can be elusive (that is, very difficult to identify) and therefore can prompt extensive and even persistent human disagreement. A contrary suggestion that allows such disagreement to preclude the reality of facts gives human disagreement too much reality-making power. Reality in general does not depend on human agreement; in fact, it can withstand, without any real difficulty, extensive and persistent human disagreement. The same holds for human knowledge: it can be genuine even in the face of widespread human disagreement. Such disagreement in an area does not, by itself, undermine justified or evidence-based true belief (of the kind suitable to knowledge) in that area. Disagreement can arise as a result of various factors that do not challenge the reality of truth, knowledge, or even evidence in the area of disagreement.

Going to an extreme, some people suggest that the central claims of religion and theology are purely subjective in being just a matter of personal taste, with no factual significance whatever beyond such taste. Analogously, I claim that vanilla ice cream is the best, but my daughter claims that chocolate ice cream is the best. Still, we respect each other's tastes, without insisting that one of us is right and the other wrong about the taste of ice cream. Fights over correctness about taste, accordingly, very rarely erupt inside or outside ice cream shops. (School cafeteria food fights are, of course, another messy matter altogether, stemming from ulterior student schemes and conflicts of various sorts.)

Perhaps theology belongs just in ice cream shops, in virtue of being just a matter of taste, without any further factual significance. Perhaps indeed, but the story regarding theology is definitely more complicated than our identifying the best taste of ice cream. One important but very sad consideration is that people do sometimes fight and even kill each other over theology, including over relatively minor doctrinal points of theology (see Juergensmeyer 2003, for a sample of the troubling details). For instance, violent disputes over the theologically proper mode of baptism as an initiation rite have left some unfortunate people murdered by drowning, even in the name of a holy and gracious God. At this point, theology and the taste of ice cream diverge, and theology fares far worse, and far more dangerous. In this respect, theology may be a serious social hazard, more dangerous than anything offered in an ice cream shop.

Theology, one might suggest, could be a matter of personal taste in two ways. First, the *content* of a theological claim, with regard to what the claim is *about*, could be just a person's taste involving personal likes and dislikes. When I claim, for example, that vanilla ice cream is the best, I might be saying simply that *I like the taste* of vanilla ice cream more than the alternative flavors (chocolate, pomegranate, peanut butter, banana, grapefruit, green tea, and so on). The previous statement may be true regarding my claim about ice cream, but an analogous claim for theology does not represent anything near the norm for theological statements. Typically, one's affirmation that God exists, for instance, is not offered as just a remark about one's taste. Instead, it ordinarily aims to acknowledge that a unique creative agent (that is, God) is real, even real beyond (and prior to) any human taste. In offering God as creator, theists typically propose that God exists prior to the emergence of humans and their tastes, and that this God has unmatched causal powers. Accordingly, some theology appears not to be reducible in its affirmed content to claims of taste involving human likes and dislikes. This appears to be an empirical fact.

A second approach to theology as taste-based proposes that the ultimate *support* for theological statements reduces to personal taste, and nothing more. Even if one talks about a God whose existence is independent of humans, according to this approach, one will have to settle for support or evidence for such talk that amounts to just personal taste involving one's likes and dislikes. This would be a bad cognitive situation indeed for theology, because its support would then be highly subjective. Its support would be akin to my subjective, taste-based support for claiming that vanilla ice cream is best. Such a subjectivist approach, however, might not capture the true story about theology in general. Perhaps some evidential support in theology actually takes us beyond mere personal likes and dislikes after all. This book aims to identify what kind of cognitive support is actually enjoyed by some theology, beyond human likes and dislikes. In particular, it introduces a distinctive kind of evidence appropriate for the reality of a God worthy of worship.

Many sane, educated, and generally trustworthy people claim not only that God exists, but also that they have genuine *knowledge*, including justified true belief, that God exists. Because claims are typically cheap and easy, however, the claim to know that God exists prompts the following response, usually sooner rather than later: *how do they know?* This common four-word question, although irksome at times, is perfectly intelligible and even valuable as far as it goes. It seeks an explanation of how the belief that

God exists exceeds *mere* belief or opinion, and achieves the status of genuine knowledge. In particular, this question typically seeks an explanation of how, if at all, the belief that God exists is *grounded, justified, reasonable,* or *evidence-based* regarding affirmation of its truth.

A plausible goal behind our four-word question, at least for many inquirers, is to acquire truth in a manner that includes an *adequate, well-grounded,* or *trustworthy indication* of true belief. These truth-seeking inquirers aim not only to avoid false belief and lucky guesswork, but also to minimize *the risk* of error in their beliefs (at least in a way befitting to acquiring truth while avoiding falsehoods). We should aim for the same, as people who seek to acquire truth (and to avoid error) but who are faced sometimes with facts and other realities at odds with our opinions, even our confident and long-held opinions. In seeking truth about God's existence, in particular, we therefore should seek truth based on adequate *evidence* for God's reality. Such evidence, *if* available, would indicate (perhaps fallibly) that it is true that God exists, or in other words, that God is real rather than fictional. Harking back to our wilderness parable, we ideally would find some genuine cognitive support or evidence for any claim to the reality of a rescuer; likewise for any claim to the reality of God. This would save us from relying just on guesswork or wishful thinking in our inquiry.

In treating any question about God's existence, we should begin with some clarity regarding what (or whom) we are asking about: in this case, *God's* existence. Are we asking about a *morally indefinite* but strikingly powerful creator? Many academic writers on theism, "mere theism," deism, atheism, and agnosticism inquire about the existence of such a creator, *whatever the creator's moral character may be.* (For one of many troublesome examples in circulation, see Dennett 2006, pp. 240–6.) The creator in question, as far as such inquiry is concerned, may turn out to be an evil tyrant or at least a morally indifferent slouch. This kind of inquiry, however earnest and rigorous in its search for a creator, may rest on a misleading bias regarding God's character. In any case, such inquiry would be significantly different from inquiry about the existence of a God who is *worthy of worship and thus morally perfect, including perfectly loving toward all persons, even enemies*. Let's begin to clarify the latter kind of inquiry, given that it refuses to lower the bar for being God and thus for questions about God's existence.

3. THE TITLE "GOD"

As suggested previously, we should approach the question about human knowledge of God's existence by asking specifically what, or (better) whose, conceivable existence we are considering. More directly, what exactly do we *mean* by the tiny but important term "God"? Our response will determine, at least in part, the actual value of our question and its suitable means of answer. Clearly, if the question of human knowledge of God's existence lacks value and thus does not matter, then we should change the subject to something else, advisedly to something worthwhile. Many people, however, contend that this question actually has unsurpassed, life-or-death importance, given what they mean by the term "God." In this case, at least, one's meaning of a term matters significantly and thus deserves careful attention. Philosophical and theological questions about God often suffer from a seriously vague conception of God, resulting typically from undue abstractness in the assumed idea of God. Perhaps some people use theological abstractness to divert attention from a potential divine moral challenge to wayward humans; at least, we should keep this possibility in mind.

In keeping with a prominent traditional usage, we can fruitfully use the term "God" as a most exalted *title* rather than as a proper name. This allows us to talk intelligibly about whether God exists, even if God does not actually exist and even if we disavow knowledge that God exists. A title, such as "the Queen of Chicago," can be perfectly intelligible even if it has no actual titleholder. (For the record, Chicago has no city queen, but the meaningfulness of the previous title is not thereby threatened; that title is not gibberish, after all.) Semantic meaning, in this and other cases, does not require naming. As a result, our use of "God" as a title saves us from unfair dismissal of agnostics and atheists by a naming fiat. Nothing is gained, in any case, by trying to name one's genuine critics out of business. That quick strategy would be too easy, given that it could be used by anyone at will, even by one's critic. Two could play that unhelpful game.

The title "God," on the proposed usage, signifies (that is, connotes) a being worthy of worship, even if such a being fails to exist and therefore even if the title fails to refer to an actual thing. Worthiness of worship is, of course, maximally morally demanding. It requires inherent (or self-contained) moral perfection, including perfect moral righteousness, and such perfection in an agent demands, in turn, a perfectly loving character, including perfect love toward one's enemies. (See Luke 6:27–36 and Matthew 5:38–48 for a distinctive and influential notion of God, originating in Jewish soil and enduring in Christian thought, that explicitly includes divine love of enemies.) An agent's selfish failure to love would block that agent from having a morally perfect character, however powerful and knowledgeable that selfish agent may be. In addition, the required unselfish love would be purportedly redemptive rather than merely sentimental or romantic, because it would *actively seek* the well-being of all persons. Talk may be cheap and easy, but the kind of love in question would not be, at all.

Let's say that a being is worthy of worship if and only if that being, having inherent moral perfection, merits worship as unqualified adoration, love, trust, and obedience. Of course, humans can worship a morally defective powerful being, perhaps out of human fear of harmful threatening power, but the being in question would not be *worthy* of worship. People, to their own detriment, often worship false gods, despite the unworthiness and unreliability of those gods. The results of such misguided worship do not include lasting human satisfaction, whatever else they include. Indeed, such worship is typically a recipe for frustration and other trouble. It follows that worship can be dangerous, and we therefore should not take worship lightly. What we worship may be, in the end, a matter of life or death for us, even if we fail to recognize this.

Given the exalted moral standard for worthiness of worship, we readily can exclude most claimants to the preeminent title "God" on the ground of moral deficiency. Moral defects bar a candidate from the status of being God, automatically and decisively. (The list of failed candidates seems almost endless, and therefore we now may postpone an actual list. Readers can easily supply their own lists, for their own anticounterfeit purposes.) People sometimes casually use the term "God" in ways contrary to worthiness of worship, but this empirical fact does not challenge the value of the current morally demanding usage. Part of the value of the current usage is that it allows us to engage some central theological concerns of traditional monotheism (particularly of Judaism, Christianity, and Islam) without arbitrarily dismissing atheists and agnostics by a naming fiat. Clearly, people cannot name or postulate God into existence via refusing to imagine that God does not exist. Likewise, people cannot define or postulate God out of existence, as if a mere human definition could block the actual existence of God. The topic of God's existence is more resilient than such quick ploys suggest.

We can have an intelligible title, such as "God," but have no ground whatever for acknowledging the reality of an actual holder of that title. As a result, we arguably need some *indication* of the reality of an agent worthy of worship to avoid mere wishful thinking in human belief that God exists. In particular, we arguably need *evidence* of the reality of perfect love in a morally impeccable agent toward all agents, given that worthiness of worship includes perfect love toward all agents. The required power of perfect love in an agent includes the agent's *intention* to bring about unselfishly what is good, and only what is good, ultimately for *all* affected persons, even those who are the agent's enemies. Perfect love thus underwrites the amazing and rare phenomenon called *enemy-love*, and hence does not settle for love just for one's friends, colleagues, or helpful associates. This accounts for its very rare occurrence among humans, including religious and educated humans.

An agent's genuine, morally righteous love aims to culminate in beneficial intentional actions toward others, and thus it must be rooted in one's *intentions* to love in action. Because intentions to love, when real, operate at the very heart of an agent, particularly at the heart of an agent's motivation, perfect unselfish love would reside ultimately in an agent's motivational center, or "heart" (*kardia*, in ancient Greek). This position is assumed in the Jewish scriptures in Deuteronomy 6:4–6, for example, and in the Christian New Testament in Mark 12:29–30, for example. We humans, it is arguable, cannot create this rare power of unselfish love ourselves, but God, as perfectly loving, would seek noncoercively to introduce, proliferate, and sustain this unselfish power among all humans, at their motivational centers (see, for instance, 1 John 4:7–9, 19). Humans therefore would depend on God for this unusual power, even if some humans mistakenly would take credit for it themselves. Such mistaken self-credit, we shall see, is a common source of one's failing to apprehend salient evidence of God's existence.

Ideally, by divine hope, all capable agents willingly would receive divine love from God and then manifest it from the heart toward all agents, even (perhaps with difficulty) toward their worst enemies and harshest critics. Mere human agents, as suggested previously, would manifest such love in a manner dependent on God, but God would do so inherently, as a matter of inherent but still praiseworthy moral character. This consideration suggests a distinctive kind of theology: *kardiatheology*, as theology aimed primarily at one's motivational heart, including one's will, rather than just at one's mind or one's emotions. Such theology accommodates Henry Sidgwick's astute observation, in keeping with Jesus's Sermon on the Mount/Plain, that "inwardness, rightness of heart or spirit, is the special and pre-eminent characteristic of Christian goodness" (1902, p. 114).

Divine self-revelation or self-manifestation to humans, it is arguable, would fit with kardiatheology in aiming non-coercively to realize divine perfect love in human hearts rather than just to expand human reflection or information. A God worthy of worship would not be in the business of just expanding our databases or simply giving us an informational plan of rescue from our troubles. Divine self-revelation and its corresponding evidence therefore would seek to transform humans *motivationally*, and not just intellectually, toward perfect love and its required volitional cooperation with God. In this respect, a God worthy of worship would have important *practical* interests regarding human intentions and actions, beyond merely theoretical interests regarding human judgments and beliefs. This widely neglected consideration, we shall see, underwrites a distinctive account of the evidence for God. It also fits well with the prospect that a perfectly loving God would want humans to become living, personifying evidence of God's reality, in willingly receiving and reflecting God's profound moral character for others. (Chapters 2 and 4 return to the cognitive significance of kardiatheology and personifying evidence of God.)

Let's consider the plausible view that divine self-revelation to humans would include a manifestation and an offering of divine perfect love to humans for their own good. Given this view, we inquirers about God's existence should identify, at least in general, what an actual indication of such a manifestation and an offering would look like. Perhaps the indication in question will be subtle, elusive, and puzzling in order (a) to avoid intimidating, coercing, or indulging humans and (b) to offer a profound existential, motivational challenge to wayward humans. God therefore would have definite purposes in offering evidence of divine reality to humans, and these purposes would guide the kind of evidence offered and the way it is to be received. We may call this *purposively available evidence* of divine reality, because it would be offered in accordance with definite divine purposes for humans. Returning to the wilderness parable, we need to consider whether the needed rescuer has a special moral agenda of transformation for lost humans, for their own good. Our time in the wilderness may thus be more purposive and adventurous than we initially supposed. God could be profoundly at work in one's wilderness troubles even if one fails to acknowledge or appreciate this.

4. BIAS IN INQUIRY

As previously noted, a widespread bias in human expectations of God is that God would be revealed to humans as a morally indefinite creator, in a way that sets aside or postpones moral issues regarding humans relative to God. In asking about a morally indefinite creator, however, inquirers might miss out on available salient evidence of an ethically robust God who is no morally indefinite creator but who is inherently morally righteous and challenging, particularly toward wayward humans. Inquirers might miss out on such evidence because they are looking for God in all the wrong places, especially in the supposedly morally indefinite places. The bias invites this largely ignored issue: are we humans in a position on our own to answer the question of whether God exists, without our being morally challenged by God, if God exists? Once we raise this issue, we can plausibly allow our list of potential cognitive options to be expanded.

Perhaps the true God, being morally perfect, is, in fact, intentionally elusive and even obscure regarding the ethically casual issue of whether there is a morally indefinite creator. One of God's aims with divine elusiveness would be to highlight a more urgent question for humans: namely, *who* exactly is (worthy of being) in charge here as the proper moral authority over the universe, including over all humans? A related urgent question in need of focus may be: exactly *how* is God in charge over this deeply morally troubled universe? A morally *definite*, perfectly loving God could use such questions to prompt us to ask seriously: to *whom* are we humans as responsible agents ultimately morally accountable, even with regard to how we inquire about God? Will we let God be truly God (and thus morally robust, challenging, and authoritative) even in the area of human inquiry about God's reality? If so, we would allow God (at least in principle) to take the initiative in seeking humans, on God's terms, even before humans seek God.

We harmfully jump the gun, philosophically speaking, when we pursue the question of God's existence as if God is morally indefinite and thus not intentionally elusive toward any human pursuit of a morally indefinite creator. Indeed, our jumping the gun in this manner may involve a kind of *cognitive idolatry* whereby we use cognitive standards that displace God's cognitive and moral supremacy, including God's authority over the actual manner of divine self-manifestation and corresponding evidence for humans. Such idolatry inevitably would be harmful to inquirers by distancing them from needed suitable knowledge and evidence of the true God. Once again, we need to consider allowing God to be God, and thus authoritative and morally challenging, even in the cognitive domain.

Jesus may have had a challenge to cognitive idolatry in mind with this otherwise puzzling prayer of gratitude for divine hiding:

At that time Jesus said, "I thank you, Father, Lord of heaven and earth, because you have *hidden* these things from the wise and the intelligent, and have revealed them to infants; yes, Father, for such was your gracious will. All things have been handed over to me by my Father; and no one knows the Son except the Father, and no one knows the Father except the Son and anyone to whom the Son chooses to reveal him." (Matt. 11:25–7, NRSV, italics added; cf. Luke 10:21–2, 1 Cor. 2:4–14. Subsequent translations from the Greek New Testament are my own unless otherwise noted.)

Jesus portrays his divine Father as hiding divine ways and means from people who are pridefully "wise and intelligent" in their own eyes, if only because they are not suitably ready to receive God's message. He suggests that God is intentionally elusive, even to the point of hiding, relative to people who oppose God's authority and morally righteous ways. This suggestion agrees with a longstanding teaching of the prophetic tradition in the Hebrew scriptures, including Isaiah 45:15: "Truly you are a God who hides himself, O God of Israel, the Savior" (NRSV). God, then, may be more challenging than many humans have supposed.

If we take Jesus and the Hebrew prophetic tradition seriously, we should expect God to be morally righteous, perfectly loving, and thus (for redemptive purposes) at times elusive toward wayward humans. God then would be anything but a morally indefinite creator. People, however, are sometimes not ready and willing to receive God's self-manifestation aright, with due honor, gratitude, and submission. Accordingly, God would offer needed challenges of various sorts to humans, and some divine hiding would offer one such challenge (see Rom. 1:18–23, John 12:39–41; cf. Moser 2008, Chapter 2). In this regard, we should expect God to be a moving target, and not an object for casual or convenient human inspection, speculation, or entertainment. God's morally profound character and aims would preclude God's joining in human intellectual games that ignore or short-change serious human moral needs. We must be wary, then, of morally neutralizing or otherwise domesticating God in our inquiry about God's existence. Accordingly, for our own good, we should steer clear of the aforementioned bias in our inquiry.

A perfectly loving God would have morally definite purposes toward humans, including the purposes to invite and
to encourage able-minded humans to enter into cooperative fellowship with God and thereby to become loving as
God is loving, even toward resolute enemies. As suggested,
therefore, God would make evidence of divine reality purposively available to humans, that is, available in a way that
serves God's perfectly loving redemptive aims for humans.
These aims would include a call from God to humans to
yield to and obey God as authoritative Lord, and this call
would seek, noncoercively, to engage humans at a level of
motivational depth, rather than at a superficial level. This
God therefore would contrast sharply with the relatively
aloof creator postulated by deism or by morally indefinite
theism. Human inquiry about God should be prepared to
follow suit, in agreement with its potential subject of inquiry.
As a result, it should be open to a divine expectation that
humans themselves become, in cooperative interaction with
God, personifying evidence of God's reality, in willingly
receiving and reflecting God's powerful moral character for
others. We shall clarify this neglected but crucial lesson.

5. DIVINE EVIDENCE

On reflection, we should expect a perfectly loving God to
offer any divine self-manifestation and accompanying evidence to humans as a matter of *divine cognitive grace* rather
than human meritorious earning or even humanly controllable evidence. In other words, divine self-manifestation and
its corresponding evidence would come to humans as a
humanly unearned gift, if they come at all, and humans
would not be in charge or in control of how or when the
gracious gift is offered to them. Being anchored in such
a gracious gift, human knowledge and evidence of a perfectly loving God would differ importantly from the kinds
of human knowledge and evidence that have humanly controllable objects, such as lab specimens, kitchen appliances,
or patio furniture pieces.

The divine gracious gift in question, in its invitational call to humans, could and would make noncoercive demands on humans for the sake of reconciling humans to God. Indeed, we should be open to God as the one who initiates the process of human knowledge of God's reality via purposive divine self-revelation that includes such an invitational call to humans. In that case, we would be open also to the need for human responsiveness to God's call to humans. Part of this responsiveness, we shall see, would include human willingness to become living, personifying evidence of God's reality, in willingly receiving and reflecting God's moral character for others.

Given divine moral perfection, a *willingly obedient* human response to divine demands to receive and to practice divine love would be the suitable way for a human to receive the divine gift on offer. Accordingly, we should expect the availability of some evidence of divine reality to be sensitive to the will of its intended human recipients. Inquiry about divine reality would move then to a new level, beyond mere reflection and inference, to human obedience and disobedience, particularly toward our becoming personifying evidence of God's reality. What once seemed to be a merely intellectual inquiry would become morally and existentially loaded for us inquirers about God.

A key question for us is: *who* is inquiring about the existence of God? More specifically, *what kind* of person is inquiring about divine reality, a person willing to yield to (and thus reflect) a perfectly loving God or a person unwilling to yield (and thus reflect)? A perfectly loving God, accordingly, would turn the tables on human inquirers by asking about *their own status*, particularly their own moral position, before God. In particular, are they *willing* to become personifying evidence of God's reality and thus to receive and to reflect God's moral character for others, thereby bringing God's presence near to others? In any case, inquiry about divine reality would no longer be a casual, morally indefinite matter akin to a spectator sport. It would become morally loaded and humanly humbling if approached aright. Inquirers about God's existence, even inquirers among philosophers and theologians, typically overlook this important cognitive consideration about a God worthy of worship.

We shall begin to reorient inquiry about God's existence by asking with due seriousness the following questions. What if God would be perfectly loving even in offering to humans any divine self-manifestation and corresponding evidence of divine reality? What would available evidence of God's existence then be like? How would it call us inquirers to account before God, and how would it bear on what we, ourselves, are reflecting in who we are? How might one's lacking evidence of divine reality then concern primarily one's own moral character and attitudes toward God rather than the actual availability of such evidence? Philosophers and theologians have not given adequate attention to such important questions, but we shall begin to correct this deficiency. In doing so, we shall allow for a fair hearing of a case for reasonable, well-grounded belief that a perfectly loving but elusive God actually exists.

As explanatory disciplines, philosophy and theology routinely introduce and explore "what if?" questions for the sake of entertaining explanatory hypotheses. Accordingly, we do well to extend the previous list of questions a bit to identify some areas in need of explanation regarding human knowledge of God's existence. What if we humans, in our moral imperfection and our resistance to unselfish love, are typically not ready and willing to receive God *on God's morally challenging terms*? What if human pride, including our desired self-sufficiency, obscures our apprehending (a) who God truly is, (b) the reality of God's authoritative call to us, and (c) the lasting good that God wants for us? What if divinely desired human knowledge of God is not a spectator sport at all, but rather calls for willingly obedient human knowledge of God *as authoritative Lord* (rather than as a morally indefinite creator)? In that case, such knowledge would demand human volitional yielding to God as Lord, at least to some extent.

The knowledge of God in question would require that we be willing to become personifying evidence of God's reality, in virtue of our willingly receiving and reflecting God's moral character for others. We thus should consider an important distinction between *spectator* knowledge of God's reality (that does not challenge a human will to yield to God or to become evidence of God's reality) and *authoritative*, invitational knowledge of God's reality (that invites a person to cooperate with God's will and thereby to become personifying evidence of God's reality, including evidence of God as an intentional agent). The latter kind of knowledge, although widely neglected by philosophers and theologians, is critically important to our inquiry.

What would become of evidence of God's reality if we found that spectator knowledge of God's reality is unavailable to humans? Could there still be salient evidence and knowledge of God's reality available to humans? There definitely could be, as long as the relevant evidence and knowledge would fit with God's distinctive character and purposes. The evidence in question would be purposively available to humans, in keeping with God's perfectly loving, morally challenging purposes for humans. Its being apprehended by humans would be sensitive then to the attitudes, including volitional attitudes, of humans toward God's character and purposes. One such attitude, we shall see, concerns whether humans are willing to become personifying evidence of God's reality, in response to a divine call. In keeping with the cognitive importance of such audience receptivity, Jesus speaks of the need for "eyes to see and ears to hear" regarding the evidence of divine intervention, including through himself (see Mark 4:22–3).

Some people assume that God would have a magic cognitive bullet in divine self-revelation whereby God *guarantees* that the divinely offered evidence of God's existence will actually be willingly received by humans. Sometimes this dubious assumption is clothed in talk of "divine sovereignty," but this approach, in any case, involves a serious mistake. Analogously, a sincere person's telling the truth to others does not guarantee that the truth thereby told is actually willingly received by the intended audience. Intended recipients of evidence can fail to be willing recipients owing to their unreceptive, resistant ways. In particular, it can be painful for people to acknowledge a humbling truth about themselves, and therefore they might opt not to accept this truth. Clearly, unselfish love (exemplified in an invitation to unselfish morally good fellowship) offered to a person need not be received or valued by that person. Accordingly, unreceptive humans would be able to block any supposed magic cognitive bullet on God's part.

We have suggested a cognitively important question of this form: "in connection with giving evidence to humans via divine self-manifestation, what if God wanted valuable feature X?" As responsible inquirers about God's existence, we should attend to various questions of this form, given that such questions can reliably guide and even correct human expectations about any divine evidence. Our questions about the evidence for God's existence then would be sensitive to what X involves in our question – that is, to what God would want to bring about in offering the relevant evidence to humans. Our questions would include, for instance, a question of this sort: if God desired to use divine self-manifestation noncoercively to challenge human selfishness and pride, including self-righteousness, and to transform humans toward unselfish, morally righteous love whereby they become personifying evidence of God's reality, then what would the relevant evidence of divine reality look like, at least in general? Philosophy of religion, theology, and general human inquiry about God have suffered from a lack of attention to such a question. A correct answer to this question, however, would be invaluable for sincere people inquiring about evidence and knowledge of God's existence.

A perfectly loving God would seek noncoercively to have others willingly receive and then manifest God's perfect love at the level of their motivational center, or heart, for the sake of building and sustaining God's kingdom community. Divine perfect love would be inherently community-building in that way, whatever else it includes. This would involve the aforementioned kind of kardiatheology aimed at the human heart, rather than just a theology of the mind or the emotions, and it would include humans' willingly becoming personifying evidence of God's reality in response to a divine call. Accordingly, certain kinds of controllable or morally neutral evidence expected or demanded by many humans would not fit at all with what a perfectly loving God seeks. Divine massive fireworks displays in the sky overhead, for instance, would not do the desired job, however entertaining they may be for some humans. As a result, we should not expect God to offer such relatively superficial displays, despite some familiar human desires and demands to the contrary. Instead, we should expect something morally more profound and more challenging. Perfect love, after all, would be anything but morally superficial or casual, especially relative to wayward human tendencies.

A perfectly loving God would desire and noncoercively promote that *all people*, both individually and collectively, willingly receive divine love and thereby worship God and live in loving fellowship with God (and with each other) from their heart, for their own good. The desired fellowship would include noncoerced human *volitional (that is, will-based) cooperation* with God, particularly cooperation with God's advancement of unselfish love toward all people, even toward God's enemies. To that end, God would want people to be cooperatively related to God on perfectly loving terms that exclude selfishness and pride and advance unselfish love toward all agents.

Being related to God on God's terms would include people in a morally transformative divine–human relationship that increasingly replaces human selfishness and pride with human reception and promotion of divine morally righteous love. It would also include their becoming personifying evidence of God's reality wherein they willingly receive and reflect God's powerful moral character for others. These people would be individually in an I–Thou relationship and collectively in a we–Thou relationship with God – that is, in the second person toward God, as *Thou*. They thereby would receive divine love and, on that basis, they would adore, love, trust, and obey God directly, and, ideally, wholeheartedly. Evidence of divine reality, anchored in divine cognitive grace, would conform to such distinctive divine purposes and thus would be purposively available to humans. It therefore would not be just a matter of speculation or entertainment for spectators.

The transformative relationship in question would include an initiating and sustaining divine call via human conscience: specifically, a divine call away from human selfishness and pride, including self-righteousness, and toward human cooperation in (receiving and manifesting) divine perfect love and its morally righteous requirements. This follows from the fact that divine perfect love would be *invitational* in that it would invite people into volitional fellowship with God and thereby with others who have similar aims. This invitational call would be directed at human conscience for the sake of motivational and existential personal depth, and it thereby would invite one to be sincerely disclosed, or revealed, before God for the sake of honest transformation. In particular, it would seek free disclosure of who one truly is morally and who one morally ought to be by the exalted standard of a perfect loving God. God thus would seek a relationship of human transformation toward God's perfect love, in divine–human volitional fellowship. Being purposively available, evidence of divine reality for humans would emerge from and fit with the same divine desire for human transformation in divine–human cooperation. A key result of such transformation would be humans who become personifying evidence of divine reality, including evidence of God as an intentional agent.

The divine evidence in question, indicating divine invitational *agape*, would itself be invitational because it includes a call to humans to enter into volitional fellowship with God. This evidence would also be authoritative in virtue of indicating an authoritative call to humans from an authoritative God. The divine authority thereby indicated would include God's being inherently worthy of human love, trust, and obedience, given God's inherent morally perfect character and intentional agency. The relevant evidence would contrast with any kind of spectator evidence that makes no demand or call on the direction of a human will or life, such as either observational evidence from design or order in nature or theoretical evidence concerning the need for a first cause of experienced contingent events. Let's acknowledge, then, a conceptual distinction between authoritative invitational evidence and spectator evidence. We shall see how this distinction bears importantly on various approaches to human knowledge of God's existence.

Given the anticipated role of invitational evidence, we shall confront three important questions about God's existence. First, if God's existence is elusive, why should we suppose that God exists at all? Second, if God actually exists, why is God elusive, particularly if God seeks to communicate with people for their own good? Third, what are the implications of divine elusiveness for supposed knowledge and evidence of God's reality? This book approaches these questions on the basis of a new account of knowledge and evidence of divine reality that challenges the main competing approaches to God's existence, including those of nontheistic naturalism, fideism, and natural theology.

This book recommends an analogue of Aristotle's wise advice, in his *Nicomachean Ethics*, to look for precision in each class of things *just so far as the nature of the subject matter admits*. The analogue is this: we should let our understanding of evidence, and thus of knowledge, regarding a subject matter (in particular, God) be guided by the nature of the subject matter and the actual corresponding features of our evidence regarding that subject matter. Accordingly, we should not be guided by some dubious antecedent cognitive standard, such as a standard that requires either human control of relevant evidence or the absence of a moral challenge to inquirers. In following the suggested analogue, we will characterize evidence regarding a subject matter (including God's existence) in a manner true to the nature of the subject matter in question and to the reality of our corresponding actual evidence concerning that subject matter. This will save us from wishful thinking and other forms of bias in connection with our topic.

Evidence of God's reality is, by definition for this book's purposes, evidence that a morally perfect intentional agent worthy of worship actually exists. Whether such evidence is available to humans remains to be seen. Where, in any case, might we find such evidence? In nature? In history? In philosophical arguments? In ourselves? Somewhere else? Famously and confidently, Bertrand Russell anticipated his response if he were to meet God after his death: "God, you gave us insufficient evidence." This simple question arises: insufficient for *what*? Russell might have considered a bit of cognitive modesty in the presence of an authoritatively and morally perfect God. In that case, Russell instead would have asked: "God, what morally impeccable purposes of yours led to your being subtle and elusive in the evidence of your reality available to humans?" It is disappointing that Russell showed no awareness of such an important question for a reasonable truth-seeker regarding divine reality. Perhaps we have a sign here that Russell had his own questionable agenda, even an ax to grind, in treating questions about God's existence. I suspect that we do.

In contrast with Russell, we will entertain the following question neglected by many skeptics: if a perfectly loving God would choose to give humans evidence of God's reality, what parameters or distinctive features for the evidence would God observe? A plausible answer is that God would impart the relevant evidence in a manner that is morally commendable as well as morally beneficial for receptive humans. Specifically, God would seek to benefit human *wills* and not just human thoughts or emotions, given the key role of wills in morally relevant motivation, decision making, and action. In this regard, the pertinent evidence would be *volitionally* and thus morally significant. In effect, it would aim to have humans themselves become personifying evidence of God's reality, in willingly receiving and reflecting God's moral character, including divine intentional agency, for the sake of others. This book contends that, in neglecting this consideration, the positions of nontheistic naturalism, fideism, and natural theology face serious problems. In general, then, the book recruits some neglected but important ideas from philosophical theology to illuminate religious epistemology in a way that highlights its moral and existential significance for all inquirers about God.

The book develops analogues of the previous wilderness parable to elucidate a distinctive volitional, purpose-oriented approach to evidence of divine reality, in contrast with the aforementioned competing approaches. The *reality* of the frequencies activating the ham radio found in the miners' shack does not depend, of course, on our tuning in to those frequencies. The radio frequencies are real and actually available to people even if all of us are fast asleep at our radios. We, in fact, are bombarded with radio waves at all hours, even when we are altogether unaware of them. Similarly, the *available evidence* of the reality of the radio waves is independent of our tuning in to them. In general, our not actually *having* (received) evidence does not entail that it is not *available* to us. Of course, our failure to turn on the ham radio can leave us with no received evidence of the reality of the radio transmissions in our area. Still, the distinctive available evidence of ham radio activity *can* be acquired by all who seek it in the right way, with the help of a radio. That evidence is definitely *available* to us, and it may be crucial to our being rescued from our wilderness predicament.

Developing the wilderness parable, the book contends that we should expect evidence and knowledge of divine reality to be purposively available to humans – that is, available only in a manner suitable to *divine* purposes in self-revelation. In addition, it contends that these divine purposes would include the noncoerced transformation of human wills toward God's will, for the sake of human moral improvement as well as human fellowship with God. This lesson generates a major shift in our understanding of human knowledge and evidence of divine reality, because it demands that inquirers become sensitive to the character and purposes of an authoritative, perfectly loving God in a manner that challenges and reorients human wills. Indeed, it demands that human inquirers themselves become personifying evidence of God's reality, in willingly receiving and reflecting God's moral character for others and thus bringing God's presence near to others.

6. OVERVIEW

As suggested previously, this book contrasts and assesses four important competing approaches to religious knowledge: *nontheistic naturalism* (as in the recent works of, for instance, Daniel Dennett, Richard Dawkins, and E.O. Wilson), *fideism* (as suggested, for example, in some influential writings of Søren Kierkegaard, LudwigWittgenstein, Karl Barth, Rudolf Bultmann, and certain advocates of Reformed epistemology), *natural theology* (as represented, for instance, in first cause, design, and fine tuning arguments for God's existence), and *volitional theism* (as hinted at by Blaise Pascal and developed at length in Moser 2008). Each of the four competing approaches receives its own expository and evaluative chapter, and the concluding chapter attends to some potential defeaters, particularly in religious diversity and in evil, against the book's volitional theism.

Chapter 1, "Nontheistic Naturalism," gives a fair hearing and a firm challenge to some influential versions of nontheistic naturalism about human knowledge. The naturalism in question recommends agnosticism, if not atheism, regarding divine reality on the basis of a demand for a certain kind of supporting evidence. The evidence demanded is naturalistic in virtue of being continuous, or of a piece, with the natural sciences, at least in terms of underlying methodological support. Chapter 1 elucidates this notion of "naturalistic," and gives attention to a familiar argument from the explanatory success of naturalism in the sciences.

The familiar argument in question, particularly as represented by Dennett in various works, concludes that *all* cognitively good explanations are naturalistic (roughly, continuous with the natural sciences) and thus ultimately nonintentional or nonpurposive in terms of what they acknowledge as real. This monopolistic inference, according to Chapter 1, fails to convince, and even lacks support from the natural sciences themselves. Chapter 1 also discusses how evidence from religious experience bears on naturalism, particularly with regard to the human variability of such evidence. The chapter contends that one person's lack of salient experiential evidence of divine reality cannot plausibly be generalized to the universal conclusion that everyone lacks such evidence. This leads to a firm challenge for many religious skeptics.

According to Chapter 2, "Fideism and Faith," fideism, as represented by Kierkegaard, Barth, and Bultmann, is driven by a twofold attempt to exempt religious beliefs from a need for supporting evidence and thereby to sidestep skeptical worries about religious beliefs. An underlying assumption, at least by Kierkegaard, is that the commitments of religion involve a kind of faith very different from inquiry in philosophy and the sciences. Even if this is correct, however, Chapter 2 contends that traditional monotheism, as represented in Judaism, Christianity, and Islam, includes *truth-claims* about reality and therefore must distinguish these claims from claims that are evidently false and from claims that lack any indication of their being true.

The neglect by fideism of needed religious cognitive support, according to Chapter 2, leaves religious commitment open to a problem of cognitive arbitrariness and thus cognitive irrationality. The chapter examines some attempts of fideism to avoid this problem, but concludes that the problem stubbornly persists for fideism. The chapter also considers a version of fideism suggested by a recent approach to the "proper basicality" of religious belief in so-called "Reformed epistemology." The chapter recommends against any confusion of *evidence* for a belief and an *argument* for a belief. Even if a religious belief can be "properly basic," and thus not in need of a supporting argument, it does not follow that such a belief needs no supporting evidence. In addition, according to Chapter 2, we would do well to avoid a kind of fideism about argument support that divorces rational belief from potential support from an argument.

Chapter 3, "Natural Theology and God," examines a non-purposive approach to evidence for religious belief found in much natural theology, including in some first cause, design, fine tuning, and ontological arguments for God's existence. The chapter contends that this approach is too objectivist, because it relies on a spectator approach to evidence that disregards important volitional tendencies of inquirers in the appropriation of any relevant divine evidence. The chapter clarifies the significant distinction between spectator evidence and a kind of authoritative evidence that includes a volitional challenge to inquirers.

Chapter 3 contends that we should expect evidence offered to humans by a God worthy of worship to be authoritative evidence rather than spectator evidence. If this is so, we can identify a critical deficiency in the familiar approaches to evidence for religious belief in traditional and contemporary natural theology. The chapter argues, in this connection, that standard natural theology fails to accommodate a key feature of a perfectly loving God: divine elusiveness stemming from perfectly loving divine purposes to transform inquirers morally and volitionally. Such natural theology also neglects the significance of personifying evidence of divine reality wherein a human, as an intentional agent, becomes evidence of God's existence in virtue of willingly receiving and reflecting God's moral character for others. In addition, the chapter identifies some salient benefits of the fact that reasonable religious belief does not depend on natural theology.

According to the volitional theism of Chapter 4, "Personifying Evidence of God," we need to ask what kind of divine self-manifestation and self-revealing evidence we should expect of a perfectly loving God worthy of worship. Part of the answer, as suggested previously, is that such a God would aim to influence not just human thoughts or emotions but also human wills, particularly regarding human desires and aversions, likes and dislikes, and loves and hates. Pascal was right in this connection, specifically in suggesting that God would self-hide and self-reveal for this important will-oriented, morally relevant end. (The same idea is suggested by John 12:20–41.)

A central divine purpose would be human transformation of a morally significant kind, whereby humans non-coercively become willing to love and to forgive as God loves and forgives, even their enemies, and thereby themselves become personifying evidence of God's reality. The needed volitional transformation would include attunement, or cooperation, of a human will with God's moral will, for the purpose of removing human selfishness and its destructive consequences as a means to building genuine community under divine moral authority. The volitional theism of Chapter 4 is doubly volitional: in acknowledging that evidence of God's reality among humans manifests God's will, and in characterizing such evidence as being suitably appropriated via the yielding of a human will to God's will, for the sake of one's becoming personifying evidence of God.

Chapter 4 contends that the needed volitional attunement of a human will with God's will includes a kind of direct human knowledge of divine reality that goes beyond mere propositional knowledge that God exists. This direct knowledge involves human experiential acquaintance with distinctive, morally relevant volitional power inherent to God's character. A salient feature of this divine power is a genuine offer of forgiveness to offenders against God, even enemies, without the condoning of wrongdoing. Chapter 4 explains that the morally transforming effects of one's willingly receiving such an offer can increase one's evidence of divine reality. The chapter's approach to evidence and knowledge of God's existence thus contrasts sharply with the naturalist, fideist, and natural theological approaches examined in Chapters 1–3. It illustrates that inquirers themselves may be under scrutiny and even moral challenge in their inquiry about God, for the sake of their becoming personifying evidence of God's reality.

Chapter 5, "Diversity, Evil, and Defeat," attends to some influential proposed defeaters of evidence of divine reality, including alleged defeaters both from the disunity – and even inconsistency – among religious explanations offered by the world's various religions and from the extensive evil in the world. One important lesson concerns the need to acknowledge human cognitive limits, particularly limits on what we humans are in a position to explain regarding any divine purposes in allowing various kinds of evil and religious disagreement. According to Chapter 5, given such limits, we humans should not expect to be able to offer a comprehensive account of either the religious disagreement or the extensive evil in the world, even if *some* religious disagreement and *some* evil can be seen to serve a divine purpose. One important result of the chapter is our increased – if still limited – understanding of the significance of elusiveness in evidence of divine reality available to humans.

Overall, then, this book invites us to inquire about God's existence in a new way that involves us morally and existentially as inquirers. We might think of ourselves as being under inquiry in our inquiry about God's existence. In doing so, we shall experience a major shift in epistemological questions about God, given that they then become questions that involve us as responsible agents, too. We now can see that the scope of this book differs from that of its predecessor, *The Elusive God*. Whereas the latter booked focused on the basis and details of volitional theism, the present book develops volitional theism against a background that includes critical assessment of prominent competing positions.

1

∾

Nontheistic Naturalism

"I think that sometimes, out of the corner of an eye, 'at the moment which is not of action or inaction', one can glimpse the true scientific vision; austere, tragic, alienated, and very beautiful. A world that isn't *for* anything; a world that is just there."
— Jerry Fodor 1998, p. 169.

Many philosophers, among others, have appealed to the sciences as a basis for challenging either the truth or the rationality of belief that God exists. We shall explore whether this common strategy actually succeeds in its challenge. Jerry Fodor elaborates on "the true scientific vision" in connection with biology, as follows: "All that happens is this: microscopic variations cause macroscopic effects, as an indirect consequence of which sometimes the variants proliferate and sometimes they don't. That's all there is; there's a lot of 'because' out there, but there isn't any 'for'" (1998, p. 168). "The true scientific vision" therefore denies that there is a purposive God or a purposive Mother Nature, or a purposive anything else, for that matter. If we return to the wilderness parable of the Introduction, we would identify "the true scientific vision" as entailing that a purposive rescuer is not part of the true scenario at all, for better or worse. Many would dare to suggest that this is, indeed, for the worse when one is lost deep in a wilderness canyon.

Even so, "the true scientific vision" merits our attention now.

Historically, according to Fodor, ". . . God was dead a century or so before Darwin turned up. . . . But Darwin made it crystal clear that the natural order couldn't care less. It wasn't God that Darwin killed, it was Mother Nature" (1998, p. 186). Accordingly, "the true scientific vision," by Fodor's lights, makes do without God and Mother Nature; indeed, it proceeds without any supernatural or natural purposive "for." It leaves behind purpose of any kind for the sake of uniformly *non*purposive causal explanation of the world. Among twentieth-century philosophers, Bertrand Russell boldly offers such an austere scientific vision in his famous essay, "A Free Man's Worship" (1903), and many philosophers of a materialist persuasion follow suit (see the relevant essays by W.V. Quine, Daniel Dennett, and Paul Churchland in Moser and Trout 1995, or the essays in Parts II, III, and V of Lycan 1999; Chapter 3 returns to the significance of Darwinism for natural theology).

If "the true scientific vision" sets the standard for all of reality, and thus for all genuine knowledge of reality (as many philosophers hold), we have a straightforward challenge to the truth of theism and to any knowledge that theism is true. If "the true scientific vision" also sets the standard for rational belief about reality, it will raise a definite challenge to rational belief that God exists. Specifically, if there are no purposes, then there is no purposive God and hence no God (as worthy of worship) at all. In that case, there will be no genuine knowledge that God exists, even if many people (for whatever reasons) mistakenly believe that God exists. Rational belief that God exists will also face serious trouble in the final analysis.

This chapter explores and undermines the challenge of "the true scientific vision" to belief that God exists. It does so in connection with certain disputed questions about the reality of purposes and of purposive – that is, intentional – explanations.

1. SCIENCE AND PURPOSE

One can argue plausibly that the natural sciences do, indeed, leave behind explanatory talk of purposes and acknowledge only nonpurposive causes and explanations. If we consider explanations in physics, for example, we find only non-purposive explanations of various sorts. Some such explanations are nonprobabilistic (say, in Newtonian kinematics), and others are probabilistic (say, in quantum statistical mechanics), but all such explanations are free of reference to purposes and thus to purposive agents. The same holds for chemistry, geology, and biochemistry, among other natural sciences. We find no explanations in these quarters of this form: "An agent purports, aims, or intends to bring about X." That form of purposive, or intentional, explanation would take us to the domain of the *social* sciences or the domain of commonsense explanation, beyond the domain of the natural sciences proper.

Someone might propose biology as an exception in the natural sciences that involves genuine purpose, given its use of some important language ("selection," "function") that seems purposive. Such biological language as "selection" and "function," however, is not intended in its strict use to signify actual purposes, goals, or intentions at work in biological explanation. Any appearance to the contrary is nothing more than a mere "manner of speaking," that is, rough shorthand for strict talk of something nonpurposive. Mother Nature is, in fact, no intentional Mother at all in the official explanations offered by biology. More generally, a key assumption of the natural sciences, if only methodologically, is that those sciences are explaining not the actions of purposive agents but, instead, events and processes (rather than intentional actions) resulting from nonpurposive causes, at least proximally if not distally or ultimately. (On the conditions for intentional actions in general, see Mele and Moser 1994; cf. Moser 1993, Chapter 5.)

One might add that the natural sciences seek only non-purposive causes and explanations *given the adopted purposes of the natural sciences*, that is, as a result of what these sciences aim to accomplish. This, however, would raise two immediate questions. First, do the natural sciences seek only nonpurposive causes and explanation *just* as a unified methodological strategy and thus merely as a *practical expedient* for natural scientific explanation? Or are the natural sciences instead committed to a theory of what exists (an ontology) that, in virtue of being "natural," excludes irreducible intentional actions and purposive agents? Many (but not all) scientists will answer no to the latter question and yes to the former on the ground that the natural sciences do not, by themselves, exclude the existence of God and all other purposive agents. The natural sciences, according to these scientists, are logically compatible with the existence of God and other purposive agents, although these sciences, *by practical or methodological expedient*, do not rely on explanations that refer to God or to any other irreducible purposive agent.

If the natural sciences were actually committed to an ontology that excludes purposive agents altogether (and thus God, too), we could properly demand adequate evidence to justify this bold exclusion. Such a demand, of course, would yield a difficult task for the natural sciences, or at least a task not yet fulfilled on the basis of the needed evidence. The dominant testimony of scientists themselves supports this unsurprising observation. Even so, many writers uncritically assume the bold exclusion in question.

The second immediate question concerns the aforementioned talk of the adopted *purposes* of the natural sciences, or of what the natural sciences *seek*. Such talk seems irredeemably intentional, goal-directed, and purposive, and therefore at odds with an attempt to rid the natural sciences of anything purposive in their explanations. If we attribute specific purposes to the natural sciences in connection with their explanatory *aims*, then we cannot consistently portray the natural sciences as being completely free of all purposes. As a result, it may seem that the relevant talk of purposes will have to be shorthand for something nonpurposive, if the natural sciences are to be free of purposes.

It is difficult to identify the needed replacement (long-hand) language, because purposes seem not to have any close cousins that can readily stand in as nonpurposive substitutes. Specifically, we have no obvious nonpurposive replacements that function (if only in our explanations) in the ways purposes do, particularly in setting *goals* for inquiry. Even so, any claim that talk of purposes is just short-hand will readily invite the question of what this shorthand is actually shorthand *for*, and the answer will need to steer clear of purposive scientific explainers. This need remains to be met, and an appropriate strategy for success (nonpur-posively understood, of course) is less than clear.

If we were to drop talk of purposes altogether, we would need (in the scenario at hand) a means of limiting the scope of the natural sciences to nonpurposive phenomena without involving talk of the "purposes" or "aims" of the natural sciences. This would seem to take us back to a disputable ontological claim that excludes God and all other irreducible purposive agents from the domain of what is real. In that case, however, we evidently move from the frying pan to the fire. It is, after all, no small task to exclude irreducible purposive agents from the domain of what is real. Clearly, it is not a lesson of the sciences, explicitly or implicitly, that this exclusion has been accomplished. In fact, the needed supporting evidence for such an exclusion seems not to be forthcoming, after all.

One might try to avoid both the frying pan and the fire by distinguishing between the purposes of natural *scientists* and the features of natural scientific *explanations*. The general idea is just this: natural scientific explanations are char-acteristically free of purposive language and commitments, given the aim of natural scientists *qua* natural scientists to avoid purposive language and commitments in their natural scientific explanations. This idea may seem promising, at least until we ask how the scope of natural scientific explanations is related to the (evidently intentional) conduct of natural scientists themselves. After all, natural scientists, among many others, do seem to *aim for* good explanations of various phenomena. In addition, given the evident intentional phenomena involved in humans (intentionally) explaining certain phenomena and in other seemingly purposive human activity, we seem to be left with an irreducible dualism in kinds of explanation: purposive explanations and nonpurposive explanations. This dualism suggests that the natural sciences fail to supply *the* true scientific vision, even if they supply an important *part* of the true vision. The reality of the remaining part(s) of the vision, including the social sciences where intentional explanation flourishes, will challenge any alleged explanatory monopoly by nonpurposive natural science.

If "the true scientific vision" feels like a liberating epiphany to some theorists (Fodor calls it "very beautiful," whereas Russell calls it "alien and inhuman"), the social sciences appear to throw cold water on the (nonintentional) party, even without apologies. Psychology and sociology, for instance, are up to their necks – even up to their very minds – in purposive language and explanations. If we take away desires, intentions, and decisions, we thereby undermine intentional explanation and take away the social sciences as we know them, including psychology and sociology. Suddenly, our domain of explanation would become very limited, and the resulting limitation would seem arbitrary at best.

Psychology without intentional action collapses into physiology and neurology (and perhaps related natural sciences); likewise for sociology. Intentional explanation then loses its footing, and in that case, psychology and sociology will have to forgo their distinctive mode of explanation via intentions and desires. If this were to take place, we might say that the social sciences (as well as everyday explanations) have been sacrificed to the natural sciences, even though the exact "purpose" of the sacrifice is unclear or at least not compelling. Perhaps an excessive standard of ontological or methodological "simplicity" is at work, a standard that ultimately runs roughshod over actual data needing explanation. In any case, the main casualty will then be intentional explanation, including the explanatory role of irreducible intentional agents. We therefore should briefly explore the significance of intentional – that is, purposive – explanation.

2. PURPOSIVE EXPLANATION

Let's think of an *explanatory strategy* as just a mode of explanation – that is, a mode of answering certain explanation-seeking questions that typically include certain why-questions, how-questions, or what-questions. A well-defined explanatory strategy, like any well-defined "strategy," must include certain specified ends and certain necessary conditions for appropriately achieving those ends. The phenomena selected as needing explanation may be description-dependent (say, certain parts of language) or description-independent (say, certain features of the world independent of humans). Neither option challenges the relevance of the aforementioned ingredients of a well-defined explanatory strategy. Whatever explanatory goals and necessary conditions are adopted, a theorist must accept a semantically significant (or an interpreted) vocabulary – a *conceptual apparatus* – for formulating those goals and necessary conditions. This conceptual apparatus also plays a crucial role in formulating acceptable explanatory hypotheses in accordance with an explanatory strategy.

A conceptual apparatus yields a domain of discourse pertinent to an explanatory strategy. It consists of an acceptable vocabulary that can underwrite standards for the kinds of vocabulary pertinent to an explanatory strategy. Lacking such a conceptual apparatus, an explanatory strategy could proceed with virtually *any* vocabulary, however arbitrary, disparate, and disjoint. It could explain, for example, the same phenomena by employing vocabulary from quantum theory, ancient Babylonian theology, Freudian psychology, and voodooism – perhaps even all in one convoluted explanation with unmatched disunity. Well-defined explanatory strategies, however, seek a kind of *explanatory unity* that disallows such an "anything goes" convoluted approach to explanation. (On unification as a fundamental goal of scientific explanation, see Friedman 1974 and Kitcher 1981, 1989.)

The general explanatory strategy in the natural sciences – for example, physics, chemistry, geology, and biology – is relatively well defined, although not algorithmic. It includes, at any given time, a conceptual apparatus and a set of necessary conditions that exclude an "anything goes" approach to explanation. It excludes, for example, natural-scientific explanation of physical phenomena by voodooism and ancient Babylonian theology, and this explains why scientific publications such as *Science* and *Scientific American* are free of voodooism and ancient Babylonian theology. Such publications, in addition, would not regard this omission as an explanatory deficiency at all.

An explanatory strategy is individuated, or singled out, by its conceptual apparatus and necessary conditions. Accordingly, if we make sufficient changes in its conceptual apparatus or necessary conditions, we thereby change the explanatory strategy. The natural sciences, on this approach to individuation, represent one general explanatory strategy, whereas intentional, or purposive, explanation represents another. (We shall continue to use talk of "intentional" explanation and talk of "purposive" explanation interchangeably.) The intentional vocabulary of purposive explanation – with its talk of beliefs, desires, intentions, purposes, and goals – is significantly different from the vocabulary of the natural sciences. Given their general explanatory strategy, the natural sciences will not settle for explanation in such purposive vocabulary. This is part of what makes them *natural* sciences (rather than, say, *social* sciences), and this holds true even if natural scientific explanation does not enjoy strict causal laws (throughout), but settles instead for statistical laws (in at least some areas).

Events needing explanation can be identified, of course, in ways neutral between differing explanatory strategies, sometimes with just the neutral demonstratives "this" and "that." Such neutral identifications typically are rather uninformative, but they can still be helpful in a quest for explanation. They can enable us to speak intelligibly of two different explanatory strategies bearing, at least potentially, on the same phenomena – for example, phenomena described by a psychologist in purposive terms as "my intentionally calling my Cavalier King Charles spaniel." In particular, we can speak topic-neutrally of certain events occurring at a certain time that are explainable, at least in principle, by both a natural-scientific strategy and an intentional strategy. We need not assume that the competing explanations are equally good or correct in such a case.

Can a natural-scientific explanatory strategy and an intentional explanatory strategy, if they are truly independent of each other, individually fully explain the same phenomena? If, following Donald Davidson (1963), we take intentional explanation to include a causal component (say, because mental events, such as decisions, sometimes have a causal role in explanation), then we must confront an apparent problem. Jaegwon Kim contends that "two or more complete and independent [causal] explanations of the same event or phenomenon cannot coexist" (1989, p. 89).

Kim's "simple argument for explanatory exclusion for causal explanations" runs as follows:

Suppose that [causes] C and C* are invoked as each giving a complete explanation of [an event] E. Consider the two questions: (1) Would E have occurred if C had not occurred? and (2) Would E have occurred if C* had not occurred? If the answer is a "yes" to both questions, this is a classic case of overdetermination, and . . . we can treat this case as one in which either explanation taken alone is incomplete, or else exempt all overdeterminative cases from the requirement of explanatory exclusion. If the answer is a "no" to at least one of the questions, say the first, that must be because if C had not occurred, C* would not have either. And this means that . . . the two explanations are not independent explanations of E (1989, p. 92).

As a first response, we should hesitate to treat cases of causal overdetermination automatically as cases of incompleteness in the individual explanations (for relevant discussion, see Marras 1998). The relation between the two kinds of cases is more complicated than this.

Let E be some event or set of events described topic-neutrally – for example, "this event occurring right now." For instance, we might let E represent the events described topic-neutrally that a psychologist would describe in purposive language as "my intentionally calling my barking spaniel." Let C be an intention-based causal explainer of E from an intentional strategy – an explanation in terms of my beliefs, desires, and intentions, including my aim to bring my barking spaniel from outside into the house, in order to give my stressed neighbors some needed relief. Further, let C* be a physical causal explainer of E from a natural-scientific strategy – say, an explainer in neurophysiological terms that does not appeal to my beliefs, desires, or intentions. Let's suppose also that we have no definitional or nomological (law-based) reduction between C's being an explainer of E and C*'s being an explainer of E. In this respect, we have independent explainers. The issue at hand is whether these two explainers, if complete, are possible at the same time.

If we accept both an intentional strategy and a natural-scientific strategy to explain E, we should answer yes to Kim's questions (1) and (2). We then have, from the standpoint of the two accepted strategies, a case of causal and explanatory overdetermination. Kim (1989, p. 91) evidently holds that any explanation that would fail to mention either of the two causes in such a case of overdetermination would fail to give the complete causal picture, and therefore would be an incomplete explanation. Accordingly, Kim suggests that neither the intentional strategy nor the natural-scientific strategy would offer a complete explanation in such a case.

Kim's approach to explanation apparently allows us to maintain both an intentional explanatory strategy and a natural-scientific explanatory strategy toward certain events (if neutrally described). The price paid in such cases is that neither strategy will be complete in Kim's preferred sense of "complete." This, however, is a small price, if it is a price at all. The lack of completeness for each accepted strategy will only be relative to the applicability of a different explanatory strategy accepted by us. Such *relative* lack of completeness takes nothing away from an individual explanatory strategy considered from its own standpoint and its own correctness. Rather, it indicates simply that different explanatory strategies are accepted by us and are applicable to the same phenomena needing explanation. This is no theoretical defect for an explanatory strategy. It is simply an indication that a theorist can use different accepted explanatory strategies for the same phenomena (described topic-neutrally).

Kim's concern is this: "Two explanations of one event create a certain epistemic tension, a tension that is dissipated only when we have an account of how they, or the two causes they indicate, are related to each other" (1989, p. 92). Our two explanatory strategies for E relate to each other as follows: they differ by way of conceptual apparatus, wielding irreducibly different vocabularies, and therefore they are conceptually independent of each other. In addition, they are not complete for us in Kim's sense of "complete," because they both are accepted by us and apply to the same phenomena described topic-neutrally. That is, they answer explanation-seeking questions about the same phenomena described topic-neutrally. On my construal of Kim's standards for avoiding epistemic tension, these considerations save us from explanatory exclusion by removing the epistemic tension. These considerations, furthermore, do not block the possibility of our establishing empirical correlations between events as intentionally described and events as (purely) physically described.

Kim applies his standards for explanatory exclusion in a very different manner. For example, he writes:

The explanatory exclusion principle provides a simple explanation of why the two theories [of "vernacular psychology" and "neuroscience"] ... compete against each other and why their peaceful coexistence is an illusion. For vernacular psychology and neuroscience each claim to provide explanations for the same domain of phenomena, and because of the failure of reduction in either domain, the purported explanations must be considered independent. Hence, by the exclusion principle, one of them has to go (1989, p. 101).

Kim adds, by way of a proposed reconciliation, that the way to save vernacular psychology is to focus only on its normative role in evaluating actions, and to stop regarding it as a competitor to neuroscience that generates law-based causal explanations and predictions (1989, p. 106). This proposal, however, seems to rob intentional explanation in psychology of its genuine explanatory value and to relegate it to a domain of evaluation without explanation. Some theorists offer an analogous proposal for religion and natural science: specifically, let religion be a matter of ethics but not of factual reality, and let the sciences handle factual reality (see, for instance, Gould 1999; for misgivings, see Dennett 2006, p. 30, and Dawkins 2006, pp. 55–8).

Kim's position on explanatory exclusion is less than compelling at best. His argument just quoted is invalid by his own standards. Explanatory independence is *not* sufficient, but is only necessary, for explanatory exclusion. Explanatory completeness, on Kim's account, is also necessary for explanatory exclusion, but his argument neglects this decisive consideration. Kim, moreover, has provided no reason to assume that vernacular psychology and neuroscience are complete in the relevant sense. Many of us accept vernacular psychology and neuroscience as explanatory strategies for the same phenomena, neutrally described. We therefore plausibly can, and would, answer yes to Kim's aforementioned questions (1) and (2) concerning causal overdetermination. We plausibly can deny, then, that vernacular psychology and neuroscience are complete in the relevant sense proposed by Kim.

A denial of completeness for vernacular psychology and neuroscience gains plausibility once we acknowledge a certain kind of relativity in the "completeness" of an explanation. Neither vernacular psychology nor neuroscience is complete in the relevant sense, if we accept an explanatory strategy relative to which each of those explanatory approaches leaves some explanation-seeking questions unanswered. Vernacular psychology raises certain explanation-seeking questions (for example, concerning beliefs, desires, and intentions) that are not raised or answered at all by neuroscience. More to the point, neuroscience does not offer any explanations in the language of beliefs, desires, and intentions. No one should be inclined to deny this empirical fact.

Clearly, neuroscience raises certain explanation-seeking questions (for example, concerning neuronal/synaptic functioning and other neurophysiological factors) that are not treated by vernacular psychology. For better or worse, vernacular psychology does not operate in the language of neuroscience, and this is an unsurprising empirical fact. If, for example, we seek an explanation in neuroscientific terms of the neuronal/synaptic functioning in my brain while I intentionally call my spaniel into the house, vernacular psychology will not serve our purpose at all. We then will need to look elsewhere. Still, it does not follow that vernacular psychology has to do only with "normative" considerations in "evaluating actions," and not with factual reality. Such an inference clearly would be invalid.

As for Kim's proposed reconciliation, we should hesitate to relinquish vernacular psychology as a basis for predictions and causal explanations. Perhaps, at bottom, Kim fears a kind of causal dualism in which both mental causes and physical causes are (acknowledged as) genuine. Even so, there is nothing inherently wrong with causal dualism, and such dualism is, in fact, cognitively reasonable if it earns its keep by its unmatched explanatory power relative to the whole range of our experience and evidence. In particular, many (if not all) of us have found considerable success in using vernacular psychology to predict various occurrences and to give causal explanations of various phenomena.

Let's consider a specific case involving the following events needing explanation.

(a) At 9:00 A.M. every Monday between September 1 and December 1, at least a dozen university graduate students and I converge on Room 334 of Crown Center of Loyola University Chicago.

(b) The students carry with them copies of some recent books on the philosophy of religion, the psychology of religion, and epistemology.

(c) From 9:00–11:30 A.M., the students and I utter sentences employing vocabulary from the philosophy of religion, epistemology, vernacular psychology, and neuroscience.

(d) At 11:30 A.M., the students and I depart from Room 334 of Crown Center.

We can describe these events in terms that are more obviously topic-neutral; this would not affect the point at issue.

As it happens, we are able to explain and to predict such events as (a)–(d) *only* by relying on an intentional, or purposive, explanatory strategy. Neither neuroscience nor natural science in general is up to the job, and one can give only a questionable promissory note that this inadequacy will change in the future. In particular, I now must rely on an explanation in terms of the beliefs, desires, decisions, and intentions of my students and myself. My students desire (and intend) to earn a university graduate degree, and I desire (and intend) to help by providing some of the academic means. My students and I believe that by meeting at the specified time to discuss the psychology and epistemology of religious belief, we can contribute to their fulfilling the degree requirements. So far, then, the relevant explanatory factors are highly intentional, and have little, if anything, to do with neuroscience or natural science.

My students and I have decided (that is, have settled on the plan) that we will contribute to fulfilling their degree requirements by, among other things, meeting at the specified time to discuss the psychology and epistemology of religious belief. We have not made any conflicting decisions that override or otherwise challenge the former decision. As a result of such factors, according to an intentional explanation in terms of the beliefs, desires, decisions, and intentions of my students, events (a)–(d) occur. Without such an intentional explanation, we would be at a loss to account for events (a)–(d), and abstract worries about a threat from causal dualism should not be allowed to obscure this fact.

Our intentional explanation of events (a)–(d) attributes causal efficacy to such familiar intentional phenomena as believing, desiring, deciding, and intending. It appeals to such causally relevant phenomena to explain and even to predict the occurrence of certain ordinary events represented by (a)–(d). Such causal intentional phenomena now play an indispensable role for us in explaining and predicting the events in question. We have no replacement explainers at hand, or even a sketch of replacement explainers. This is a fact partly about us as agents who formulate explanations, of course, but it is nonetheless a fact of the matter, at least so far as we know.

We have no reason to suggest that physicalists (or naturalists) and intentionalists should always agree in their explanations and predictions. Rather, the point is that *intentional* explanation and prediction sometimes are our only available means of explaining and predicting certain occurrences. It is very doubtful, as just suggested, that anyone could explain or predict the events represented by (a)–(d) solely on the basis of contemporary natural science, including neuroscience. Kim's proposal for reconciliation therefore would have us relinquish our best available explanation and predictive basis of the events in question. This is a proposal with an obvious explanatory loss and no corresponding benefit. Accordingly, we should decline this proposal. (For additional support for the genuine explanatory value of intentional psychology, see Horgan and Woodward 1985.)

Suppose that we accept that neuroscience can (at least in principle) explain the events represented by (a)–(d), if described topic-neutrally, and that its explanations are altogether nonintentional. In that case, neither neuroscience nor vernacular psychology would be complete for us in Kim's sense of "complete." This consideration, however, takes nothing away from the explanatory value of either strategy. It simply indicates that we accept different explanatory strategies applicable to a certain set of phenomena needing explanation. My suggested approach to explanatory completeness, as noted previously, acknowledges a certain kind of relativity to the explanatory strategies accepted by a theorist or group of theorists.

A theorist who rejects intentional explanatory strategies might accept only a natural-scientific explanatory strategy, and no alternative explanatory strategy. Such an eliminative naturalist would have a difficult time explaining many macro-aspects of our daily lives, including what appear to be our intentional actions aimed at certain goals. For instance, explaining the aforementioned events (a)–(d) under the descriptions offered would become a serious problem. In addition, in such eliminative naturalism, theology in general would go by the board as something without a genuine grip on reality. Even so, the natural-scientific strategy would be complete, at least in principle, *for the eliminative naturalist* who accepts no alternative explanatory strategy. Kim's alternative understanding of explanatory completeness seems not to acknowledge such relativity, but in this regard it is obscure on the exact conditions for completeness.

If we relinquish intentional explanation altogether, three options remain for the social sciences, given their acknowledgment of intentional actions (for supporters of each option, see Moser and Trout 1995). First, one might try to *reduce* the social sciences to the natural sciences by showing that explanations in the social sciences are ultimately (that is, in what they genuinely contribute) just explanations in the natural sciences. This option is now widely acknowledged as hopeless, although a few wishful philosophers and scientists have tried to keep the pipe dream alive. At least, no one has shown how intentional explanation (say, in sociology or in psychology) can be adequately captured by nonintentional explanation (say, in biology or in chemistry). In particular, no one has shown how familiar explanatory talk of intentions (or of intentional, purposive agents) reduces, without semantic loss, to talk of something nonintentional.

On the second option, a theorist proposes that we simply *eliminate* intentional explanations as irretrievably false, without bothering to seek a reduction to nonintentional explanations. This option is highly controversial, however, because no one has shown that intentional explanations and therefore the corresponding social sciences are irretrievably false (in their acknowledging intentional actions or intentional agents). Indeed, barring a fear of causal dualism, one must wonder what would motivate one to "want" to eliminate intentional explanations. In any case, even eliminative naturalists seem to have their (intentional) wants, given their desired and promoted strategies for explanation.

The third option proposes that we continue to use intentional explanations when convenient but acknowledge that they are *just* a useful *manner of speaking* that is, strictly speaking, false. Such pragmatism about intentional explanation (which is at least suggested by Kim's proposed reconciliation) may seem helpful at first glance, but it faces two serious problems. As suggested previously, one problem is that no one has offered a defensible case that intentional explanations and the corresponding social sciences are, strictly speaking, false. In addition, such a case does not seem to be available to us, given the evident reality of purposive phenomena. The other problem is that we inquirers naturally want to explain *why* intentional explanations are actually useful, when they are useful. Are they useful, at least in part, because they portray something *real* – namely, intentional agents, attitudes, and actions? An affirmative answer is arguably a live option in the social sciences and in everyday intentional explanation. In any case, we do well to separate two variations on naturalism that bear on intentional explanation: ontological naturalism and methodological naturalism. Let's briefly explore these two variations.

3. ONTOLOGICAL NATURALISM

Ontological naturalism comes in many different forms, but the variations share the following thesis that may be called *core ontological naturalism:* every real entity consists of, or at least owes its existence to, the objects acknowledged by what would be the completed empirical sciences. We may think of the latter objects as the objects of a *natural* ontology. Ontological naturalism is a general position about what actually exists, and therefore is a metaphysical view. It is directly neither an epistemological view about how we know something nor a semantic view about the meaning of terms. Instead, it directly concerns how things actually are, and therefore is, properly speaking, ontological. (I use the terms "ontological" and "metaphysical" interchangeably.)

Ontological naturalists typically (but not always) endorse some kind of materialism, or physicalism, about real things. In that endorsement, they hold that the completed empirical sciences will support materialism. One influential understanding of "material" (or "physical") is that something is material (or physical) if and only if it is extended in space. Given this understanding, *strict materialism* is the view that everything that actually exists is extended in space, and therefore nothing nonspatial exists. *Loose materialism*, in contrast, is the view that all *particular* things that exist are extended in space, but this view allows for the existence of nonspatial universals (which are not *particular* things, strictly speaking), such as abstract properties and mathematical sets. Still, strict materialism and loose materialism (even taken individually) entail that God, characterized as a nonspatial spirit who is not a universal, does not exist.

The aforementioned general portrayals of strict and loose materialism seem straightforward, but the relevant notion of *spatial extension* evidently depends on the very notion of "material" that is in need of clarification. In other words, the notion of spatial extension seems to involve the notion of physical, or material, space. If that is so, conceptual circularity will threaten the suggested characterization of materialism. We cannot truly clarify our talk of "material" with more talk of "material." Something else is needed. (We are, as suggested, using the terms "material" and "physical" interchangeably.)

The problem at hand is that the notion of spatial extension is actually the notion of something's being extended in *physical* space, or being *physically* extended. We can coherently conceive that something (say, a personal spirit) has *temporal* extension, in virtue of extending over time, even though that thing is not extended at all in physical space. In other words, we face no self-contradiction in holding that something is temporally extended but is not a physical thing. The proposed characterization of materialism needs revision, then, to talk of *physical* space or *physical* extension. In that case, however, a problem of conceptual circularity threatens. Even if there is no strict circularity here, the notion of being extended in physical space seems too close, semantically, to the notion of being material to offer genuine illumination. Minimally, we need some clarification of the talk of spatial extension, if such talk is to clarify our understanding of what is material. We now can leave that project, however, as homework for materialists.

A second prominent construal of "material," in keeping with the ultimate base acknowledged by naturalism, invokes the empirical sciences as a source of clarification. The general idea is that the language of the (hypothetically completed) empirical sciences determines what it is to be material, or physical. On this view, a predicate such as "is an electron" signifies a physical item if and only if the empirical sciences, in their hypothetically completed form, rely on that predicate in their descriptive and explanatory formulations. This strategy may seem promising at the start for naturalists, because it lets the empirical sciences themselves ultimately clarify what it is to be physical.

Three difficulties are noteworthy. First, the empirical sciences currently lack an exhaustive list of truths about the physical world and therefore are definitely incomplete. In addition, it is not clear that they will ever have such an exhaustive list, given the tremendous complexity of the physical world. Such incompleteness allows for there being predicates that the empirical sciences do not rely on, but that nonetheless pick out something real in the physical world. It is questionable, then, whether the empirical sciences have a monopoly on predicates signifying real physical items. Second, the empirical sciences use mathematical and logical predicates that evidently do not signify physical items at all. For example, the predicate "is a member of a (mathematical) set" does not signify a physical item, according to standard mathematical interpretations. Third, invoking "the empirical sciences" raises the problem of specifying exactly when something is an "empirical" science. Such specifying would be no small task, given (a) the actuality of such theoretical empirical sciences as cosmology and particle physics that rely on highly theoretical entities, and (b) the inclusion of the social sciences, including their intentional vocabulary and explanations, in the empirical sciences. In any case, it would not help now to portray an empirical science as a discipline that investigates, in a special way, only the *material*, or *physical*, world, because we are seeking an elucidation of the relevant notion of being material (or physical).

The exact conditions for what it is to be material, or physical, resist easy specification, and the same holds for the category of being empirical. Is social psychology, for example, an empirical science? Social psychologists, as previously suggested, often use intentional vocabulary (for example, talk of beliefs, desires, intentions, fears, and hopes) that does not obviously signify (just) material things. As a result, we would need clarification of the sense in which social psychology is "materialist," if it is an empirical science in the relevant sense. In general, ontological naturalists who base their materialism on the empirical sciences would do well to characterize what it is to be an empirical science without relying on talk of what is material or physical. This would save them from a clear threat of conceptual circularity. (For other difficulties in giving an adequate characterization of materialism, see Crane and Mellor 1990, and their follow-up contribution in Moser and Trout 1995, pp. 85–9.)

Ontological naturalists who are materialists oppose various forms of ontological pluralism, including ontological dualism – the view that there are two irreducible kinds of things that actually exist. A very influential kind of ontological substance dualism, stemming from René Descartes, affirms that there are mental substances (particularly, thinking and willing individuals) as well as physical substances (particularly, material substances), and that mental substances do not depend for their existence on physical substances. Proponents of such Cartesian dualism must specify, among other things, the sense in which mental substances do not *depend* for their existence on physical substances. They typically allow for relations of *causal* dependence between mental substances and material substances, but they deny that mental substances are part of the ontological realm of material substances. According to Cartesians, a mental substance is different in ontological kind from a material substance. If there is a coherently conceivable ontological distinction between minds and material bodies, then materialism, understood as entailing mind–body identity, is not conceptually, or analytically, true – that is, true just in virtue of the meanings of the terms "mind" and "material body."

An inference from a coherently conceivable ontological distinction between minds and material bodies to an actual ontological distinction between minds and material bodies *in reality* creates trouble. The latter actual distinction entails that actual minds are not material bodies. Such an actual ontological distinction goes beyond a distinction between kinds, concepts, or definitions; it entails a difference between actual particular *things*. The inference in question would need to accommodate this fact.

Even if it is not conceptually (or otherwise necessarily) true that minds and material bodies are identical, according to many philosophers, it may still be *contingently* true (and thus possibly false) that minds are material bodies. According to these philosophers, an identity relation between minds and material bodies may hold as an actual matter of fact even if it does not obtain as a matter of kind, concept, definition, or necessity. Other philosophers deny that the notion of contingent identity is coherent, and accept an inference from the coherent conceivability of an ontological mind–body distinction to an ontologically real distinction between minds and bodies. We need not endorse either position here. According to most contemporary materialists, the coherent conceivability of the falsity of materialism does not challenge the actual *contingent* truth of materialism about minds. The contingent truth of such materialism, according to most contemporary materialists, is truth enough.

Ontological naturalists who are materialists reject Cartesian ontological dualism, particularly its implication that a human mind consists of a nonphysical substance different in kind from material bodies. They also reject the Cartesian view that some mental properties are actually exemplified by certain *nonphysical things* – that is, things not extended in physical space. Materialists are uniformly *monistic* in their views that all actually existing individuals are material, and that the only things that exemplify mental (or psychological) properties are material things. These two fundamental materialist views, according to most contemporary materialists, are contingently true and justifiable empirically, not *a priori*. These materialists acknowledge that the evidence for these two views must come from factors dependent on human experience. They hold, accordingly, that neither reason nor definition alone can produce the needed evidence.

We should contrast the following two contrary options about the relation between ontological naturalism and materialism: (a) ontological naturalism is logically neutral regarding materialism and therefore is logically compatible with ontological dualism, and (b) ontological naturalism logically entails materialism and therefore is logically incompatible with ontological dualism. Given option (a), a defense of materialism on the basis of ontological naturalism should appeal to supporting evidence beyond naturalism, and that evidence presumably would be independent empirical evidence. Given option (b), an appeal to ontological naturalism in defense of materialism would need to be an appeal to something irreducible to materialism, because materialism would then be a logical prerequisite of ontological naturalism. An appeal to materialism to support materialism would convince no one. Many, if not most, contemporary ontological naturalists prefer option (a) over option (b).

W. V. Quine has opposed option (b) as follows:

> ... nowadays the overwhelming purposes of the science game are technology and understanding.... The science game is not committed to the physical, whatever that means.... Even

telepathy and clairvoyance are scientific options, however moribund. It would take some extraordinary evidence to enliven them, but, if that were to happen, then empiricism itself – the crowning norm... of naturalized epistemology – would go by the board. For remember that that norm, and naturalized epistemology itself, are integral to science, and science is fallible and corrigible (1990, pp. 20–1).

Quine suggests that naturalism anchored in science is *not* logically committed to physicalism (or materialism) or even to empiricism. Quine's use of "science" here is definitely not restricted to *empirical* science in the usual sense, because it allows that empiricism could "go by the board" in science as the result of our discovering extraordinary evidence of parapsychological phenomena. He does not regard such potential extraordinary evidence as entailing our moving either outside of science or against science. Instead, he finds such potential evidence compatible with science as a fallible (or error-capable) pursuit of human understanding on the basis of evidence.

Naturalists of Quine's persuasion endorse fallibilism about science (owing to its error-capability) with good reason, given the enormous shifts in the scientific understanding of reality that have occurred early and late in the history of science. A commitment to absolute space as the basis for material reality led many theorists, at least in earlier times, to oppose theories of space–time relativity. Likewise, an *a priori* commitment about the materialist or the empiricist nature of science could bring naturalists directly into conflict with the best contemporary science humans have to offer if science develops in certain novel nonmaterialist directions. As just noted, accordingly, Quine's own avowed constraints on the ontology of the sciences permit (under certain extraordinary conditions) the acknowledgment of parapsychological processes as being scientific, and Quine's constraints on scientific methodology permit (again, under certain extraordinary conditions) the rejection of empiricism. The sciences, as portrayed by Quine, permit (under certain extraordinary conditions) even *non*empirical methodologies to ground belief in *non*physical things or processes. Quine, then, is no monolithic ideologue for empiricism or materialism.

It is now unclear how the nonempirical methods employed in traditional metaphysics, including the metaphysics of God, can be ruled out by Quine's liberal naturalism, as long as those nonempirical methods are fallible and yield human understanding. If the sciences are the fallible pursuit of human understanding, and there is no requirement that the objects of such understanding fall within the range of empirical experience, then there is no requirement that the scientific pursuit of human understanding must be fully delimited by empiricism. The scientific pursuit can then include even fallible theology that advances human understanding. This will come as an odd result, at best, for many naturalists. Even so, it is a (seldom noted) result of Quine's liberal naturalism as just summarized. Perhaps theology does not yield technology, but the same is true of much widely accepted empirical science. It is arguable, however, that some theology yields fallible human understanding and, in that respect, is akin to the sciences.

The odd result for naturalists of Quine's persuasion stems from their reliance, particularly in opposing traditional metaphysics, on their portrayal of science as pretty much any "fallible and corrigible" pursuit of understanding. Specifically, they offer no reason to think that science, as merely a fallible pursuit of understanding, must exclude fallible metaphysics, even the fallible metaphysics of God. Contrary to Quine's liberal naturalism, then, many philosophers anchor naturalism in *empirical* science rather than just in the fallible and corrigible pursuit of understanding. This is in keeping with the fact that naturalists typically limit good scientific explanation to *empirically oriented* explanation, and thereby intend to exclude theology from science.

Without digressing to the complex task of supplying a precise account of "empirically oriented" explanation, let's construe "empirical science" broadly to encompass any scientific discipline housed in a typical college of natural or social sciences. Accordingly, astronomy is in, and astrology out; psychology is in, and parapsychology out. Anthropology is in, but philosophy and theology are out, given their customary place in the humanities or the arts, as a result of their being insufficiently empirical to be empirical sciences. Our criterion is rough, of course, but it enables us to take some definite steps.

Ontological naturalism comes in *eliminative*, *reductive*, and *nonreductive* forms, as follows:

(i) *Eliminative ontological naturalism*: every real entity is included in the ontology of the hypothetically completed empirical sciences, and any language independent of those sciences is eliminable from discourse without any cognitive loss.

(ii) *Noneliminative reductive ontological naturalism*: every real entity either is included in the ontology of the hypothetically completed empirical sciences or is reducible to something included in that ontology.

(iii) *Noneliminative nonreductive ontological naturalism*: every real entity either (a) is included in the ontology of the hypothetically completed empirical sciences, (b) is reducible to something included in that ontology, or (c) supervenes, without reduction, on entities that fall under (a) or (b).

The relevant talk of *supervenience* in (iii) has received many technical analyses from philosophers (see, for instance, the essays in Savellos and Yalçin 1995), but the key idea in the present context is that some features of the world are nonreductively based on certain objects of the empirical sciences. Perhaps the fluidity of water is supervenient in this manner, and perhaps mental events are, too. If we bracket discussion of abstract entities, such as mathematical sets, proponents of (i) have included W.V. Quine (1957), Paul Churchland (1979), and Daniel Dennett (1987). J.J.C. Smart (1963) and E.O. Wilson (1987), among others, have represented (ii). Donald Davidson (1970) and David Papineau (1993), among many others, have supported variations on (iii).

Some philosophers favor naturalism for some domains, but hold certain views that are incompatible with positions (i)–(iii). They offer, as one example, a version of naturalism that acknowledges the existence of nonphysical abstract objects (for instance, abstract propositions or mathematical sets) that neither consist of nor are grounded, whether by reduction or by supervenience, in the objects of an ontology of empirical science. Even so, they hold that all "particular" (as opposed to "abstract") things consist of or at least are grounded in the objects of empirical science, and this underwrites their endorsement of naturalism for some domains.

Ontological naturalism invites a straightforward question: why should we hold that empirical science has a monopoly on the ontological basis for real things or even for real "particular" things? Clearly, there is no logically or conceptually *necessary* connection between empirical science and the ontological basis for real things. We can coherently imagine the reality of many things (including such objects as mathematical sets and abstract propositions) that have no apparent ontological basis in the objects of empirical science. As a result, naturalism calls for an answer to the previous question about a monopoly, and that answer should offer a necessary or at least a universal connection between empirical science and the ontological basis for real things. The answer will need to speak to the following issue in particular: given the remarkable diversity of the kinds of real objects, including the real objects experienced by humans, why should we suppose that empirical science offers the *exclusive* ontological basis for those objects? Empirical science would appear, at least at first glance, to offer a rather narrow basis for the wide-ranging set of real things.

If ontological naturalism is true, then God does not exist, because God (if God existed as a nonphysical spirit) would not consist of or be grounded in the objects of empirical science. If traditional monotheism is true, God is an individual personal agent (and not an abstract object) whose existence does not depend on the objects of empirical science. According to such monotheism, the objects of empirical science resulted from divine creation. As a result, if such monotheism is true, there is at least one real thing that does consist of or depend on the objects of empirical science, and hence ontological naturalism is false.

If someone knows that ontological naturalism is true, then that person has the basis for knowledge that traditional monotheism is false. This basis involves the fact that such naturalism logically entails that traditional monotheism is false. After careful attention to the available pertinent evidence, however, I am unaware of anyone's having such a basis, and therefore I find ontological naturalism to be doubtful at best. In any case, a proponent of ontological naturalism must provide adequate cognitive support for such naturalism, and this task is demanding by any standard. The immediate question is this: what kind of actual evidence excludes God's existence in the manner suggested? In particular, what kind of actual evidence from empirical science thus excludes God's existence? It is very difficult to identify candidates for such evidence, even after careful investigation.

Might God not hide from the domain of scientific evidence and even be elusive toward humans for various good purposes? Might God not want to make it clear that God is not a scientific object or any kind of humanly controllable or conveniently predictable object? We can think of various good purposes that could underlie such divine elusiveness (as we shall see in Chapters 3 and 4), and it would be presumptuous at best to suppose that our scientific evidence precludes such purposes or otherwise excludes God's existence. Some philosophers steer clear of ontological naturalism, as a result, and look to a methodological variation on naturalism. Let's briefly consider that variation.

4. METHODOLOGICAL NATURALISM

Going beyond the immediate concern of an ontology of what is real, the term "naturalism" picks out a range of views about the nature of legitimate *inquiry* that are logically independent of ontological naturalism. These views share the following position, which we may call *core methodological naturalism*: every cognitively legitimate (or rational) method of acquiring or revising beliefs consists of or is grounded in the hypothetically completed methods of the empirical sciences (that is, in "natural" methods). This is not ontological naturalism, because claims about the cognitively legitimate *methods* of acquiring or revising beliefs are not the same as claims about what *actually exists*. In agreement with most naturalists, we may understand talk of the "methods of the empirical sciences" broadly, to encompass the kinds of "lay scientific" observation and belief formation that underlie ordinary perceptual beliefs.

Methodological naturalism offers a kind of variety analogous to that of ontological naturalism. We thus may distinguish:

(iv) *Eliminative methodological naturalism*: all terms, including empirically disputed terms (for example, normative and intentional terms), employed in cognitively legitimate methods of acquiring or revising beliefs are replaceable, without cognitive loss, by terms employed in the hypothetically completed methods of the empirical sciences.

(v) *Noneliminative reductive methodological naturalism*: all terms, including empirically disputed terms, employed in cognitively legitimate methods of acquiring or revising beliefs either are replaceable, without cognitive loss, by terms employed in the hypothetically completed methods of the empirical sciences or are reducible (by, for example, either definition or entailment) to terms employed in those methods.

(vi) *Noneliminative reductive-and-nonreductive methodological naturalism:* all terms, including empirically disputed terms, employed in cognitively legitimate methods of acquiring or revising beliefs either (a) are replaceable, without cognitive loss, by terms employed in the hypothetically completed methods of the empirical sciences, (b) are reducible to terms employed in those methods, or (c) are neither replaceable nor reducible in the manner of (a) or (b) but instead have referents that supervene upon those of the terms employed in the hypothetically completed methods of the empirical sciences.

W.V. Quine suggested (iv) in his early work, and Donald Davidson suggested a version of (vi). Perhaps a reductionist such as J.J.C. Smart or E.O. Wilson would endorse (v). The talk of "empirically disputed" terms in (iv)–(vi) connotes terms deemed by some to be insufficiently empirical to figure in the empirical sciences. Normative terms (say, from ethics) and mentalistic terms (say, from psychology) are familiar instances of empirically disputed terms. In (iv)–(vi), the notion of "cognitive" may be taken in the broadest sense, to include knowledge proper (however analyzed in detail), justified belief, and even evidence for a belief. In other words, methodological naturalists claim that the hypothetically completed methods of the empirical sciences define or otherwise ground the only sorts of inquiry that yield knowledge, justified belief, or even evidence for a belief.

Contrary to many textbooks on science, we lack a simple recipe to characterize precisely the methods of the empirical sciences. The actual sciences are methodologically complex by any standard, and their methods do not reduce to recipes. Perhaps the best we can do is to refer to the methods employed in our best physics, chemistry, astronomy, geology, biology, anthropology, psychology, sociology, and so on. The debate will turn, quite naturally, to what exactly is included in "and so on" or in our "best" empirical sciences.

This will lead quickly to complex topics in the philosophy of science, but we need not digress. Our main point is that an accurate understanding of the methods of the sciences is no simple matter.

We may acknowledge that the methods of the empirical sciences, however fallible and whatever specifically they include, are designed to achieve truth rather than falsehood. We also may recognize that the methods of the empirical sciences seek various cognitive virtues, such as fruitful explanation and predictive success, at least in some areas. Even faced with the concerns of skeptics about acquiring truth, we should acknowledge that the methods in question are *intended* to achieve truth, regardless of whether they actually succeed. The turbulent history of the empirical sciences illustrates conclusively that they do not always succeed. That limitation, however, does not preclude intended truth in the methods of the empirical sciences. Characteristically, scientific methods are intended to achieve truth, even when they fail. We may assume, accordingly, that a scientific method is cognitively relevant at least in that it aims for true (rather than false) results on the basis of supporting evidence. Some people evidently hold that the methods of the sciences have a monopoly in this area, but this view, we shall see, faces a serious problem by its own standard, given that it is not, itself, a scientifically justified view. We turn now to a troublesome dilemma for naturalism.

5. A DILEMMA FOR SCIENTISM

Our dilemma will bear on positions (i)–(vi), given that it bears on the aforementioned core statements of naturalism satisfied by those positions, namely:

Core ontological naturalism: every real entity either consists of or at least owes its existence to the objects acknowledged by the hypothetically completed empirical sciences (that is, the objects of a natural ontology).

Core methodological naturalism: every cognitively legitimate method of acquiring or revising beliefs consists of or is grounded in the hypothetically completed methods of the empirical sciences (that is, in natural methods).

These are core statements of ontological and methodological naturalism, and they offer the empirical sciences as the criterion for metaphysical and cognitive genuineness. They entail ontological and methodological *monism* in that they acknowledge the empirical sciences as the *single* standard for genuine metaphysics and cognition. These core positions therefore promise us remarkable explanatory unity in metaphysics and cognition. Still, we must ask: is their promise trustworthy? For brevity, let's call the conjunction of these two positions *Core Scientism*, while allowing for talk of both its distinctive ontological component and its distinctive methodological component.

Core Scientism is *not* itself a thesis offered by any empirical science. In particular, neither its ontological component nor its methodological component is a thesis, directly or indirectly, of an empirical science or a group of empirical sciences. Neither component is endorsed or implied by the empirical scientific work of physics, chemistry, astronomy, geology, biology, anthropology, psychology, sociology, or any other natural or social empirical science or any group thereof. As a result, no research fundable by the National Science Foundation, for instance, offers Core Scientism as a *scientific* thesis. In contrast, the National Endowment for the Humanities would be open to funding certain work centered on Core Scientism, perhaps as part of a project in philosophy, particularly in philosophical metaphysics or epistemology.

Core Scientism proposes a universality of scope for the empirical sciences (see its talk of "every real entity" and "every cognitively legitimate method") that the sciences themselves consistently avoid. Individual sciences are typically distinguished by the particular ranges of empirical data they seek to explain: biological data for biology, anthropological data for anthropology, and so on. Similarly, empirical science as a whole is typically distinguished by its attempt to explain all relevant *empirical* data and, accordingly, by the range of all relevant empirical data. Given this typical constraint on empirical science, we should be surprised indeed if the empirical sciences had anything to say about whether entities *outside* the domain of the empirical sciences (say, in the domain of theology) are nonexistent. At any rate, we should be suspicious in that case.

Sweeping principles about the nature of cognitively legitimate inquiry in general, particularly principles involving entities allegedly outside the domain of the empirical sciences, are not the possession or the product of the empirical sciences themselves. Instead, such principles emerge from philosophy or from some product of philosophy, perhaps even misguided philosophy. Accordingly, Core Scientism is a philosophical thesis, and is not the kind of scientific thesis characteristic of the empirical sciences. The empirical sciences flourish, have flourished, and will flourish without commitment to Core Scientism or to any such philosophical principle. Clearly, furthermore, opposition to Core Scientism is not opposition either to science (regarded as a group of significant cognitive disciplines) or to genuine scientific contributions.

Proponents of Core Scientism will remind us that their scientism invokes not the current empirical sciences but rather the hypothetically completed empirical sciences. Accordingly, they may be undisturbed by the absence of Core Scientism from the theses of the current empirical sciences. Still, the problem at hand persists for Core Scientism, because we have no reason to hold that Core Scientism is among the claims or the implications of the hypothetically completed empirical sciences. A general problem is that specific predictions about what the completed sciences will include are notoriously risky and arguably unreliable (even though this robust fact has not hindered stubborn forecasters of science).

The often turbulent, sometimes revolutionary history of the sciences offers no firm basis for reasonable confidence in such speculative predictions, especially when a sweeping philosophical claim is involved. In addition, nothing in the current empirical sciences makes it likely that the completed sciences would include Core Scientism as a thesis or an implication. The monopolistic hopes of some naturalists for the sciences, therefore, are hard to anchor in reality.

The problem with Core Scientism stems from its distinctive monopolistic claims. Like many philosophical claims, it makes claims about *every* real entity and *every* cognitively legitimate method for acquiring or revising beliefs. The empirical sciences, as actually practiced, are not monopolistic, nor do we have any reason to think that they should or will become so. Neither individually nor collectively do they offer scientific claims about *every* real entity or *every* cognitively legitimate method for belief formation. Advocates of an empirical science monopoly would do well to attend to this empirical fact.

The empirical sciences rightly limit their scientific claims to their proprietary domains, even if wayward scientists sometimes overextend themselves, and depart from empirical science proper, with claims about every real entity or every cognitively legitimate method. (The latter claims tend to sell trendy books, even though they fail as science.) Support for this observation comes from the fact that the empirical sciences, individually and collectively, are *logically* and *cognitively* neutral on such matters as the existence of God and the veracity of certain kinds of religious experience. Accordingly, each such science logically and cognitively permits the existence of God and the veracity of certain kinds of religious experience. We have no reason, moreover, to suppose that the hypothetically completed empirical sciences should or will differ from the actual empirical sciences in this respect. Naturalists, at any rate, have not shown otherwise; nor has anyone else. This comes as no surprise, however, once we recognize that the God of traditional monotheism does not qualify or function as an object of empirical science. Accordingly, we do well not to assume, without needed argument, that the objects of empirical science exhaust the objects of reality in general. An analogous point holds for the methods of empirical science: we should not assume uncritically that they exhaust the methods of cognitively legitimate belief formation in general.

Proponents of Core Scientism might grant that it is not, itself, a claim of the empirical sciences, but they still could propose that Core Scientism is cognitively *justified* by the empirical sciences. (A "claim" of the empirical sciences is, let us say, a claim logically entailed by the empirical sciences, whereas a claim justified by the sciences need not be thus logically entailed.) This move would lead to a focus on the principles of cognitive justification appropriate to the empirical sciences. Specifically, what principles of cognitive justification allegedly combine with the (hypothetically completed) empirical sciences to justify Core Scientism? More relevantly, are any such principles of justification required, logically or cognitively, by the (hypothetically completed) empirical sciences themselves? No such principles of justification seem logically required, because the (hypothetically completed) empirical sciences logically permit that Core Scientism is not justified. Whether such principles of justification are cognitively required depends on the cognitive principles justified by the (hypothetically completed) empirical sciences, and the latter matter clearly remains unsettled. We have, at any rate, no salient evidence for thinking that the (hypothetically completed) empirical sciences will include or justify cognitive principles that justify Core Scientism. The burden for delivering such evidence is squarely on naturalists, and it remains to be discharged.

Minimally, the empirical sciences rely on abductive cognitive principles that certify inferences to a best available explanation of pertinent phenomena. The empirical sciences, after all, are in the business of best explanation regarding empirical phenomena in various domains (physics, chemistry, astronomy, geology, biology, and so on). Even so, their domains of pertinent phenomena to be explained are not, individually or collectively, monopolistic in the manner required by a straightforward abductive justification for Core Scientism. For example, those domains of empirical phenomena do not preclude, individually or collectively, every kind of religious experience suitable to abductively justified belief that God exists; nor do they otherwise exclude (grounded belief in) the reality of God. As a result, the abductive cognitive principles accompanying the empirical sciences will fall short of justifying Core Scientism, given the latter's dubious monopolistic assumptions.

More generally, any domain of evidence outside the scope of the (hypothetically completed) empirical sciences will raise potential problems for the abductive justification of Core Scientism, given its dubious monopolistic assumptions. In particular, a God who is outside the domain of the empirical sciences could supply a kind of experiential evidence that does not fall under the category of the empirical sciences, perhaps because the evidence supplied by God is too elusive to be scientific in any typical sense of "scientific." The sciences do not preclude this coherent option; nor should we as theorists regarding the sciences and the reality of God. (Chapters 3 and 4 explore this option further.)

By way of reply, some philosophers may propose that Core Scientism is constitutive of the hypothetically completed empirical sciences *properly understood*. The proposal, more specifically, suggests that the proper understanding of "empirical science" involves Core Scientism as a *definitive* ingredient. This would amount to an attempted vindication of Core Scientism by semantical, or definitional, fiat. The relevant claim would be that it is just part of the proper understanding of what "empirical science" means that Core Scientism is correct. Mere definition then would do all of the heavy lifting here.

The proposed solution is too arbitrary to be satisfactory. It offers nothing to block opponents of Core Scientism from making an analogous move, whereby a position contrary to Core Scientism becomes part of the *proper understanding* of "empirical science" as a definitive ingredient. For example, one might as well build a theistic design hypothesis into the "proper understanding" of what "empirical science" means. (I do not recommend this, of course, but the logical point holds.) Two, then, can play the unconvincing game of semantical fiat in this connection. Of course, one might object that a theistic design hypothesis is insufficiently empirical to figure in the proper understanding of "empirical science." In that case, an opponent of Core Scientism might direct a similar objection to the ontological and methodological components of Core Scientism. If the proper understanding of "empirical science" rests on semantical fiat alone, Core Scientism will run afoul of various available contrary proper understandings of "empirical science." In other words, Core Scientism would need a different line of defense if arbitrariness is to be avoided.

Naturalists sympathetic to either pragmatism or some kind of antirealism about truth may try to rescue Core Scientism by rejecting any characterization of scientific and philosophical understanding as "truth-seeking." Pragmatists insist that the purpose of inquiry is to produce (theoretically) "useful" beliefs rather than to uncover truths. In addition, antirealists typically claim that the purpose of inquiry is to produce consensus of a certain sort regarding various claims or at least to pursue any of a number of other nonalethic goals (that is, goals other than truth). (Pragmatism and antirealism face decisive self-referential problems, but we need not digress here; for the problems, see Moser 1993, Chapter 1, and Alston 1997.) The relevant problem with pragmatism and antirealism emerges from their assumptions about "the" purpose of inquiry. We have no reason to suppose that there is such a singular, specific thing as "the" purpose of inquiry or that truth is irrelevant as a goal of inquiry, particularly in the sciences. Even if inquiry has nonalethic goals of the sort favored by pragmatists and antirealists, it can (and often does) still have truth as a central goal, particularly in the sciences.

Like theorists engaged in the empirical sciences, we are concerned with legitimate inquiry *in those cases where* inquiry is directed to the discovery of truth (and the avoidance of falsehood). The fact that some standards (whether naturalist or otherwise) would govern inquiry with goals other than truth is no surprise, but it has no bearing on the dispute over naturalism offered as a view about the nature of legitimate truth-seeking inquiry. It *may* be "useful" (assuming that this term avoids undesired alethic implications – no small task, actually) for some purposes not to posit nonphysical objects or not to employ nonscientific methods. Still, even if this were useful relative to those purposes, this fact would be irrelevant to the current dispute over Core Scientism as defined previously. Therefore, we need not concern ourselves further with pragmatist or antirealist defenses of Core Scientism.

We now can raise a troublesome dilemma for Core Scientism. Either Core Scientism is not, itself, a thesis included in or even justified by the (hypothetically completed) empirical sciences, or its justification depends on a special commitment to the "proper understanding" of "empirical science." In the first case, Core Scientism is self-defeating; that is, it fails by its own standard. In the second case, Core Scientism is philosophically harmless, because it rests just on definitional fiat rather than on a significant independent reality. In either case, however, Core Scientism is philosophically ineffectual, and is no real threat to an ontological commitment to God's existence.

The self-defeat of Core Scientism would result from its failing to be included in or even justified by its own proposed single standard for methodological and ontological integrity – the (hypothetically completed) empirical sciences. By its own standard, in that case, Core Scientism would suffer defeat. If, however, Core Scientism is to be rescued via semantical (or definitional) fiat, as a desideratum for the proper understanding of "empirical science," it becomes harmlessly stipulative, with no firm basis in reality beyond stipulative definition, such as in the reality characterized by empirical science. In that case, Core Scientism loses its ontological and cognitive bite by its own standard, because it becomes divorced from the ontological and cognitive successes of the actual empirical sciences. Given this dilemma, Core Scientism becomes philosophically innocuous on its own standard, because it then has no significant reality behind it. As a result, a commitment to God's existence is not thereby threatened. In the end, we do well to let Core Scientism collapse of its own weight, because it takes nothing of significance down with it. Science, in particular, will flourish without it.

6. THEISM BEYOND SCIENTISM

Scientism aside, we have found no reason to regard the empirical sciences as a threat to belief that God exists or to the claim that it is reasonable (for some people) to believe that God exists. Of course, by "empirical science," we mean empirical science that is not monopolistic regarding ontology or cognitive method, and this includes our best actual empirical science. If everything real, known, or knowable is scientific or otherwise natural, but God is not part of what is scientific or natural, then God will be excluded from the domain of what is real, known, or knowable. Rudolf Bultmann (1966, p. 274) has commented, however, that "philosophy leaves fundamentally free the possibility of a word spoken to [humans] from beyond," where "from beyond" means "from God." At least, philosophy apart from Core Scientism leaves this possibility free. The same is true of empirical science, although it is a common but implausible mistake among naturalists to conflate empirical science and Core Scientism. Actual empirical science, in any case, leaves free the possibility of a word spoken to us from beyond, and this empirical fact, on reflection, should come as no surprise.

Clearly, the history of empirical science exhibits remarkable explanatory success, along with its many failures in truth seeking and explanation. The history of physics, astronomy, biology, and chemistry supplies abundant examples on both fronts. This history of science is mixed indeed, but the paths of explanatory success are clear and convincing. Can any intellectually capable person (at least beyond dogmatic skeptics) suggest with a straight face that our best sciences offer no explanatory success at all? This seems doubtful at best. Even so, the history of explanatory success in empirical science does not recommend Core Scientism in any way. In particular, this success does not underwrite a monopoly for a natural ontology of science, as if it called for a sweeping philosophical position in materialist metaphysics. As a result, the explanatory success in empirical science does not undermine, or otherwise challenge, belief that God exists.

At a minimum, we have no reason to think that if God exists, God must or even would be available to ordinary scientific investigation. In particular, if God, being worthy of worship, is inherently purposive, then God may have certain purposes that call for divine elusiveness relative to scientific investigation and (at times) to scientific investigators themselves. In particular, God's elusiveness may yield a kind of *variability* in religious experiences among humans, and in corresponding evidence, that undermines any sweeping claiming that scientific evidence or methodology has a monopoly regarding evidence or knowledge. In that case, the absence of religious experience from scientific evidence would not recommend skepticism about God's existence for all people, particularly for those people who have suitable religious experience and corresponding religious evidence.

As a matter of empirical fact, the evidence in empirical science does not attend, in any serious way, to religious experience that is sensitive to the volitional tendencies of human persons. In particular, such religious experience is sensitive to humans' willingness to receive and to reflect

God's moral character for others and thereby to become personifying evidence of God's reality, including evidence of God's intentional agency and moral character. Perhaps such religious experience is either insufficiently empirical, in a scientific sense, or too elusive to attract serious attention from empirical science. (Chapters 3 and 4 return to this important but widely neglected theme.)

Recall Fodor's aforementioned "true scientific vision" according to which "there's a lot of 'because' out there [in the world], but there isn't any 'for'" (1998, p. 168). Theorists can effectively pursue Fodor's "true scientific vision" to see how far it can be pushed as a comprehensive explanation, as long as this pursuit avoids an implausible assumption of an ontological monopoly for the objects of empirical science. The latter assumption would exclude agents themselves and their intentional actions from the ontological picture, and thereby would preclude the very role of agents (intentionally) pursuing Fodor's true scientific vision. We then would be unable consistently to recommend the intentional pursuit of Fodor's "true scientific vision" or even natural scientific explanations.

In the absence of a monopolistic ontological assumption for the actual world, Fodor's "true scientific vision" (regardless of its dubious truth) can illuminate the nature of an imagined world without intentional agents and intentional actions. There will be, of course, no intentional agents in that world for whom the vision is illuminating, but from outside that imagined world, an intentional agent can apprehend the strangeness of the vision of an altogether nonintentional world. The actual world, thick with intentional agents and actions, is definitely *not* that world, and this should come as no ontological or cognitive embarrassment for us. Indeed, if we are in a predicament akin to the wilderness parable of the Introduction, we should value not only intentional agents lost in the wilderness canyon, but also any prospective intentional agent who can serve as our needed rescuer.

It would be unwise indeed (and dangerous, too) to value otherwise.

A big question remains: if the claim that God exists neither is part of empirical science nor is justified by empirical science, what is its actual status relative to empirical science? More specifically, what kind of rational support, if any, does this claim enjoy? Is its support compatible with the kind(s) of rational support found in empirical science? If so, is there room for peaceful coexistence, after all, between science and religious commitment that acknowledges God's existence? We shall see that there is, but first we need to consider a position that, in the philosophical tradition of Immanuel Kant, tries to leave room for such religious commitment by abandoning hope of its having any (decisive) *cognitively* rational support – that is, the kind of rational support fitting for genuine knowledge. Science may enjoy such rational support, but, according to the fideist position to be explored in Chapter 2, religious commitment must earn its keep in some other, noncognitive way. We shall see that such a fideist requirement faces serious trouble, quite aside from the actual cognitive status of theistic belief. Fideism, we shall see, will not deliver a successful alternative to scientism.

2

❧

Fideism and Faith

"The certainty in the religious life is bound up with the autonomy of that life, its uniqueness and its independence of other knowledge. Our natural modes of rational certainty are but points of attachment, or under-agents for the certainty of faith; they are not germs of it, and they are not tests of it.... Our ultimate authority, then, which justifies every other authority in its degree and measure, is the Creator of the New Humanity as such."

– P.T. Forsyth 1913, pp. 135–6.

In the wilderness parable of this book's Introduction, some people lost in the wilderness gorge named "Hells Canyon" disown any need of a *well-grounded*, or *trustworthy*, indication of either a rescuer or a plan to reach safety. Nonetheless, they are committed to a rescuer who will bring them to safety. Perhaps their commitment is motivated by what seems either prudent or morally advisable to them. In any case, their belief in a rescuer is not accompanied by acknowledgment of a need for well-grounded, or trustworthy, evidence to support their belief. This position is akin to *fideism* about theistic belief, the view that belief in God does not depend for its acceptability on well-grounded, or trustworthy, supporting evidence.

We shall use "well-grounded" and "trustworthy" to signify something's *meriting*, or *being worthy of*, trust or reliance, either as a (possibly fallible) basis for a truth-affirming commitment or as a (possibly fallible) supported truth-affirming commitment, such as a supported belief. Such trustworthiness for a belief is not objective reliability relative to how the world actually is, but is, instead, relative to a person's available truth indicators, or evidence. It requires, accordingly, not the truth of a supported belief, but rather the worthiness of a belief's being held on the basis of its supporting truth indicator, or evidence. Even if some false beliefs enjoy this kind of trustworthiness, given their supporting evidence, not all beliefs do, even all true beliefs. The support for many beliefs, even many true beliefs, fails to yield trustworthiness, and therefore recommends due suspicion rather than commitment toward the relevant beliefs as true.

Theistic fideism might seem to try to achieve its desired theological benefits by simple theft instead of honest toil. A leap without trustworthy evidence, in other words, seems too easy, if not outright arbitrary and dangerous. Even so, some religious theorists hold that humans must approach God *only by faith*, and that faith in God involves – or at least may involve without deficiency – a leap without trustworthy supporting evidence. Some fideism appears to be a (severe) reaction to a cognitive standard similar to the methodological naturalism presented and challenged in Chapter 1. If faith in God does not need support from trustworthy evidence at all, then it will not be troubled by cognitive demands similar to those associated either with methodological naturalism or with the sciences themselves. Perhaps, in that case, neither methodological naturalism nor the sciences themselves will pose a threat to faith in God. Fideism, in any case, evidently makes faith in God a cognitively different kind of entity from knowledge in the sciences, and some religious theorists deem this an important source of safety (that is, freedom from challenge) for theistic belief.

According to Jewish and Christian theism, God authoritatively invites and highly values human *faith in God*. What exactly, however, is such faith? What, in addition, is its primary value? Is it a virtue of some sort, perhaps even a moral virtue? How, furthermore, is human faith in God related to human knowledge and evidence, and how does it contrast with so-called human "works"? This chapter explores such questions, in order to put theistic fideism and human theistic faith in an illuminating theological, cognitive, and moral context. More specifically, it will identify some serious deficiencies of fideism, while suggesting that human faith in God need not be similarly deficient. Accordingly, we should not confuse human faith in God with fideism about human faith in God. Fideism, at its core, is a controversial view about the relation between human faith in God and evidence of God's existence; it denies that the acceptability, even the cognitive acceptability, of such faith requires such trustworthy evidence.

1. FAITH

The term "fideism" comes from the Latin word for faith, "fides," and we can illuminate fideism by attending to some of the important features of human faith in God. According to the Hebrew Bible, God's valuing of human faith became apparent in very early times, even before the origin of national Israel and Judaism. In particular, Genesis 15:5–6 states: "He [God] brought him [Abram] outside and said, 'Look toward heaven and count the stars, if you are able to count them.' Then he said to him, 'So shall your descendants be.' And he believed the LORD; and the LORD reckoned it to him as righteousness" (NRSV). The Hebrew word translated "believed" derives from the same root as that of our English word "Amen." Accordingly, we might offer this paraphrase: "Abram 'amen-ed' the Lord, and the Lord counted it for him as a right relationship with the Lord." The word "trust" is among the best in the English language for the "amen-ing" relationship in question. Various translations of the Hebrew Bible (for example, the NEB,

REB, NAB, and NJB translations) use language that helpfully captures the object of Abram's faith: "Abram put his
faith *in the LORD*...." We may treat "faith in God," "trust
in God," and "belief in God" as interchangeable phrases in
such a context.

The kind of faith ascribed to Abram in Genesis 15 is no
mere intellectual or psychological matter. It involves the central purpose and direction of Abram's life relative to God's
redemptive promise and call to him. The best language for
such faith is "entrusting oneself to God." Accordingly, we
should consider this paraphrase: "Abram entrusted himself to the Lord, and the Lord counted this self-entrusting
by Abram as a right relationship of Abram with Himself." The relevant self-entrusting, as exhibited in Genesis
15–25, required Abram's *living obediently* into an ongoing
and future-directed relationship with God as the authoritative promise-giver and promise-keeper, and therefore his
faith was itself dynamic and ongoing (or diachronic) rather
than static (or synchronic). This self-entrusting exceeded
intellectual assent, given that it was life-involving, and not
just mind-involving or just action-involving. In particular,
Abram was entrusting *himself* to God, for the present and
for the future, relative to God's unique promise to bless
all the families of the earth through him (that is, Abram),
even though it was unclear to him exactly how this promise
would eventually be realized (see Gen. 12:2–3, 13:16; for
similar notions of entrusting oneself to God, see Ps. 31:5,
Luke 23:46, 1 Pet. 2:23, 4:19).

According to Genesis 15, God calls Abram into a self-
entrusting relationship, and then responds to Abram's
entrusting himself to God by crediting this entrusting commitment to God (and God's promises) as righteousness –
that is, as a right relationship with God. In other words,
God thereby offers a means to exercise mercy rather than
condemnation toward rebellious and wayward humans,
without condoning either their rebellion, including their
supposed self-righteousness, or any other wrongdoing of

humans toward God. God therefore seeks, in the Genesis narrative as well as in other key biblical narratives, the redemption of humans via the human response of faith, or self-entrustment, toward God and God's promise. (Section 3 of this chapter returns to this important lesson.)

According to various biblical writers, the temporal order in the divine process of crediting righteousness to humans via faith, or entrusting oneself, is crucial and irreversible. Mercifully, God moves first, both with a redemptive promise for the needed good of humans and with a corresponding authoritative invitation to humans to entrust themselves wholeheartedly to God. Specifically, God calls Abram into a needed relationship *before* Abram calls God (see Gen. 12:1–3). We therefore might say, in this connection, that "in this is love, not that we loved God, but that he loved us. . . . We love, because he first loved us" (1 John 4:10, 19). God's promise and corresponding invitation to humans manifest divine love, as various biblical writers have noted (see, for instance, Hos. 11:1–9, Rom. 5:1–11, 9:25–33, Heb. 5:1–10, 6:13–20). According to these writers, we are called by God to put our faith in, or entrust ourselves to, the God who first loved us. This distinctive theme of divine *grace*, or unearned gift, appropriated through faith as self-entrustment, emerges in the Hebrew Bible and in the Christian New Testament. (Sections 3 and 4 of this chapter clarify this theme.)

2. PHILOSOPHY AND FAITH

The topic of faith in God has attracted extensive controversy throughout the history of philosophy, at least from Socrates to the present. One important lesson of this ongoing controversy is that the notion of faith "in God" is not reducible to the idea of faith "that God exists." If faith that God exists is just belief that God exists, it is merely a psychological attitude toward a judgment or a proposition. That is, it is simply *de dicto*, related to a propositional dictum: namely, to the statement that God exists. In contrast, faith *in God* is best understood as having a *de re* component (specifically, involving a relation to something agent-like) that is irreducible to a judgment or a proposition. In particular, faith in God relates one to *God*, and not just to a judgment or a proposition about God. Some writers, under the influence of Søren Kierkegaard, would say that human faith in God involves a distinctive "I–Thou" relationship between a human and God that is not reducible to *de dicto* belief that God exists. What exactly such an I–Thou relationship consists in has been a topic of controversy in the philosophy of religion. Clearly, given its *de re* component, this is not faith regarding merely historical or propositional information of any sort. (For relevant discussion, see Farmer 1942, Chapter 2, Brunner 1964, Moser 2008, Chapter 3. For an influential discussion of the I–Thou relationship influenced by Kierkegaard 1992 [1846], see Buber 1958 [1923].)

Writing under the pseudonym "Johannes Climacus" in *Concluding Unscientific Postscript*, Kierkegaard emphasizes the importance of the "inwardness of faith." He proposes that such inwardness "cannot be expressed more definitely than this: it is the absurd, adhered to firmly with the passion of the infinite" (1992 [1846], vol. 1, p. 214; subsequent page references to Kierkegaard are to this volume). He adds that the relevant inwardness, in contrast to "objective faith" as "a sum of tenets," includes "... placing [a person] decisively, more decisively than any judge can place the accused, between time [namely, human finitude] and eternity [namely, God] in time, between heaven and hell in the time of salvation" (p. 215). As a result, according to Kierkegaard's Climacus, "... an objective knowledge about the truth or the truths of Christianity is precisely untruth. To know a creed by rote is paganism, because Christianity is inwardness" (p. 224). Faith in God, Kierkegaard's Climacus maintains, involves a commitment to mystery (in the presence of God in human inwardness) that does not go away or yield to explanation, nonparadoxical description, or philosophical resolution (cf. pp. 213–14).

Human philosophical speculation about God and God's purposes, according to Climacus, "is a temptation, the most precarious of all" temptations (p. 214). The speculative philosopher who seeks an explanation of God's ways, he claims, is *not* the prodigal son who comes home to his waiting divine Father. In contrast, the speculative philosopher is "the naughty child who refuses to stay where existing humans belong, in the children's nursery and the education room of existence where one becomes adult only through inwardness in existing, but who instead wants to enter God's council, continually screaming that, from the point of view of the eternal, the divine, the theocentric, there is no paradox" (p 214). As a result, the speculative philosopher refuses to acknowledge God *as God* (cf. p. 156).

Kierkegaard's Climacus makes his antispeculative point in connection with divine forgiveness of human sins. He proposes that "the simple wise person," even after reflection on God's forgiveness of human sins, would say: "I still cannot comprehend the divine mercy that can forgive sins; the more intensely I believe it, the less I am able to understand it" (p. 228). On this basis, Climacus concludes that "... probability does not seem to increase as the inwardness of faith is augmented, rather the opposite" (p. 228; cf. p. 211). This fits with his suggestion that Christian faith "... is not a matter of knowing" objectively (p. 215). Climacus's underlying assumption is that "if I am to apprehend God objectively, I do not have faith; but because I cannot do this, I must have faith" (p. 204). In addition, Climacus holds that in faith "the individual existing human being has to feel himself a sinner," and such feeling is subjective (as "the deepest pain") rather than objective (p. 224).

Faith in God, according to Kierkegaard's Climacus, does not require comprehending God or God's mysterious ways. If "comprehending" means "fully understanding," this position of Climacus's is compelling, or at least worthy of serious consideration. We should not expect cognitively limited humans to be able to comprehend God or God's purposes in the sense of "being able fully to explain God or God's purposes." Even so, we should be careful about the implications of this position for well-grounded faith in God, particularly in connection with Climacus's following remark: "Faith [in God] has ... two tasks: to watch for and at every moment to make the discovery of improbability, the paradox, in order then to hold it fast with the passion of inwardness" (p. 233). This remark yields a dubious message, because it suggests that the inwardness of faith is antithetical, or at least inversely proportional, to reasonable or well-grounded belief as evidence-based, probably true belief.

At times, Kierkegaard as Climacus suggests that his talk of the "absurd" and the "paradox," with regard to the inwardness of faith, is just talk of an eternal, "infinite" God entering temporal, finite human history, particularly in the divine incarnation in Jesus as a human with historical existence. He writes: "The eternal truth has come into existence in time. That is the paradox. . . . What, then, is the absurd? The absurd is that the eternal truth has come into existence in time, that God has come into [such] existence, has been born, has grown up, etc., has come into existence exactly as an individual human being. . . . " (pp. 209–10; cf. pp. 213, 217). *If* this is all Kierkegaard means, his talk of "paradox," "absurdity," and "contradiction" is potentially very misleading, because it suggests much more than this when taken at face value.

The Christian proclamation of divine incarnation in Jesus is surprising and mysterious indeed, but it is not, strictly speaking, absurd or contradictory. Any suggestion to the contrary should deliver a careful demonstration of the alleged contradiction in this proclamation, but it is at best doubtful that this requirement can be met. Kierkegaard's Climacus portrays the claim of divine incarnation in Jesus as " . . . contain[ing] the contradiction that something that can become historical only in direct opposition to all human understanding has become historical," and he adds that "this contradiction is the absurd, which can only be believed" (p. 211). In the methodology of Climacus, " . . . the point is . . . to do away with . . . reliabilities, demonstrations from effects, and the whole mob of pawnbrokers and guarantors, in order to get the absurd clear – so that one can believe if one will" (p. 212). We do not find here, then, an invitation to well-grounded, evidence-based faith in God. On the contrary, we find resistance to such an invitation.

Climacus's talk of contradiction as "direct opposition to all human understanding" is evidently to be taken at face value, as involving a conflict with what we humans can understand. Even so, Kierkegaard's Climacus has not shown that Christian faith, including commitment to divine incarnation in a human, harbors a literal contradiction. He evidently assumes that God as eternal cannot enter temporal existence but nonetheless has actually done so. Specifically, he speaks of the "dialectical contradiction" as " . . . the historical that has been able to become historical only against its nature . . . " (p. 578). Still, Kierkegaard's Climacus has not shown that, according to Christian faith, God as eternal cannot enter temporal existence or that this is against God's nature; accordingly, he has not shown that a contradiction is present. The Christian view that God has entered temporal existence in Jesus is surprising and mysterious by any ordinary standard, but its original proponents, as represented in the New Testament, seem not to have offered it as contradictory. More to the point, we have no good reason to offer it as literally contradictory, particularly if divine eternality is logically compatible with historical divine incarnation. Accordingly, the suggestion of Kierkegaard's Climacus to the contrary fails to convince.

If Christian faith presents us with a literal contradiction, then it presents us with something that cannot be literally true. A literal contradiction is not only false, but also necessarily false. So far as we know, the earliest proponents of the Christian proclamation of divine incarnation in Jesus did not offer their proclamation as necessarily false. On the contrary, they evidently were offering a message they claimed to be *true*, that is, a proclamation of divine incarnation that, they claimed, actually occurred. As a result, a literal contradiction would pose a serious problem for their message; in particular, it would undermine the prospect, and thus the actuality, of their proclamation's being true. Accordingly, Climacus's talk of "contradiction" seems foreign to the cause of the earliest proponents of the Christian proclamation of divine incarnation in Jesus. The same holds for Kierkegaard's talk of the incarnation as "a sign of contradiction" in his later work, *Practice in Christianity* (1848), which he regarded as his "most perfect and truest" writing. Kierkegaard himself evidently held the view of contradiction represented in *Concluding Unscientific Postscript* and *Practice in Christianity*, at least during the time of those works, despite his use of pseudonyms.

Kierkegaard's understanding of faith in God, as represented by Climacus, appears to sacrifice not only the (possible) truth of the message of God's intervention in human affairs, but also the general accessibility of that message throughout history. In particular, his understanding of the "inwardness of faith" in God evidently blocks people who existed before the incarnation in Jesus from having faith in God as the human means of receiving divine grace. This, of course, is an excessively narrow approach to faith in God. Abraham (aka Abram), for instance, should be a candidate for faith in God, in keeping with Genesis 15 and Romans 4, even if (quite naturally, given his historical location) he did not believe in the divine incarnation in Jesus or in any contradiction, or absurdity, regarding God's intervention in Jesus. (For relevant discussion, see Käsemann 1971, Chapter 4.) Abraham's not believing in a contradiction about divine incarnation, in other words, should not disqualify him from having faith in God.

Faith in God, as suggested previously, is plausibly regarded as a human response of entrustment of oneself, now and into the future, to God and God's promises, and not as an acceptance of a contradiction or an absurdity.

As illustrated by the case of Abram in Genesis 15, faith in God can have (at least in principle) a cognitive basis in the human experience of God's intervening in human lives with redemptive actions and thereby calling people to trust and obey God. In fact, faith in God *should* be grounded in trustworthy supporting evidence of that distinctive kind in order to avoid becoming just wishful thinking, misleading dogmatism, distorting bias, or some other kind of cognitively arbitrary commitment. Cognitive arbitrariness is harmful in this connection because it leaves faith as unguided by a trustworthy indication of what is true and therefore as a prime candidate for a species of distorting bias or misleading dogmatism. Fideism about faith in God, we shall see, suffers from the deficiency of failing to protect against this serious problem.

Ideally, human faith in God is cognitively grounded in humanly experienced evidence of its divine personal object: namely, the God who authoritatively calls humans before they call God. (On the relevant cognitive basis as purposively available authoritative evidence, see Chapters 3 and 4 and Moser 2008.) Faith in God therefore should not be characterized as an inward embracing of contradiction or absurdity, because that approach to faith undermines the important need for supporting evidence of the truth of any proposition accepted in faith. Kierkegaard's portrait of faith as contradictory or absurd, accordingly, is misleading and harmful if taken at face value. Even so, Kierkegaard is correct about the independence of human faith in God from philosophical speculation or theoretical speculation in general. If such faith is a human response of self-entrustment to an experienced divine intervention, such as a divine call, then it does not depend for its existence on philosophical speculation or any other kind of speculation. In addition, Kierkegaard was right to contrast genuine faith in God with rote memory of tenets and with empty ritual in practices, but he went to an implausible and dangerous extreme in welcoming contradiction in faith.

Kierkegaard's Climacus suggests that Socrates manifested and recommended a kind of "existential inwardness" analogous to faith, given his focus on human existence and what it means for humans to exist (pp. 204–7). Even if he did manifest this (and it may be impossible to verify), we should hesitate to compare Socrates favorably to Jesus regarding the latter's emphasis on faith in God. The difference between them is, in the end, vast and irreducible, and the key difference stems from the distinctive role of God in the theology of Jesus.

Jesus, as the self-avowed authoritative Son of his divine Father (see Mark 12:1–12, Matt. 11:25–7, Luke 10:21–2), commands people to have faith as obedient and loving entrustment of themselves to his Father (see Mark 11:22), on the basis of God's purportedly redemptive intervention in human lives. Such entrustment of oneself moves outward obediently in self-giving love, by divine command, toward God and thereby toward others. It transcends mere discussion and mere passionate subjectivity in order to personify, and thereby to represent, the value of a life of faithful obedience under divine authority. The intended result is human personification and reflection of God's moral character for others, in the manner exemplified and commanded by Jesus (see Matt. 5:14–16). Accordingly, the apostle Paul speaks of "faith [or trust, in God and Jesus] working through love (*agape*)" (Gal. 5:6). Such outgoing faith in God is a consistent focus of Jesus as the representative of his divine Father, and it is absent from Socrates as represented by Plato (and from Kierkegaard writing as Climacus in the *Concluding Unscientific Postscript*). In this respect, the difference between Jesus and Socrates regarding human faith in God is more substantial than any similarity.

Kierkegaard has captured an important dimension of faith in God in his emphasis on human *decision*, or *resolution*, regarding God's call (pp. 116, 129–30, 221–2). As Climacus, he remarks that "the speculative thinker . . . believes only to a certain degree – he puts his hand to the plow and looks around in order to find something to know" (p. 230). The self-entrustment central to faith in God requires a definite commitment to God, and this commitment demands a human decision to yield oneself to God, now and into the future, relative to God's authoritative will and promises. In this respect, faith in God is a kind of self-giving obedience, even morally virtuous obedience because it is morally excellent in at least one respect, as we shall see. It therefore is a mistake to oppose faith in God to human obedience, although such faith is irreducible to individual obedient actions apart from self-entrustment to God. Even so, the required decision and commitment need not be cognitively arbitrary or otherwise unreasonable. They can rest on salient evidence supplied by divine intervention in human experience.

In the wake of Kierkegaard, many writers have latched on to his language of a "leap" of faith, and have suggested that faith in God cannot have supporting evidence. Rudolf Bultmann is a clear proponent of this view. In explaining John's Gospel on the topics of human faith and divine revelation, he writes: " . . . the man called to have faith can ask for no credentials, no legitimation, no 'testimony' (*marturia*) to the validity of the word of the revelation. . . . The paradox is that the word of Jesus does not find its substantiation by a backward movement from the attesting word to the thing attested. . . . , but finds it only in a faith-prompted acceptance of the word" (1955, p. 68). Bultmann's fideism becomes explicit as follows: "Every authentication of the Word [of God] is rejected; it is itself 'witness', and there is no other witness beside the Word which man acting under his own control could first test and find correct, so that he could then decide to believe" (1969, p. 304). Bultmann, like Kierkegaard, thus divorces faith from any supporting evidence that could serve to test the veracity of a faith-commitment.

Karl Barth has also echoed Kierkegaard in fideist remarks about faith in God. He writes: "The Gospel of salvation can only be believed in; it is a matter for faith only. It demands choice.... To him that is not sufficiently mature to accept a contradiction and to rest in it, it becomes a scandal – to him that is unable to escape the necessity of contradiction, it becomes a matter for faith" (1933, p. 39). In addition, according to Barth, "the Gospel does not expound or recommend itself. It does not negotiate or plead, threaten, or make promises" (1933, p. 38–9). Here, again, we find no place for evidence in support of the veracity of a faith-commitment. The emphasis on human choice, or decision, displaces any role for supporting evidence. This theme from Kierkegaard, echoed in Bultmann, Barth, and many others, leaves us with fideism about faith in God. As a result, we should wonder how one is to handle questions, even for oneself, about the veracity of a faith-commitment.

Of course, a person can make a faith-commitment in the absence of supporting evidence. For instance, one can make a faith-commitment that Black Beauty will win at the racetrack, even though one has no supporting evidence for his commitment to this particular horse. Even so, it would be odd indeed if a faith-commitment *could not* be supported by, or recommended on the basis of, evidence for the veracity of the commitment. Kierkegaard, Bultmann, and Barth, however, have suggested that there is an *incompatibility* between faith in God and supporting evidence. Their suggestion evidently stems from their view that the nature of faith in God is inherently paradoxical, contradictory, or absurd. The latter view, however, is anything but obvious, and we do well to remain suspicious of it, particularly in the absence of compelling support. The view emerges from Kierkegaard's needlessly extreme view of God as being "infinite" in a manner that makes a divine historical incarnation a "contradiction." Kierkegaard, Bultmann, and Barth should have found due warning of their mistake in the fact that none of the biblical writers calls people to embrace a contradiction or anything else that is necessarily false.

Contrary to Kierkegaard, Bultmann, and Barth, we have characterized human faith in God as human *self-entrustment* to God, now and into the future, in response to human experience of God's redemptive intervention in human lives. Such faith as entrustment of oneself to God is arguably a needed motivational anchor for human *faithful actions* toward God and others, in obedience to God. It includes one's general *receptive volitional commitment* to receive any manifested and offered divine power of redemptive unselfish love as a gracious gift and thereby to obey God in what God commands and promises. In such faith, accordingly, one will commit oneself to personify and to reflect God's distinctive moral character, including divine unselfish love, for others. On this personally interactive basis, one can, oneself, become personifying evidence of divine reality and thus reflect God's moral character for others.

A faith-commitment of oneself to God can be firmly in place even if one occasionally disobeys God and thereby, on occasion, violates one's *general* self-commitment to God. Such a volitional self-commitment, when actually carried out by a person in action, includes that person's submitting his or her will to God's authoritative will in a particular case of action, just as Jesus did in Gethsemane (see Mark 14:32–8) and Abram did in the context of Genesis 15. This kind of faith-commitment is arguably morally virtuous because it includes human reception of divine moral excellence, particularly divine unselfish love. In contrast, mere belief that God exists can be altogether selfish, and therefore need not be virtuous at all in that respect (see James. 2:19). As a result, we should not confuse such belief with genuine faith in God.

Faith in God includes, at its core, one's *obediently receiving, and volitionally committing oneself to,* God and what God graciously offers for the sake of both reconciled fellowship with God and human reflection of God's moral character. A life of faith in God therefore is inherently a life that obediently receives, and volitionally entrusts oneself to, God and God's authoritative call to reconciled divine–human fellowship. The obedient receptivity of faith in God toward God's call leads to the kind of human transformation that enables a human to become suited to divine–human fellowship and to reflect God's moral character. In short, such obedient receptivity enables one to become personifying evidence of God's reality as one receives God's moral character and lives obediently into the future. Faith in God is therefore forward-looking, given divine plans and promises for the future. It is, accordingly, akin to hope in God, as is indicated in some of Paul's letters (see Rom. 4:17–18, 2 Cor. 1:9–10; cf. Ridderbos 1975, pp. 248–52).

It would be misleading at best to contrast human faith in God with human obedience to God's call to reconciled divine–human fellowship. Such faith is inherently an obedient response of volitional self-commitment to receive and to follow agreeably an authoritative divine call that offers lasting forgiveness and reconciled fellowship. Faith in God, accordingly, is a means to reconciled fellowship with God for the sake of receiving and reflecting God's moral character for others. Abraham, the biblical exemplar of faith in God, is thus called a "friend" of God, given the role of fellowship with God in his faith in God (see 2 Chron. 20:7, Isa. 41:8, James. 2:23). He also entrusted himself to God, as his obedient response to God's authoritative call. The friendship in question therefore preserves God's unique authority and thus is not reducible to a friendship among equals.

The receptive feature of faith in God, toward an experienced divine call, arguably excludes a characterization of such faith in terms of pure imagination or wishful thinking, and points instead to a kind of experiential cognitive support. This lesson, if secured, counts directly against fideism, because the lesson portrays faith *in* God as being responsive to a kind of intervention in human experience that can, and arguably sometimes does, qualify as trustworthy evidence. Exactly what such evidence is evidence *of* will be, of course, a matter of dispute among philosophers, as pretty much everything else is. Even so, we have a basis for contrasting faith in God with unconstrained fantasy or guesswork, and for finding a trustworthy *ground* for faith in God in the thing(s) to which such faith is a response. This consideration merits our attention as a warning against conflating faith *in* God with mere belief that God exists. In addition, it counts against any kind of fideism (familiar from Kierkegaard, Bultmann, and Barth) that portrays faith in God as irreconcilable with supporting evidence. We will explore this important consideration in connection with a distinctively Christian understanding of faith in God.

3. CHRISTIAN FAITH

We can turn to Paul's letters in the New Testament for a distinctively Christian nonfideist approach to faith in God. Paul uses talk of *obedience* (of a special kind) and talk of *belief/faith* interchangeably in some important contexts that can illuminate our understanding of faith in God (see, for instance, Rom. 10:16–17; cf. Rom. 1:5, 6:16, 16:26, Gal. 5:5–7). Likewise, as the authoritative model for Paul, Jesus acknowledged a necessary role for human obedience to God's will in order for humans to enter God's kingdom (see Matt. 7:21, 16:24–6, 19:16–22, 21:28–32; cf. Matt. 6:24–9). In addition, Jesus *commanded* that his followers have faith in God and in the Good News of divine redemption via himself (see, for instance, Mark 1:15, 5:36, 11:22; cf. John 14:1). A positive response therefore would be obedience of a definite sort.

The "obedience of faith" mentioned by Paul (in Rom. 1:5, 16:26) is deep-seated *attitudinal obedience.* It includes one's obediently receiving, and volitionally committing and yielding oneself to, God as perfectly authoritative and good, for the sake of living into and reflecting God's redemptive offer of new life, including volitional fellowship with God. We may call such faith in God *obedience of the heart,* in keeping with Paul's illuminating remark that "with the heart one believes unto righteousness" (Rom. 10:10). This obedience of the heart includes, at its core, one's entrusting oneself to God, now and into the future, as one's authoritative source of life. Accordingly, the obedience of faith is no mere intellectual assent to a statement or even mere belief that God exists. It is not simply *de dicto*, because it has an irreducible *de re* component, given that it is faith *in* God. (For one of many failures to appreciate this feature of Paul's understanding of faith in God, see Buber 1951, pp. 97–8; for more accurate approaches, see Käsemann 1971, Chapter 4, Ridderbos 1975, Chapter 4, and Segal 1990, Chapter 4.)

As suggested, one's heart-based obedience of faith can be, for various reasons, imperfectly represented in one's corresponding actions. In other words, we can entrust ourselves to God in faith but still make occasional moral mistakes, including serious moral mistakes. Indeed, a self-commitment to God as authoritative Lord could genuinely accompany such moral failings and enable those failings to be seen for what they are: moral failings before God. In addition, a perfectly loving God, such as the God represented by Jesus in his Sermon on the Mount (see Matt. 5:38–48), would seek to attract and to transform the very center of human motivation, that is, the motivational "heart" (*kardia*) of a person. This consideration lends support to the distinctive kind of theology mentioned in the Introduction: *kardiatheology*, as theology aimed primarily at a person's motivational heart, including the person's will, rather than just at a person's mind or a person's emotions. Such kardiatheology seeks to bear on human attitudes, including faith as obedient self-entrustment from the heart, that are motivationally more significant than mere beliefs, thoughts, and emotions.

Christian faith in God, in keeping with the teaching of Jesus and Paul, should be understood in terms of kardiatheology. In particular, it should be understood as a willing, obedient entrustment of oneself to God that involves one's motivational heart and that therefore is inherently action-oriented. This understanding stands in clear contrast with intellectualist approaches that portray faith as only belief that something is the case, and with subjectivist approaches that fail to make faith in God action-oriented. In addition, if we regard a moral virtue as a motivating moral excellence of a person, we may understand kardiatheology as promoting moral virtues of the heart, anchored in fellowship with God, the ultimate source and sustainer of human moral virtues. Faith in God is significant among those moral virtues, and, in the perspective offered here, it can also be *cognitively* virtuous given that it enables a person to receive some otherwise unavailable evidence of divine activity. The latter point fits with (one fruitful reading of) the Augustinian thesis that "I have faith [in God] in order to understand." (Chapter 4 returns to this cognitive theme; see also Dickie 1954.)

Many theologians have disregarded the important idea of faith in God as including a general volitional commitment to receive and to follow God and God's authoritative call to fellowship. They therefore have neglected the status of human faith in God as a distinctive kind of obedience of the human heart to God's call and will. The importance of kardiatheology has been obscured accordingly, as has the importance of humans, themselves, becoming personifying evidence of God's reality in receiving and reflecting God's moral character for others. Some Christian theologians fear that, given such an approach, faith would be confused with human "works" that are not only unnecessary for but also incompatible with any *grace*-based divine redemption of humans.

The heart-based "obedience of faith" is not what Paul calls "works" in contrast with faith. Instead, Paul thinks of "works," at least in Romans 4:4 and Romans 9:30–3, as what one does to *obligate* God or to *earn* (or to merit) a certain status from God. In contrast with an ordinary use of the term "works," the word is a technical theological term in Paul's remarks in Romans 4 and 9. It signifies a contrast with the divine redemptive *grace* (*charis*= gift) that is to be received by faith, or self-entrustment, toward God, the gift-giver of salvation. Paul highlights the role of grace in a way that makes grace inseparable from the grace-*giver*, given his view that the needed power of redemption for humans is from God and is not a human product or a humanly controllable possession (see 1 Cor. 1:18–29, 2 Cor. 1:8–10; cf. Käsemann 1971, p. 82).

In keeping with faith in God as obedient entrustment of one's heart to God, Paul says the following about identity markers for God's redeemed people: "For neither circumcision counts for anything nor uncircumcision, but *keeping the commandments* of God" (1 Cor. 7:19, RSV, italics added). In Paul's understanding, God's commandments include not only the divine love commands issued by Jesus (Mark 12:28–31; cf. Gal. 5:14), but primarily the gospel of Jesus Christ itself, in virtue of its authoritatively calling people to "the obedience of faith" in God and Jesus (see Rom. 16:26; cf. Matt. 28:18–20). Accordingly, after presenting the Good News of divine grace as gift-righteousness through Jesus (Rom. 3:21–6), Paul speaks of "obedience which leads to righteousness" (Rom. 6:16, RSV). He characterizes this obedience as one's being "obedient from the heart," and he suggests that it underlies one's "having been set free from sin" (Rom. 6:17–18, RSV). These remarks cohere with Paul's talk of the "obedience of faith" (Rom. 1:5, 16:26), which is best understood in terms of one's general volitional entrustment of oneself, at the level of one's heart, to God and God's call to new life as one obediently receives the transformative gift of reconciled fellowship with God.

Contrary to some theistic predestinarians, Paul acknowledges an indispensable *human role* in the (human reception of) divine redemption of humans. This role includes human receptivity of faith in God; more specifically, it includes the human *obedient reception of*, and *volitional commitment to*, the Good News gift of divine righteousness exemplified in Jesus. In this connection, Kierkegaard was right to stress the role of human decision or commitment in faith in God. Paul avoids extreme divine sovereignty that forecloses a crucial role for human volitional response (on which see Meadors 2006), and states *why* Abraham and many other humans are reckoned with divine righteousness. Specifically, *their faith*, as their response of entrustment of themselves to God, is reckoned to them as divine righteousness (see Rom. 4:16–25). If Paul were an advocate of extreme divine sovereignty, he would have mentioned only God's predestinarian role, but clearly he does not do so. Following Jesus, he therefore can, and does, offer a robust conception of universal divine love for humans, even for human enemies of God.

The human rejection of faith in God, according to Paul, will exclude some humans from life with God (see Rom. 11:20; for a similar theme outside Paul, see Heb. 11:6). The divine redemptive gift offered without coercion falls short of its salvific goal in the absence of being voluntarily received by human faith, or self-entrustment, toward God. When, however, this gift is received by human faith, and divine righteousness (including right relationship with God) is thereby credited to a human, we have an actual divine gift of righteous reconciliation of humans to God. As a result, salvation by divine grace through faith does not rest on an acknowledged fiction. Instead, Paul portrays such salvation as resting on a divine unearned gift of reconciliation appropriated by human faith (see Rom. 5:1–11). God's righteousness includes divine power to enable such grace-based reconciliation and salvation (see Käsemann 1961, Way 1991, Chapter 4).

Following a common reading of Ephesians 2:8, one might think of faith in God, itself, as a divine gift, but in that case there would still be a crucial role for human volitional response in *willingly receiving* this gift. In any case, Paul, in the wake of Jesus, thinks of human faith in God as the human means of receiving the unearned gift of divine redemptive grace and new, reconciled life (see Rom. 4:16). He also thinks of such faith as something that humans willingly can reject by adopting resolute distrust in God (*apistia*, Rom. 4:20). Abraham, according to Paul, did not fail in that way relative to God and God's redemptive promise, despite Abraham's occasional acts of disobedience. In Paul's grace-based theology, "*that* is why his faith in God was 'reckoned to him as righteousness'" (Rom. 4:22, RSV, italics added; cf. Gal. 3:6–9). Such faith resists any motive for human boasting, earning, or self-credit before God, because it is just the human means, for Jews as well as Gentiles, to receive the gracious gift of redemption promised by God, including the gift of divine–human fellowship via God's Spirit (see Rom. 3:29–30, 5:2, Gal. 3:14). Paul therefore reports that God's crediting of righteousness to humans "depends on faith" in God, "in order that the promise [of redemption] may rest on grace," that is, on the grace-giver (Rom. 4:16, RSV).

Paul links human faith in God to human reception of God's Spirit, which, according to Paul, is reception of the Spirit of the risen Jesus (see Rom. 8:9). More specifically, he thinks of human faith in God, in terms of obedience of the heart, as the means of receiving God's empowering Spirit whereby divine love commands can actually be obeyed by a human in virtue of the power of divine love in one's receptive heart (see Rom. 5:5, Gal. 3:2–5,14, 5:5–7,22). This empowering Spirit, according to Paul, leads a willing human noncoercively to love as God loves by "killing the deeds" antithetical to divine love (Rom. 8:13). Of course, Paul does not confuse killing evil *deeds* and killing *people* who perform evil deeds. Instead, Paul echoes the command issued by Jesus to follow his divine Father in loving people who do evil deeds, even one's evil enemies (see Rom. 12:19–21, Matt. 5:43–8).

Paul thinks of humanly received divine love, via self-entrustment to God, as empowering the human *fulfillment* of (the main purpose of) God's law when such love is lived out toward God and others (see Rom. 13:8–10, Gal. 5:15; cf. 2 Cor. 3:5–8, Gal. 6:2, Matt. 5:17, 20–2). God's offering, as a gracious powerful gift, what the divine love commands require of humans underwrites Paul's Good News of God's inviting humans into God's kingdom, via the crucified and risen Jesus. This Good News, according to Paul, is "the power of God for salvation to everyone who has faith [in God]" (Rom. 1:16, RSV; cf. 1 Cor. 4:20). In this perspective, such faith is a crucial means to transfer needed power to humans from God, and this power, being divine, transcends all merely human sources and possessions. According to Paul, this is the saving power of God's Spirit, the Spirit received only as a God-given gift via the human self-entrustment of faith, and not by human earning. This self-entrustment approach to faith, in making faith a response to an experienced intervention rather than a blind leap, reveals that fideism about Christian faith is misguided in divorcing faith from a trustworthy basis. Let's briefly explore this lesson further.

4. FAITH IN ACTION

Human faith in God, as characterized by Paul, includes an affirmative human response of self-entrustment to God's redemptive call. This fits with Paul's remark that " . . . faith [in God] comes from what is heard" (Rom. 10:17, RSV; cf. Gal. 3:2). This is faith in God as a receptive response of volitional commitment to God's call heard by a person. It includes the person's *willing reliance*, grounded in experienced evidence of the call, on the God whom humans need to overcome their destructive selfishness and impending death with lastingly good life. Accordingly, this is *not* faith as guesswork or as a leap without evidence, as if faith in God were automatically defective from a cognitive point of view. Faith in God can be at least as cognitively good, well-founded, and trustworthy as one's trusting in one's best friend, and therefore need not be a cognitive embarrassment or shortcoming at all. (Chapter 4 returns to this important cognitive point.)

Our entrusting ourselves to God includes our willingly counting *on* God as our authoritative Lord, in response to God's redemptive intervention in our lives. This, of course, is no mere intellectual affirmation or ungrounded leap in the dark. Christian faith offers the life, death, and resurrection of Jesus as the focal divine intervention and the focus of the preached Good News of God's salvation for humans. As Paul expresses this: " . . . God was in Christ reconciling the world to himself . . . " (2 Cor. 5:19). Faith in God, accordingly, is for the sake of reconciliation in fellowship with God through Jesus. In counting on God as authoritative Lord, I manifest my having committed myself to God volitionally as *my* God and *my* Lord. I therefore commit, obediently, to put God's will over my own will in my life, even with regard to my impending death. This fits with the way Jesus prayed to God in Gethsemane upon his impending redemptive death by crucifixion: "Not what I will, but what *You* will" (Mark 14:36).

According to Paul, in entrusting myself to God, I commit my selfish ways to dying and even to death in order to live by God's unselfish loving ways, in fellowship with God. In short, I resolve to die to my selfishness in order to live to God and God's ways of perfect love. I thereby share, and cooperate in realizing, God's purposes for me in his calling me to faith in God. Paul understands the human reception of divine grace via such a commitment of faith in terms of "dying and rising with Christ" (see Rom. 6:1–14, Phil. 3:9–11; for the same general lesson offered by Jesus himself, see Mark 8:34–6; cf. Byrnes 2003, Gorman 2009). This process of dying and rising entails a commitment to reject selfishness, specifically any selfishness that involves exalting my will above God's will of perfect unselfish love. The relevant trust, or faith, thus includes my obediently *entrusting myself* to God as God, in response to God's authoritative call that makes a claim on me and my whole life, now and for the future. This call is, accordingly, a call to wholehearted entrustment of oneself to God, now and for the future. Nothing in one's life is to be excluded from God's authoritative call to faith as such self-entrustment.

In selfishness (the antithesis of loving others), I fail to honor God *as authoritative Lord*, because I put myself and my own ways above the superior ways of a perfectly loving God. I would not necessarily be selfish, however, in putting God's ways first in order to bring good *to myself*. Doing something good for myself is not automatically selfish on my part. *Self-interestedness* and *selfishness* are clearly not one and the same thing, and, of the two, only selfishness inevitably conflicts with the will of a perfectly loving God. We can avoid some confusion here if we replace familiar religious talk of "selflessness" with talk of "unselfishness." Selfishness threatens if I seek to fulfill my desires in ways that knowingly bring harm to others. The divine call to human faith in God, in contrast, is a call to die to human selfishness in order to live to (and thus for) the God who seeks to empower unselfish love and to overcome death for humans. This action-oriented call is a far cry from any fideist call to embrace a contradiction in passionate subjectivity.

The suggestion of Paul and various other early Christians that, in faith in God, I must die to my selfish ways to live to God may seem to rest on an unduly harsh understanding of what such faith requires. Even so, the suggestion gains some support from an empirically verifiable feature of the human condition: namely, deep-seated human selfishness, the antithesis to the unselfish love, including the love of enemies, characteristic of a morally perfect God. Obviously, selfishness is the immoral toxin inside us that leads us to hoard the wealth and other resources desperately needed by other people. We definitely need a powerful remedy, or antitoxin, and we gain nothing of significance by ignoring this urgent problem. Facing the problem of human selfishness with honesty would enable us to apprehend our genuine need of the divine power of perfect unselfish love. In addition, it thereby would encourage us to become sincerely open to any available evidence of divine reality and of any reconciliation offered by God. More to the point, it would prompt us to be attentive to any divine call for us to become, through transformation in self-entrustment to God, personifying evidence of divine reality.

If we could free ourselves of selfishness on our own, by our own controllable power, we would doubtless find much less selfishness around us and even within us, given its self-destructive effects. Even so, we cannot plausibly be encouraging about our taking care of the problem of human selfishness on our own, because we typically protect our own selfishness out of selfish fear of personal loss. Obviously, our persistent selfishness makes us morally defective (and arguably worthy of judgment) by the divine standard of unselfish perfect love. It therefore disqualifies us from being morally equivalent to God and even from deserving, meriting, or being owed redemption by God. Nonetheless, we humans have a lingering tendency to "play God" in assuming supreme authority in some areas of our lives. This tendency has harmful cognitive as well as moral consequences, because it obstructs our ability to receive available evidence of divine reality that is intended to challenge our moral deficiencies.

We humans can become inclined to ignore, if not to suppress, needed evidence of God's authoritative call in human conscience that challenges us in our selfish tendencies opposed to God. As Paul suggests, in our self-indulgent immorality, we can consistently "suppress" what God offers to us by way of corrective challenges (see Rom. 1:18). We evidently have the God-given freedom to suppress challenges in conscience, and we often exercise that freedom, even to our own cognitive and moral detriment. The relevant empirical evidence arguably is overwhelming in favor of the latter point. In addition, it does not encourage hope for humans aiming to free themselves from their tendencies to selfishness. A power beyond human powers evidently is needed.

We humans tend to consider ourselves to be authoritative lords over our lives, particularly in areas we deem crucial to our own well-being. An especially revealing area concerns how we treat our enemies who clearly threaten our own (perceived) well-being. In some cases, we ignore them, but in other cases, we seek to destroy them, at times with heavy artillery and toxic chemicals or at least with great harm to their reputations. We very rarely, if ever, offer our enemies unselfish forgiving love, the kind of merciful enemy-love found in the perfectly loving God acknowledged by Jesus's Sermon on the Mount (see Matt. 5:43–8; cf. Luke 6:27–36). Such enemy-love, however, is a crucial feature of what enables the Jewish–Christian God to be inherently morally perfect and worthy of worship, and thereby to satisfy the maximally honorific title "God."

Not just any maximally powerful being, of course, will qualify as titleholder of the *morally* demanding title "God." The title requires inherent moral perfection, and such perfection demands a perfectly loving character, even toward enemies. Once we acknowledge this, we readily can exclude as imposters a long list of proposed candidates for the titleholder, and then can focus carefully on the very small list (of one) worthy of the wholehearted self-entrustment appropriate to faith in God. In the end, the perfectly loving God represented by Jesus is the only remaining serious candidate, once we acknowledge the crucial role of enemy-love. This claim may seem implausibly bold and exclusive at first glance, but we simply have no other candidate who offers enemy-love as a standard for all concerned. The evidence from the history of religion is, if surprising, clear on this front. We, of course, might divorce the title "God" from the standard of enemy-love, but that would be a move of ad hoc moral diminution of the category of being God.

We humans are inclined to suppose that the risk of living by unselfish love (especially toward our enemies) is too great for us, because it is too threatening to our own perceived well-being. We thereby often choose contrary to the unselfish ways of a perfectly loving God, given our presumption that we know better and given our selfish fear of personal loss. (On fear as an impediment to faith, see Mark 4:40–1, 5:36.) Accordingly, we play (false) God in the arena of ethical conduct, and we proceed with destructive actions against our enemies who seem to threaten our well-being. In contrast to such selfish fear and destructive actions, faith in the true God would be inherently the volitional commitment to *let God be God* in our lives. Such faith would include the heart-based commitment to refuse to play (false) God regarding the true God's ways of perfect love, including enemy-love. If we would have such faith in God, we would decisively renounce selfishness as ultimately counterproductive and destructive, even toward enemies. Obviously, we and our relationships with other people would become very different in that case. Faith in God then would make a striking difference in action as well as in passion. The urgent question is whether we are sincerely willing to undergo the needed change.

We must face a cognitive obstacle to human faith in God, given that we humans sometimes play (false) God regarding what is to count as needed adequate evidence of God's existence. Boldly, we presume to be in a position to say, on our own authority, what kind of evidence God *must* supply regarding God's existence. We thereby reason in a questionable way, familiar from Bertrand Russell (1970), N.R. Hanson (1971), and many other philosophers, that neglects the fact that any evidence of God's existence would be purposively available to us in a manner that suits the authoritative purposes of a morally perfect God.

In general, the questionable reasoning runs as follows. If God actually exists, God would certainly be revealed in a way readily noticed by all concerned. For instance, God would be revealed with considerable signs easily acknowledged by all relevant observers. God, however, is definitely not revealed in that way. Therefore, according to many casual observers, God does not actually exist. As a result, Russell stated as follows his response if he were to meet God after his death: "God, you gave us insufficient evidence." Using the previous line of reasoning, we intentionally exalt ourselves as cognitive judge, jury, and executioner over God, and our boldly appointed cognitive standard consigns God to the hapless category of the nonexistent.

Our dubious presumption is that God must be revealed on *our* preferred cognitive terms, as if our own boldly appointed terms were cognitively above reproach. This amounts to a kind of cognitive idolatry whereby we replace God's cognitive authority with our own. In particular, we set up our preferred cognitive standards in ways that block

or undermine "reasonable" acknowledgment of God's reality. At the same time, we ignore the fact that any evidence of
God's existence would be purposively available to humans
in keeping with *God's* perfectly loving (and thus sometimes
subtle and elusive) character and purposes. Cognitive idolatry typically stems from cognitive pride wherein we play
(false) God in the cognitive domain, to our own harm. One's
epistemology matters, then, because it can interfere with
one's reception of important available evidence of God's
existence.

Obviously, we humans are imposters in playing God, in
any domain, because we fail decisively to be worthy of worship. In particular, we lack the kind of powerful divine moral
perfection that delivers not only an opportunity for lasting
life in the face of our impending death, but also an offer
of unselfish love and reconciliation in the presence of our
destructive selfishness. Divine power therefore contrasts
sharply with familiar human power, especially in supplying
what humans desperately need in their dire predicament.
We should allow, accordingly, for *cognitive grace* whereby
God freely gives us purposively available evidence of divine
reality on God's perfectly loving terms, without either our
trivializing God's morally profound character or our earning evidence or knowledge of God.

A perfectly loving God would call us to die to our playing
God in order to live obediently and lastingly in fellowship
with God as our Lord. Our playing God wreaks havoc, wherever played, because we are at most a weak and pathetic
counterfeit in place of the morally perfect and powerful true
article. In the presence of our impending physical death, a
perfectly loving God would call us to the realization that our
playing God, including in the cognitive domain, will lead
ultimately to the grave, with no happy ending. This God
would also call us to yield our selfish wills to God's unselfish
ways rather than to have our selfish wills extinguished altogether, given their destructive tendencies. Offering purposively available evidence of divine reality, God would call

us to fold now (that is, to repent) and to welcome (that is, to trust) divine redeeming power in a new Spirit-led mode of living and dying. According to the Christian Good News, the life, death, and resurrection of Jesus perfectly model this new mode of existence, receptively and obediently under the divine authority that, in perfect redemptive love, is for our good. Faith in God, as self-entrustment now and for the future, is the human means of receiving and appropriating this new mode of life under God, in fellowship with God.

Moral considerations surround and permeate faith in God, taking it beyond merely intellectual considerations. In human selfishness antithetical to divine love, we fear not getting something we want (perhaps an opportunity or a relationship), even at the expense of harming others, perhaps by blocking them from things they need. One motive at work is self-indulgent fear, which typically underwrites greed, covetousness, bias, and various other evils. Such fear haunts our natural behavioral tendencies, and looms large over much of human history, including national wars, racial and ethnic conflicts, and religious violence. More specifically, such fear can capture and enslave us at the expense of flourishing and loving human relationships, and it is always contrary to the life-giving ways of a perfectly loving God. Faith in God is a needed antidote, because such faith, as human entrustment to God, is the avenue of receiving the perfect divine love that casts out selfish fear and offers reconciled fellowship instead (see 1 John 4:18).

Ordinary knowledge of information will not free us from our selfishness or our impending death, because humans need volitional, purpose-directed *power* to move beyond selfishness and death. Clearly, contrary to Plato, we can know what is good but fail to conform to it in our desires, intentions, and actions. Selfishness is inherently a matter of the will, and therefore cognitive enlightenment by itself will not solve the human problem of selfishness. Although many philosophers and religious thinkers have overlooked this important lesson, we should acknowledge it as well as the human need of corrective power beyond intellectual illumination.

Bearing on the wilderness parable in the Introduction, human faith in God offers a place of rescue and safe refuge from our selfishness where we are set free of selfish fear even in the face of death. This is a place of divine–human *interpersonal fellowship* where humans are volitionally related and reconciled, via entrusting themselves, to a personal agent who first calls them into reconciled fellowship and new life. This call comes with the distinctive *power* of divine unselfish love. Such divine love can bring good to us, even in our suffering and dying, in ways that make selfishness undesirable, ineffectual, and even repulsive.

In our suffering and dying, we often have a clear opportunity to see that the lasting power of the salvation, or rescue, we humans need does not come from us but must come instead from God (see 2 Cor. 4:7, 12:9). According to the Christian Good News, God's authoritative power of unselfish lasting love, particularly as exemplified in the life, death, and resurrection of Jesus, *shows* us (perhaps even without fully explaining) that we do not need selfishness to receive what is vitally good for us, and that even physical death can be overcome in resurrection by God. This is a central part of the Christian Good News of powerful divine redemption by grace through faith in God and in Jesus as God's unique mediator.

In the interest of full disclosure, we humans should ask whether we are morally and cognitively *fit* or *positioned* to recognize on our own a personal power of perfect love that can liberate us from our selfishness if we are willing. We may be too far into the wilderness darkness of destructive selfishness to see on our own what we truly need to see and to do. This would recommend cognitive pessimism about *our own resources* relative to a perfectly loving God, but it would *not* be unqualified pessimism about all available resources. Fortunately, we ourselves arguably do not exhaust the available resources in this area.

Perhaps the needed divine resources are purposively available to us if we are suitably willing, in a manner that fits with divine redemptive purposes for us as people needing volitional transformation, in reconciled fellowship and life with God (see Moser 2008 for details). At least we now face this urgent question: are we humans *willing* to hear, and then to obey in the self-entrustment of faith, a call to everdeepening fellowship and life with a God who manifests and commands love toward others, even toward enemies? This life-or-death question raises the existential question of whether we are willing to be addressed by a God who offers new life on God's terms of unselfish love. This question takes us well beyond philosophy proper, into a self-defining decision each reflective human must make, however the details of one's philosophy are worked out.

5. WHITHER FIDEISM?

The previous sketch of distinctively Christian faith in God serves an important purpose in an evaluation of fideism. Specifically, it gives us a concrete standard for measuring the adequacy of fideism as an approach to faith in God. We shall see that fideism not only falls short of the standard outlined but also conflicts with it. As a result, Christian faith in God calls for an alternative to fideism. The same antifideist lesson is true, as we shall see, of any other approach to faith in God that calls for faith that can be trustworthily, or wellgroundedly, commended as true rather than false or illusory.

A perfectly loving God, in virtue of genuine unselfish love toward others, would be outgoing in intentional actions for the good of others. In addition, for the sake of genuine unselfish love toward others, such a God would encourage and even command others to be likewise outgoing in intentional actions for the good of others. As a result, such a God would expect human faith in God to be lived out in unselfish love toward others, and not in hate toward others. Accordingly, as noted previously, Paul identifies Christian faith in God as "faith [in God] working through love" (Gal. 5:6). In addition, as also suggested previously, Paul portrays Christian faith in God as a grounded human response of self-entrustment to a divine call to a new life of unselfish love (see Rom. 10:17). This call, according to Paul, is an integral part of the Christian Good News of God's redemptive plan via the crucified and risen Jesus, and it is offered as a cognitive ground for Christian faith in God.

Faith in God could not be trustworthily commended as a correct human response to be obediently lived out for the good of others if it rested just on an acknowledged contradiction or on some other kind of ungrounded commitment. The latter two options (of acknowledged contradiction and ungrounded commitment) will undermine the crucial role of a divine call, or anything else, as a trustworthiness-conferring ground for a correct human response of faith in God. More specifically, those options divorce such faith from a trustworthy grounding in a divine call to new human life with God, or in anything else. In doing so, they cut off faith in God from both what gives it trustworthy significance in a human life and a trustworthiness-conferring cognitive ground for its being correct. The result is a kind of faith that is either necessarily false (if it is contradictory) or cognitively arbitrary (if it is lacking in a cognitive ground).

Humans cannot trustworthily adopt or live out, in intentional actions aimed at manifesting unselfish love, contradictory or ungrounded faith in God. Indeed, such faith cannot be, even in principle, trustworthily commended (for adoption or practice) as correct if it is either contradictory or ungrounded. Instead, such faith will be trustworthily commended as correct only if it is *cognitively* commendable, because the faith in question commits one to *the reality* of God. As a result, questions about reality in contrast with *unreality* or *illusion*, in the case of God, emerge automatically. Accordingly, from a cognitive point of view, such faith calls for a (possibly fallible) *truth indicator* to serve as a trustworthiness-conferring ground.

Faith in God will be cognitively commendable only if it has an available basis for commendation that is neither contradictory nor cognitively arbitrary. Fideist faith that is not thus commendable relative to available truth indicators will lack needed support relative to our evidential perspective on reality, and thus will float free of our trustworthy indicators of what is real, or actually the case, rather than illusory. As a result, fideist faith will be cognitively deficient, relative to our (possibly fallible) trustworthy evidential indicators of reality, in a manner that blocks its being trustworthily commendable as correct.

If human faith in God has no truth indicator to serve as a trustworthiness-conferring ground, it will lack a trustworthy place in human thought and life. Indeed, it will then be an untrustworthy postulate that fails to earn its keep for what it actually is in a human life: namely, a definite claim on reality, particularly regarding the reality of God. Fideism makes faith in God just such a postulate in need of a trustworthiness-conferring basis regarding its being correct. In separating such faith from a trustworthiness-conferring basis that offers a (possibly fallible) well-grounded truth indicator, fideism has faith make do without a trustworthy basis for its supposedly being correct, or for its commendation as correct. It thereby makes faith untrustworthy and thus, arguably, dispensable, at least relative to our trustworthy truth indicators. In the end, fideism leads to the dispensability of faith in God, at least from the standpoint of what has a trustworthy basis or what is trustworthily commendable as correct.

Fideists cannot salvage their fideism by requiring *just some* evidential support for faith in God but not enough to make such faith more reasonable, or trustworthy, than its denial. That position would leave faith in God, at best, as a position on which people should withhold judgment (that is, neither affirm nor deny) from a cognitive point of view that demands trustworthiness. If faith in God is at best a position on which we should withhold judgment from the standpoint of trustworthiness, then we should withhold judgment on it, all things considered. A position that makes a claim about reality (such as a claim that God exists) but is not supported by trustworthy evidence (and thus is, itself, not trustworthy) should not be accepted *as true*. As noted previously, the trustworthiness in question is not objective reliability relative to how the world actually is; instead, it is relative to a person's available truth indicators, or evidence.

One might accept, of course, that an untrustworthy position is prudently or morally beneficial when adopted, but that would be a move to a domain of practical value other than either correctness in the position or trustworthiness regarding correctness in the position. For practical, noncognitive reasons, such as prudential or moral reasons, one might recommend faith in God, but that recommendation would fall short of a recommendation of either the correctness or the trustworthiness regarding *correctness* (in the *content*) of faith in God. It would be more accurate, therefore, to offer noncognitive reasons as recommending that one *act as if* one had faith in God, without recommending either the actual trustworthiness or the actual correctness of (the content of) such faith. We should distinguish, accordingly, between (a) trustworthiness regarding the *evident truth of the content* of belief or faith and (b) advisability (say, for practical or moral reasons) of one's *adopting* a belief or faith-commitment. This content–act distinction undermines pragmatist and Kantian variations on fideism, so long as a faith-commitment makes a claim on reality, such as the reality of God. (In particular, this distinction challenges the kind of Kantian fideism developed in Bishop 2007.)

Under pressure, a fideist might retreat to a nonrealist conception of faith in God that avoids any commitment to the reality of God. That, however, would be a move of troublesome desperation. Faith in God, as suggested previously, is *de re* in a manner that contrasts such faith with a mere noncognitive use of language that is free of concerns about reality as opposed to illusion. If there is no God, then there is no genuine *de re* faith *in God,* even if there is belief that God exists. Fideists, accordingly, can move to a nonrealist conception of faith in God only if they change the subject away from genuine faith in God that concerns reality as opposed to illusion. As usual, a move to nonrealism, in keeping with the case of nonrealism about truth itself, sacrifices what was originally at issue: the real existence of something. (For problems with such nonrealism in general, see Moser 1993, Chapter 1.) Such nonrealism simply relinquishes genuine faith *in God.* It also sacrifices the role of God as a needed source of real power for human transformation and redemption. (The same problem faces any version of Kantian fideism that portrays God as a moral postulate.)

In steering clear of nonrealism and its problems, fideists will be faced with a commitment to the *reality* of God that requires, from a cognitive point of view, a trustworthy truth indicator that can supply a basis for trustworthy commendation concerning the reality, rather than the illusion, of God. As suggested previously, the latter requirement leads to the demise of fideism, because it leads to a required trustworthiness-conferring ground for faith in God. Summing up, then, we can see that fideism faces a dilemma of misplaced nonrealism or untrustworthy cognitive arbitrariness regarding its implication for faith in God.

A central motivation for fideism, in the end, is just fear of the potentially corrosive effects of cognitive standards on religious belief. Kant, at least, famously offered a noncognitive approach to theistic belief that sought to escape a perceived threat from scientific or "theoretical" knowledge of reality. His general strategy was to deny knowledge in order to make room for faith in God. More specifically, he sought to fold theistic belief into the domain of morality (by making commitment to God a postulate needed by moral rationality), and then to offer morality as a function of human practical rationality understood as a kind of consistency in human willing and believing. In thus moralizing faith in God, Kant's strategy decisively isolated theistic belief from the domain of science in particular and cognition in general, and this noncognitivist lesson was not lost on subsequent Christian theology in large sectors of the Protestant tradition. (For relevant discussion, see Thielicke 1990, Chapters 10–11; cf. Wainwright 2005, Chapter 1.) A fideist fear of cognitive standards for theistic belief is misplaced, however, when it is generalized to concern all (plausible) cognitive standards. Indeed, the unfortunate result is akin to throwing out the baby with the (dirty) bath water.

The fideist mistake, in the wake of Kant and Kierkegaard, is to approach some troublesome cognitive standards as if they were representative of cognitive standards in general. For instance, the Core Scientism challenged in Chapter 1 is, indeed, a troublesome cognitive standard, given that it is at odds with any cognitive standard not grounded in the empirical sciences. In particular, Core Scientism is at odds with any such cognitive standard independent of the sciences that approves of faith in God. The crucial problem is that Core Scientism fails to meet its own cognitive standard that requires a grounding in the empirical sciences. Given this self-referential failing, Core Scientism is, at best, a cognitive standard worthy of our rejection. Even so, cognitive standards in general are not a threat to well-founded faith in God, regardless of any general fears behind fideism. We therefore should be suspicious of any general fideist attempt to set aside the primary importance of cognitive standards for faith in God, including any Kantian attempt to relegate faith in God to the domain of (the needed postulates of) practical or moral rationality (including the Kantian fideist attempt in Bishop 2007).

The task of identifying adequate cognitive standards for human belief, including faith in God, is difficult by any standard. The task is remarkably complex, and it stubbornly resists any quick and easy solution. (See Moser 1989, 1993 for some indications of the significant complexity in this domain.) Even so, this task merits our careful attention, even in connection with cognitive standards for human faith in God. The motivation is straightforward: for human faith in God to be trustworthy in human life, it must be supported by a trustworthy truth indicator, and this requires a basis for trustworthy commendation of human faith in God. The truth indicator in question will confer trustworthiness, and therefore will supply a well-founded cognitive grounding for faith in God. As a result, fideism about faith in God will be misplaced, because a trustworthiness-conferring ground for faith in God will then be available. In the end, fideism leaves faith in God as something less than a trustworthy source for finding a needed rescuer in the Introduction's wilderness parable. In doing so, fideism arguably hinders trustworthy pursuit of the question of whether human faith in God contributes to the satisfaction of the deepest human needs, including human cognitive needs. (Chapter 4 returns to the latter topic.)

6. ARGUMENT-INDIFFERENT FIDEISM

Traditional fideism rejects a requirement of trustworthy support for religious beliefs, or at least minimizes the significance of such support in some way, perhaps by allowing moral or prudential reasons to have decisive significance. In any case, one might reject traditional fideism about evidence but, following Alvin Plantinga, endorse argument-indifferent fideism: the view that belief in God can be perfectly rational even if there is no cogent argument whatever for the existence of God (see Plantinga 1983, p. 65). Many proponents of so-called "reformed epistemology" support such argument-indifferent fideism, but we shall see that this fideist position is untenable. By "cogent argument," Plantinga means "rationally convincing argument," which is not synonymous with "logically sound argument." The premises of a logically sound argument, although true, need not be rationally convincing at all. In addition, we should not confuse the idea of a cogent argument and the idea of evidence. Evidence, say from sensory experience, need not be an argument at all.

Plantinga's position rests on an account of *epistemic warrant* – that is, of that "quality or quantity enough of which, together with truth and belief, is sufficient for knowledge" (1993, p. v). He proposes that a belief has epistemic warrant only if it has been produced and sustained by cognitive faculties that (a) are functioning properly in an appropriate environment, (b) are aimed at the production of true beliefs, and (c) have a high objective probability of producing true beliefs under the appropriate conditions of belief formation. Plantinga explains his notion of the "proper function" of our cognitive faculties in terms of a "design plan" governing those faculties. Proper function of our cognitive faculties is function in accordance with the design plan for those faculties, and this design plan specifies the way those faculties function aright.

Plantinga suggests that his talk of a design plan, as a specification of every aspect of how a thing will function when it functions *properly*, does not entail that humans were designed by God. He explains: "Human beings are constructed according to a certain design plan. This terminology does not commit us to supposing that human beings have been literally designed – by God, for example. Here I use 'design' the way Daniel Dennett . . . does in speaking of a given organism as possessing a certain design, and of evolution as producing optimal design. . . . " (1993, p. 13). There is, however, a significant difference neglected by Plantinga between saying that humans are "constructed according to a certain design plan" and saying that they "possess a certain design."

Contrary to a suggestion of neutrality, Plantinga evidently builds into his ideas of proper function and design plan (and thus also into his idea of epistemic warrant) an implicit reference to an intentional designer. Dennett's idea of the design of a thing (for instance, in Dennet 1987) is arguably not irreducibly normative or purposive, but Plantinga's notions of a design plan and of proper function are. Plantinga proposes that a design plan specifies how a thing ought to function. In addition, specification of how a thing ought to function is independent of how things of that sort actually do function for the most part. Indeed, it could happen that nothing of a certain kind actually functions as it ought to function in accordance with its design plan. Plantinga holds that proper function is determined by how a thing functions normally, but he emphasizes that this is *not* a descriptive or statistical sense of "normal." As a result, any desire for compatibility with an evolutionary account of design, such as Dennett's, will ultimately fail.

Plantinga speaks of proper function as follows: "[I]t is of first importance to see that this condition – that of one's cognitive equipment functioning *properly* – is not the same thing as one's cognitive equipment functioning *normally*, not, at any rate, if we take the term 'normally' in a broadly statistical sense. Even if one of my systems functions in a way far from the statistical norm, it might still be functioning properly. (Alternatively, what we must see is that there is a distinction between a normative and a statistical sense of 'normal'.)" (1993, p. 9). Plantinga understands "proper function" in such a way that it is possible that no human actually functions in accordance with a particular aspect of the design plan for humans. As a result, this is not a merely descriptive or statistical understanding of "proper function."

Given that Plantinga's standards for proper and improper function do not stem from a generalization from actual behavior, they must find their source elsewhere. Plantinga mentions evolution and God as possible alternative sources (1993, p. 21), and he claims not to rule out evolution by definitional fiat. As noted previously, however, Plantinga requires that "proper function" be understood in relation to a normative sense of "normal," but Darwinian evolution yields only descriptive statistical norms and therefore cannot deliver a genuinely normative sense of "normal." Darwinian evolution does not yield norms to distinguish proper from improper functions as understood by Plantinga, because it produces only organisms that actually function in accordance with mutation and natural selection.

Plantinga's talk of *the* proper function of our cognitive faculties evidently makes sense only if we assume that there is some definite set of cognitive standards provided by a (consistent) designer's intentions. Without that assumption, we are faced with the relativity of when a cognitive function is proper in the context of a wide range of different, and even conflicting, standards. Accordingly, Plantinga's epistemology fares better in a supernaturalist ontology than in a naturalist ontology. Indeed, it is hard to make definite normative sense of his talk of *the* proper function of our cognitive faculties without the assumption that there is a definite set of standards for proper cognitive function provided by a (consistent) designer's intentions for our cognitive faculties. We therefore should hesitate to adopt Plantinga's talk of *the* proper function of our cognitive faculties unless we are agreeable to a supernaturalist ontology.

Many theorists will doubt that we should follow Plantinga in talking about *the* proper function of our cognitive faculties in a normative sense that presupposes a supernatural designer. Even if Plantinga's theism is true, we have no reason to suppose that intentional standards for proper function set by *humans* cannot serve human epistemological purposes. Such standards arising from humans may vary across human groups, owing to varying standards of propriety, but this will not preclude effective epistemological assessment. Variance in epistemological standards is a fact of contemporary epistemological life, and it may entail a kind of variance in epistemological concepts, at least at a level of specificity. (On the latter topic, see Moser 1993.) If we bracket the design plan of a single God (or some such supernatural agent), we shall be hard put to ignore variability in relevant epistemological standards. In that case, a kind of conventionalism and relativism about epistemological standards will merit serious consideration. Plantinga, however, does not give due consideration to the possibility that we humans are the sources of the standards for distinguishing proper and improper cognitive function, relative to our preferred cognitive goals.

Conventionalism aside, Plantinga's theism includes the following two propositions (2000, p. 438):

(1) The world was created by God, an almighty, all-knowing and perfectly good personal being (the sort of being who holds beliefs, has aims and intentions, and can act to accomplish these aims).

(2) Human beings require salvation, and God has provided a unique way of salvation through the incarnation, life, sacrificial death, and resurrection of his divine son, Jesus Christ.

Regarding the possibility and the necessity of arguments for (2), Plantinga claims:

My aim is to show how it can be that Christians can be justified, rational (both internally and externally), and warranted in holding full-blooded Christian belief. . . . Justification [taken deontologically, in terms of non-violation of intellectual obligations] and internal rationality [as proper function of one's cognitive processes given one's actual, possibly grossly misleading experiences] are easy enough. . . . External rationality and warrant are harder. The only way I can see to argue that Christian belief has *these* virtues [namely, external rationality and warrant] is to argue that Christian belief is, indeed, *true*. I don't propose to offer such an argument. That is because I don't know of an argument for Christian belief that seems very likely to convince one who doesn't already accept its conclusion. That is nothing against Christian belief, however, and indeed I shall argue that if Christian beliefs are true, then the standard and most satisfactory way to hold them will not be as the conclusions of argument (2000, pp. 200–1).

Plantinga refrains from arguing that Christian belief is true, on this ground: "I don't know of an argument for Christian belief that seems very likely to convince one who doesn't already accept its conclusion." As a result, by Plantinga's lights, a worthwhile argument for Christian belief must seem very likely to convince one who does not already accept its conclusion. We now are on very thin ice, however, quite aside from the unclear talk of an argument's seeming "very likely" to convince.

Regarding whom is to be convinced, does Plantinga mean *everyone* who does not already accept the conclusion of a proposed argument for Christian belief? If so, why should we accept that dubious requirement? It amounts to the following standard:

> (a) It is worthwhile or proper to argue that Christian belief is true only if one's argument seems very likely to convince everyone who does not already accept its conclusion.

Many perfectly worthwhile and proper arguments fail to seem very likely to convince *everyone* who does not already accept their conclusions. As a result, (a) is too demanding. For instance, Plantinga's influential free-will argument against the logical problem of evil for theism is perfectly worthwhile and proper (see Plantinga 1977), but it fails to seem likely to convince everyone who does not already accept its conclusion. Some people who do not already accept its conclusion are just too stubborn, whimsical, or outright confused to be (likely to be) convinced by the argument. This fact reflects badly on the wayward people in question, and not at all on the free-will argument in question. This argument is beyond reproach relative to its avowedly limited goal of showing consistency, despite its failure to convince all people.

Perhaps Plantinga meant not (a) but rather the following:

> (b) It is worthwhile or proper to argue that Christian belief is true only if one's argument seems very likely to convince at least one person who does not already accept its conclusion.

The problem is that (b) is too weak to yield Plantinga's desired result. It is a sad but true comment on our species that any argument, or at least any minimally nonpreposterous argument, seems very likely to convince at least one person who does not already accept its conclusion. Many people are terribly and shamelessly gullible in the face of arguments (see any television talk show audience for examples). As a result, we will be able to find, in fairly short order, at least one person who is very likely to be convinced by an argument for Christian belief but who does not already accept it conclusion. Accordingly, (b) will not support Plantinga's view that his arguing for the truth of Christian belief is not worthwhile or proper.

It seems ill-advised to base the supposed inappropriateness or lack of success of an argument for the truth of Christian belief on the argument's shortcoming in its apparent likelihood to convince certain people. In fact, Plantinga's line of argument disarms itself. His (implicit) argument for not arguing for the truth of Christian belief does not seem very likely at all to convince one who does not already accept its conclusion. By his own standard, then, Plantinga should relinquish his suggested argument against the appropriateness or success of argument for Christian belief.

What, if anything, would underwrite Plantinga's misgiving about argument for Christian belief? One might offer a diagnosis in keeping with Plantinga's evident liking for things Calvinist. The Calvinist problem here, as pretty much everywhere, is *sin*, that is, depraving and corrupting *sin*. (Chapter 4 returns to the cognitive significance of human sin.) According to Plantinga's Calvinism (mercifully free of explicit foreordained lasting condemnation of certain people), "we human beings, apart from God's special and gracious activity, are sunk in sin; . . . [as a result,] without some special activity on the part of the Lord, we wouldn't believe" (2000, p. 269; cf. p. 303). We are sunk *deeply* in sin, according to this story, so deeply that our coming to have Christian beliefs must come "by way of the work of the Holy Spirit, who gets us to accept, *causes us to believe*, these great truths of the gospel" (2000, p. 245, italics added; cf. p. 260). Plantinga notes that God's *causing* us to do something rules out our doing it freely (2000, p. 462). It follows, on his view, that no one *freely* comes to have Christian beliefs. So far, this is very Calvinist, even with intimations of God's selective irresistible grace in regeneration of the "favored" (2000, p. 254). Plantinga looks for scriptural support in Jesus's remark (John 6:44) that "no one can come to me unless the Father who sent me draws him" (2000, p. 269).

The proposed diagnosis will not survive scrutiny. One difficulty is that John's Gospel resists a Calvinist reading of divinely selected and caused regeneration. The notion of "drawing" people in John's Gospel suggests both *universality* of drawing and human *freedom* to reject or to embrace the drawing. Accordingly, Jesus remarks that "when I am lifted up from the earth, I will draw *all* (*pantas*) [people] to myself" (John 12:32). Famously, John's Gospel (3:16) teaches that God so loved the whole *world* (*ton kosmon*) that he gave his unique Son, so that *anyone* who trusts in him will have everlasting life. Taken as a whole, John's Gospel does not portray God as causing some people but not others to believe. Instead, this Gospel assumes a typical free human response of receiving or rejecting God's gracious salvation intended for all people (see John 1:11–13, 3:19–21). According to John's Gospel, in seeking genuine love from humans and thus respecting human freedom, God did not cause Jesus to obey (see John 10:17–18); likewise, God does not cause the "favored" to believe or to be faithful.

In John's Gospel and in the New Testament generally, God graciously gives humans the freedom to receive or reject God's salvation (see Meadors 2006). Otherwise, in regenerating just some favored people in moral and spiritual bondage, God would show a kind of selective love incompatible with genuine love of *all* people, including enemies. As a result, God would lack moral perfection and thus worthiness of worship, and would be inconsistent in commanding *humans* to love all of their enemies. As worthy of worship, God, of course, would be *at least* as loving as humans. In sincerely offering the gift of faith and salvation to all (and not just the favored), God would want *none* to perish but everyone to come to repentance (see 2 Pet. 3:9; cf. Rev. 3:20). This divine want would be free of harmful deceit; otherwise, its source would not be worthy of worship.

As it happens, the necessary role of human freedom in loving God has a tragic result: it results in the gracious divine want and invitation being unsatisfied in the case of some humans. The inherent risk of rejection is thus realized, tragically, by some humans in the actual world. We would have a kind of harmful deceit (or at least a pathetic notion of want) if God (i) reported his wanting the salvation of all people, (ii) could cause all people to have saving faith, but (iii) failed to cause all people to have saving faith. Neither God nor anyone else, however, can *cause* a person to love others in the manner essential to saving faith. True love is inherently resistible, for the sake of maintaining the genuine agency of the people loved. Calvinism, however well-meaning and cleanly systematic, thus distorts and underestimates the universal genuine love found in a God worthy of worship.

Calvinism aside, and contrary to Plantinga, the crucial role of God's Spirit in human faith and regeneration does not make argument for Christian truths superfluous or otherwise unnecessary. In the Christian story of divine revelation, God's Spirit can and sometimes does use arguments as pathways to (or components of) free human reception of faith in God and human regeneration by God. One's freely coming to God via the work of God's Spirit can, and arguably sometimes does, include one's coming by way of argument. Here is a quick sketch of a relevant argument to be refined and defended in Chapter 4:

1. My human life will be dominated by unselfish love toward all other people only if my selfish human fears are subdued at least for the most part.

2. My selfish human fears are subdued at least for the most part only if a perfectly loving God pours out (in response to my free reception) divine unselfish love in my heart.

3. My human life is indeed dominated by unselfish love toward all other people.

4. Therefore, a perfectly loving God exists.

This rough sketch of an argument for God's existence draws from such New Testament passages as Romans 5:5 and 1 John 3:14, 4:12–13,18. (As suggested, Chapter 4 adds some important details to this quick sketch.)

God's Spirit would not be required to use any argument, of course, but could use a good argument without reproach. I, for one, find rational support for theism in such an argument as 1–4 (when properly amplified), and many Christians testify to God's Spirit's using arguments on occasion for Christian belief. Of course, the argument 1–4 does not support the distinctive details of a Christian theology, but it can offer a theistic basis for a Christian theology, and it can be extended with further argument (as in Chapter 4) to lend support to central Christian beliefs.

Plantinga's reluctance to propose arguments for Christian belief is puzzling at best. He claims, anticlimactically, that in asking about the *truth* of Christian belief, "we pass beyond the competence of philosophy" (2000, p. 499). What, however, is the supposed problem with Christian belief from the standpoint of philosophy and argument? Even if (as Plantinga holds) Christian faith in God is a gift that must be sealed upon one's heart by God's Spirit, and we suffer profoundly from sin, how do such truths make Christian belief "beyond the competence of philosophy"? This is far from clear in Plantinga's reformed epistemology.

Our tendency not to follow God's unselfish ways on our own does not challenge the value of philosophy in itself for theology. Likewise, bad reasoners do not make reasoning itself hopeless, improper, or worthless. The *performance* of philosophers, however misguided at times, leaves unscathed the *competence* of philosophy as a rational truth-seeking and error-avoiding discipline. Philosophy done properly (unlike that, say, in Corinth in Paul's day; see 1 Cor. 1:19–29) is arguably a proper and worthwhile means to our freely discerning and welcoming the inviting and drawing righteous love of God's Spirit for all people, even for argumentative philosophers. It is not just a sophisticated tool for pollution control (as Plantinga 2000, p. 499 suggests). Christians, after all, do claim to speak wisdom (*sophia*) among the mature children of God (see 1 Cor. 2:6), even if not wisdom of this world, and the wisdom from God can sustain valid inferential patterns in arguments.

Plantinga notes often that Christian belief is not typically formed on the basis of arguments. That seems virtually undeniable and even true. Even so, philosophers, including Christian philosophers, have at least epistemological, ontological, and ethical work to do in philosophy, and this work depends on arguments of various sorts. (Otherwise, they would not have a place for such philosophical works as Plantinga's *Warranted Christian Belief*.) Plantinga proposes that God's Spirit enables believers to apprehend the glory and the beauty of the gospel in a manner that restores (to an important extent) the operation of the *sensus divinitatis*. This apprehension is not a premise in an argument, but is, instead, an *occasion* of one's forming the belief that the gospel is from God and true. Plantinga *apparently* suggests at one point that this apprehension is (on the model of perception) part of one's (nonpropositional) evidence for the gospel truths in that it is part of what makes those truths evident for one (2000, pp. 305–6). He evidently backs off this suggestion, however, in his official mood (2000, p. 326); as a result, evidentialist hopes are not encouraged by Plantinga.

My own evidentialism, as developed in this book, is moderate evidentialism, implying that justified belief in God must rest on (perhaps fallible) evidence, but *not* necessarily propositional evidence, that indicates the reality of God. (Unfortunately, however, "evidentialism" seems to be a dirty word in Plantinga's vocabulary.) Determinate non-propositional experience, for instance, can supply relevant evidence in connection with theism. (The idea of non-propositional evidence in general is developed in Moser 1989.) More specifically, various New Testament writers promise morally transforming evidence to genuine seek-ers after God, and because this promised evidence is a def-inite indicator of the reality of a perfectly loving God, it manifests God's perfectly loving character. That is, this evi-dence includes and exhibits God's profound unselfish *love* *(agape)*, even for God's enemies. Accordingly, Paul remarks that hope in God does not disappoint us (cognitively or otherwise) "because God's love has been poured out in our hearts" by God's Spirit (Rom. 5:5; cf. 2 Cor. 5:16–17; see also 1 John 4:12–13, 16, 19).

The presence of God's morally transforming love, it is arguable, can serve as a nonpropositional *cognitive* founda-tion for human knowledge of God's reality (see, for instance, Col. 2:2, 1 Cor. 8:2–3, Eph. 3:17–19.) In that capacity, it is real nonpropositional *evidence* of God's reality and pres-ence. Such morally transforming love from God can pro-duce (noncoercively) a loving character in willing people, despite their obstruction at times. This transformation *hap-pens to one,* in part, and thus is neither purely self-made nor simply the byproduct of a self-help strategy. This widely neglected supernatural evidence and sign would be avail-able at God's appointed time to anyone who is receptive toward God with due moral seriousness. Such an approach can illuminate these otherwise puzzling remarks: "We *know* that we have passed from death to life because we love one another. . . . Whoever does not love does not know God, for God is love" (1 John 3:14, 4:8, NRSV). This approach con-firms that one's theistic belief need not be based on an argu-ment or a proposition, even though it (cognitively) should be based on supporting evidence.

Given the suggested approach to nonpropositional evidence, humans would need to learn how to apprehend, and to be apprehended by, God's unselfish *love*, not just *truths about* God's love. Neither God nor God's love, of course, is a proposition or an argument, and neither is reducible to a purely intellectual entity. The (personifying) evidence of God's reality offered by character-transformation toward unselfish love in willing people goes much deeper than the comparatively superficial evidence proposed in, for example, visions, ecstatic experiences, and fancy philosophical arguments. We consistently could dismiss any such proposed evidence as illusory or inconclusive, given certain alterations in our beliefs. In contrast, genuine character transformation toward God's unselfish love does not admit of convenient dismissal, because it bears directly on who one really is, or has become, including the morally relevant kind of person one actually is, or has become. Such transformation, in any case, cuts too deeply against our natural selfish tendencies to qualify as just a self-help ploy. As a result, it arguably offers a kind of firm nonpropositional evidence that resists quick dismissal and offers a basis for theistic belief. (Chapter 4 returns to this topic in connection with personifying evidence of God's reality; see also Moser 2008.)

Plantinga's epistemology must answer this question: when exactly does an experience that occasions a belief yield *warrant* for that belief, and when not? Obviously, not all experiences that occasion a belief yield warrant for that belief; an experience can prompt an unwarranted belief under certain circumstances. Plantinga's answer, as suggested previously, invokes a feature of the cognitive faculty that yields the belief in question. According to Plantinga, that faculty must function properly in a hospitable cognitive environment according to God's design plan that is directed at truth. This view leads Plantinga to argue that agnosticism and naturalism about human origins lead to the destruction of knowledge (2000, pp. 222–40). Now, *given* the role Plantinga assigns to cognitive faculties and God's design plan in warrant, his conclusion is not a far reach. Let's suppose, however, that one dissents from that role assigned by Plantinga. What considerations can Plantinga then offer, given his argument-indifferent fideism?

Assuming agnosticism for the sake of argument, Plantinga claims that " . . . because I now do not believe that my cognitive faculties are reliable . . . , I also realize that . . . beliefs produced by my faculties are no more likely to be true than false" (2000, p. 238). This inference, however, is too quick. One might have an undefeated truth indicator (say, an auditory experience of the RoiTan cigar song, in the absence of conflicting experiences or beliefs) for a perceptual belief (that the RoiTan cigar song is being sung), even if one lacks actual reliability and even supposed reliability in one's cognitive faculty of hearing. The undefeated evidence for a belief need not derive from the general reliability of the faculty producing that belief.

General unreliability in a belief-producing faculty, such as an auditory faculty, is perfectly compatible with one's having an impeccable, or undefeated, truth indicator (or evidence) in a *particular* case of belief formation, such as an auditory belief. A generally unreliable microphone, for instance, can deliver crystal-clear, faultless singing in some cases, as seasoned singers will testify. It follows, then, that undefeated truth indicators (for example, even from nonpropositional experience) can justify a belief without general reliability in the faculty yielding the belief. In addition, defeaters of evidence are not generated by mere beliefs (in the way suggested by Plantinga 2000, p. 485). Mere belief, even if aimed at truth, can be epistemically and alethically bankrupt and hence incapable of defeating evidence. These considerations about evidence and defeat should raise doubts about Plantinga's view that agnosticism and naturalism about human origins lead to the destruction of human knowledge.

Although we should grant that Christian belief is not always formed on the basis of an argument, one must still explain the *grounds* on which Christian belief is to be *recommended as true*. Otherwise, one will be left with recommendation fideism – that is, fideism about recommending a belief, or (equivalently) what I have called "argument-indifferent fideism." Plantinga suggests that traditional theists lack reason to doubt that our cognitive faculties are designed to produce true beliefs. If, however, one doubts that our cognitive faculties yield truth, then, according to Plantinga, "you can't quell that doubt by producing an argument about God and his veracity, or indeed, any argument at all; for the argument, of course, will be under as much suspicion as its source. Here no argument will help you; here salvation will have to be by grace, not by works" (1993, p. 237). According to Plantinga, traditional theists remain unscathed here because they are not inclined to doubt the reliability of our cognitive faculties.

Regardless of what traditional theists are actually inclined to doubt, one must ask whether, and if so how, they can *justify,* or *trustworthily commend,* the assumption that their cognitive faculties have been designed by God to be reliable. Even if salvation here is by grace rather than by works, many people seeking redemption would like to justify, in some definite and trustworthy way, that the divine redeeming grace proclaimed by Plantinga is genuine *rather than spurious or illusory*. One does not have to be a friend of skepticism in general to have this common aspiration. Instead, one might simply aim to "test the spirits to see whether they are from God, because many false prophets have gone out into the world" (1 John 4:1). Many false prophets indeed have gone out and, therefore, any responsible inquirer will seek a discriminating standard.

Various and sundry (incompatible) philosophical and religious positions lay claim to authority on humans, and we need some way to distinguish the wheat from the tares, even if the two are allowed to grow together for a while. Plantinga has given us no reason to receive as genuine, rather than illusory, the divine epistemological grace he proclaims. He has left unanswered what exactly can trustworthily commend his message of alleged divine grace, including cognitive grace, to the multitudes. Personal intuitions about warrant and proper function seem to figure prominently in his account, but, notoriously, such intuitions vary among philosophers, even among contemporary epistemologists.

The real problem is Plantinga's view, amounting to argument-indifferent fideism, that belief in God can be perfectly rational even if there is no cogent argument whatever for the existence of God (1983, p. 65). As acknowledged previously, an individual believer need not base her theistic belief on an argument (given a role for nonpropositional supporting evidence), but one still could formulate an argument that identifies the needed trustworthy truth indicator and the way it supports belief in God (see the previous argument 1–4 and the refined argument in Chapter 4). More generally, whenever there is a trustworthy truth indicator for a belief, one can construct, in principle, an argument that identifies the truth indicator as support and represents the justificatory relation that enables the truth indicator to confer justification on the belief in question. If one cannot construct, in principle, such an argument, then something is suspect or missing in the alleged case of rational belief.

Argument-indifferent fideism suffers from the problem this chapter identified for fideism in general: it robs theism of a needed cognitive basis for trustworthy commendation as true. It thus treats the predicament of the wilderness parable in the Introduction as though an adopted path in Hells Canyon need not be trustworthily commended as accurate or safe. This approach smacks of a kind of cognitive arbitrariness in the area of commendation, because it manifests argument indifference in this area where many find a genuine cognitive need for trustworthy argument. Chapter 4 recruits some considerations about best explanation in evidence to show that we can actually do much better than fideism of any stripe.

We must continue our search for a trustworthy evidential basis for theistic belief. If we cannot find such a basis, we should opt for agnosticism (or perhaps even atheism) rather than for fideism. *If* our evidence for theistic belief is ultimately untrustworthy, then agnosticism will serve at least to make us face the music about this fact. Fideism, we have seen, mutes this music in a way that obscures the need of faith in God for trustworthy support and commendation. We turn now to the question of whether natural theology can satisfy this important need. We shall see that natural theology faces a major problem of its own in this connection: namely, the problem of divine elusiveness.

3

 ❧

Natural Theology and God

"Intellectual acuteness cannot discover the things of God, and the man who assumes that it can, will only be misled."

– John Oman 1928, p. 71.

The astonishing God acknowledged by Jews and Christians is not static but is dynamic, interactive, and elusive in self-revelation. In particular, this God reveals himself to some people at times but also hides himself from some people at times. As a result, this God is *cognitively* elusive; that is, the available evidence for this God's reality typically escapes human control, even regarding its reproducibility. In addition, the claim that this God exists is not obviously true or even beyond reasonable, or well-grounded, doubt (in any familiar sense) for all capable mature inquirers.

Let's think of the God in question as "the living God" in virtue of this God's being *personally interactive* with some agents, and cognitively nimble and dynamic rather than cognitively inflexible or static. We should not confuse this God, then, with an immutable Platonic form or any other kind of abstract entity or nonpersonal principle. This God, more specifically, is reportedly elusive for good reasons – that is, for reasonable divine *purposes* that fit with God's unique character of being worthy of worship and thus being morally perfect. Accordingly, we should expect any evidence of God's existence for humans to be *purposively available* to humans – that is, available to humans in a way that conforms to God's character and perfectly good purposes for them.

If one of God's main purposes is to elicit noncoerced human faith or trust *in God*, then God may seek to be, himself, the conclusive (objective) cognitive ground for human commitment to God's reality. That would be to unify *the ultimate ground* and *the object* of the desired human faith, in a manner that preserves God's cognitive centrality. In that case, God would reveal God's presence directly to willing humans, for the sake of their becoming personifying revelatory evidence of God. Part of God's cognitive aim would be to have willing humans become agents who receive and reflect God's moral character and thereby bring God's presence (rather than just theological information) near for others. The general idea is suggested in Paul's Corinthian correspondence, where he suggests that, through willing humans themselves, God disseminates knowledge of God to others, and that the Corinthians themselves are epistles, or letters, that establish the authenticity of Paul's divine Good News message (see 2 Cor. 2:14, 3:1–6; cf. 2 Cor. 4:2). This chapter identifies some significant consequences of such personifying evidence and divine elusiveness for natural theology in particular and for theistic epistemology and philosophy in general.

1. A LIVING GOD

If the living God of Jewish and Christian theism actually exists, then this God is worthy of worship. That is, this God would *merit* worship by all created persons who are capable of worshipping God. In addition, an agent would merit worship only if that agent is morally perfect – that is, morally good and altogether free of any moral defect. Of course, people can worship all manner of things, even to their own detriment, but an agent truly worthy of worship must be above reproach or defect of any moral kind.

God therefore must be perfectly loving toward all persons, including resolute enemies of God, even while hating evil attitudes and actions. If an agent failed to be perfectly loving toward other persons, then that agent would suffer a moral deficiency, and thus would fail to qualify for the maximally honorific title "God." Failing to love even one enemy, including a particularly cruel and repulsive enemy, would entail moral imperfection and therefore disqualify one from being God.

The requirement of being perfectly loving toward all persons sets a demanding moral standard for God, in keeping with Jesus's Sermon on the Mount (see Matt. 5:43–8; cf. Luke 6:27–36). In particular, it requires that God seek not only what is good but also what is *best, all things considered*, for all persons and thus what is *morally* best for them. If an agent aimed just for something less than what is best for a person, then that agent would be able to seek, alternatively, something even better for that person. As a result, that agent would not be *perfectly* loving toward that person. Being perfectly loving toward others, then, is intentionally active in virtue of seeking what is best, all things considered, for others, even for others who are one's enemies. Accordingly, such seeking aims for a certain kind of *moral transformation* in those persons who suffer moral deficiencies, such as selfishness and pride, and this transformation would include a move away from moral defects and toward what is morally best for them.

In seeking moral transformation of humans, from spiritual death to new life, God would seek cooperative fellowship with them that includes their obeying God, because such fellowship would be morally best for them. Cooperative human fellowship with God would enhance the moral depth and well-being of humans, owing to the purifying influence of God's morally perfect character. More specifically, God would seek to empower, without coercion, a moral transformation away from human selfishness and toward human unselfish love for all people, for the sake of what is morally best for humans. Such empowerment would ideally supply, among other things, morally good motives in human interaction with all people. It therefore would deliver needed moral correction and strength to humans. In addition, it would enable humans to receive and to reflect God's powerful moral character for others, thereby becoming personifying revelatory evidence of God's reality. In this way, humans would bring God's presence near for others.

In seeking to empower humans without coercion, God would aim to interact with humans via *calling* them into the needed fellowship and transformation. This divine call would include an invitation to draw humans internally (as well as behaviorally) away from selfishness, and toward God's way of moral life in unselfish love. It would be a call on our *lives*, not just on our thoughts, and it would be a call for us to live agreeably *with God*, whereby we share and reflect God's perfect moral character and thus become personifying evidence of God (cf. 1 Thess. 5:9–10, 2 Pet. 1:4). We therefore should expect this call to emerge, not superficially but deeply, particularly via conscience, where humans can be changed and motivated profoundly, including morally. God, after all, would aim to engage humans profoundly rather than superficially, for their own good. The aim would be for humans to be willingly moved and transformed by merciful divine love, for the sake of realizing and manifesting such unselfish love in and toward all persons. Accordingly, willing humans would become reflections, and hence evidence, of the moral character of God.

The importance of a divine call or invitation fits well with some of the parables told by Jesus, including the parables of the great feast (see Matt. 22:2–14, Luke 14:16–24), and we find such a call at the very start of Jesus's ministry, in his baptism and in his inaugural preaching of the Good News regarding God's intervention in human history (see Mark 1:11, 14–15). In addition, Jesus and his turbulent life, themselves, are offered by various New Testament writers as part of God's redemptive call to humans. The apostle Paul, accordingly, refers to Christians as those who were "called" by God "into fellowship" (1 Cor. 1:9; cf. 1 Cor. 1:2, 26, 7:17–24, Rom. 1:6–7, Eph. 1:18–19). More generally, first-century Christians came to be referred to as the people "called out" (from bondage and death into new life) by God – that is, as the *ekklesia* (or the church; see 1 Thess. 1:1, Matt. 16:18).

Emil Brunner puts the main point as follows: "To answer to the creative loving call of God with responsive love; this is the destiny for which man was created, and this call is the foundation of his being.... The [divine] call reaches us as the assurance which bestows upon us fellowship with God, and as the claim which calls us as God's possession to obedience [to God]" (1962, pp. 328–9). In a similar vein, Ernst Käsemann proposes: "That God has spoken to us, and does not cease to speak to us, is our only salvation; that we allow this Word to be spoken to us and dare to live by it is our sanctification and justification" (1971, p. 93). Unfortunately, the central role of the divine call to humans has largely disappeared in contemporary theology and philosophy of religion, to the detriment of accurately characterizing human experience of God.

Divine gracious love would include a call, or an invitation, to humans that can be ignored only at the expense of distorting a key intended aim of such love: divine–human fellowship and new human life that include human obedience to God for the good of humans. An urgent question, then, is whether humans are actually *willing* to be addressed by God for this purpose. The focus here is not so much on a gift as on the divine gift-*giver* and the call of this personal agent to humans. As Käsemann remarks: " ... every gift of God which has ceased to be seen as the presence of the Giver and has therefore lost its character as personal address [to humans], is grace misused and working to our destruction" (1961, p. 175). Due attention to this insight would transform religious epistemology as well as theology. We shall identify some of the important results, including their connection with natural theology.

A divine call to, and interaction with, humans would aim for our transformation as *conformation* to God's moral character, which, according to the Christian message, is imaged perfectly by Jesus. In particular, the aim would be to redirect our wills, without coercion, rather than just our minds, thoughts, or emotions. Blaise Pascal was right on this important matter of divine self-revelation. As he puts it: "God wishes to move the will.... Perfect clarity would help the mind and harm the will. Humble their pride" (*Pensées*, sec. 234, Krailsheimer edition). By insisting on the goals of one's own will, in conflict with God's will, one embraces pride and thus rejects a humble attitude toward God's will, even if one refuses to acknowledge the reality of God's will. A perfectly loving God would aim to challenge and transform any such prideful will, for the sake of bringing it into the morally better state of cooperation with God's will of unselfish love toward all persons.

God's intended deflation of human pride would work on a number of troubled human fronts, including the cognitive front. Paul's Corinthian correspondence takes up the cognitive front, among others, in stating that "... in the wisdom of God, the world did not know God through [its] wisdom.... " (1 Cor. 1:21, RSV). One must wonder, of course, how such a view bears on so-called "natural theology," and we will investigate this matter. The divine motive, according to Paul, is to "shame" those who are wise, in the know, or otherwise strong by human standards, "so that no human being might boast in the presence of God" (1 Cor. 1:29, RSV). Such divine deflation aims to unmask the weakness of human authority and strength before God, and to show that these human resources cannot give life in the face of death. We might think of this deflation as divine pollution control, or as an anticounterfeit program, including in the cognitive domain.

A life-defining example of resistance to a prideful human will emerges from Jesus in Gethsemane. Despite having acknowledged a divine call to offer up his life to God in

redemptive crucifixion for others, Jesus struggles in Gethsemane with the challenge of his impending torturous death.
In particular, he prays to God that, if it were possible, his
crucifixion would be avoided. Mark's Gospel reports his
prayer as "Abba, Father, for you all things are possible;
remove this cup from me; yet, not what I want, but what
you want" (Mark 14:36, NRSV). Accordingly, Jesus submits
his will to God's perfect will, in faithful obedience to God.
This kind of "Gethsemane struggle" would effectively serve
God's redemptive purpose to bring human wills into cooperation with God's life-giving will. Such cooperation would
manifest human life as a *God-given* gift to be guided by
divine power rather than a humanly owned possession to be
guided just by human power. Indeed, God's call to humans
would include a call to enter into such a Gethsemane struggle at every opportunity, for the sake of ongoing human
transformation toward God's will. The living God thereby
would meet humans where they actually live: that is, in real
settings made for volitional struggle against human selfishness and pride. If some humans would agreeably receive
God's self-revealing call in these settings, then God, as perfectly loving toward humans, would noncoercively extend
such a call to them, at least at fitting times when they are
ready.

We now can begin to make some sense of the kind of revelatory evidence of divine reality available to humans. In
particular, we now can appreciate that divine self-revelation
to humans would involve a divine call that includes a
human experience of *divine volitional confrontation*. Accordingly, Käsemann has remarked that " . . . God's power [in
God's "Word"] . . . speaks to us in love and judgment so that
we experience the pressure of its will . . . " (1961, pp. 176–7, italics added). More specifically, the power of God's call would
include an I–Thou confrontation of human and divine personal wills that is inherently *de re* rather than merely propositional, or merely *de dicto*. H.H. Farmer says of such a confrontation that "it is a relationship wherein the activity of

one self-conscious, self-directing will is conditioned by that of another in such wise that each remains free" (1942, p. 26). The "pressure" of God's will, then, would not be coercion of humans, but it would, nonetheless, be purposively available to human experience on God's terms, which involve volitional pressure. Such volitional power offered to us would be an opportunity for us to manifest God's power or, alternatively, to try to exclude God from his universe. We might think of all of human life as such a power transaction, from God for us or, alternatively, from us against God.

A direct authoritative call from God to humans would seek to find acknowledgment and agreeable reception in human conscience, where people can experience deep conviction and move toward cooperation with God's will and conformation to God's moral character. Human yielding to such a call would enable God's presence to emerge noncoercively with increasing salience in a human life, and it would advance human transformation away from selfishness and toward God's perfectly unselfish will. Accordingly, God would aim to use such divine–human volitional confrontation to bring about not only human volitional knowledge of God and of God's presence but also human redemption, in fellowship and new life with God. Humans themselves thereby would become living, personifying evidence of God's reality, owing to their receiving and manifesting God's characteristic moral power, the same power that guided Jesus to demonstrate God's self-giving *agape* in Gethsemane and, even more vividly, on Calvary.

The direct acquaintance of a human with God, in an I–Thou volitional confrontation, would be different in kind from an argument, because such acquaintance does not require an inference of any sort. In addition, it would be irreducible to *de dicto* truths, given its ineliminable *de re* component, which is describable as "volitional pressure." Even so, humanly experienced acquaintance with God's call could serve as conclusive evidence of God's existence for a person, in the absence of defeaters that undermine such evidence. We could illustrate this with a case in which such experiential acquaintance with an evident divine call is best explained, relative to all available evidence, by the proposition that God has actually intervened in that person's experience. Evidence is conclusive, let's say, if and only if it is sufficient to satisfy the justification condition for knowledge, in a manner free of ultimate defeat. (Chapter 4 returns to the details of such an approach.)

A longstanding myth in philosophy of religion, shrouded in dense intellectualist fog, is that epistemically justified belief that God exists must be based on a sound *argument* for God's existence. Sometimes this myth is coupled with the more widespread dark myth that evidence must consist of an argument. Of course, a proposition *for which one argues* must rest on an argument, but we should not confuse either evidence or propositions supported by evidence with propositions for which one argues. *Any* truth indicator for a proposition qualifies as evidence, even if defeasible, for a proposition, and even nonjudgment and nonargument experiences can and do qualify as such evidence. It is just an intellectualist and rationalist myth to assume otherwise, and much of traditional empiricism rightly challenges that myth. (See Moser 1989 for detailed opposition to that myth.) We need to avoid, in any case, a bias against evidence of divine reality that comes from the volitional pressure of a transcendent call and the resulting transformation of a willing human recipient who thereby becomes personifying evidence of God's reality.

The divine call in question and its resulting nonargument evidence of God's reality are not volitionally static but instead are subject to variations regarding the presence of God's purposive good will. In particular, God can retract a divine intervention or call from a person when doing so serves God's perfect will. In doing so, God would withhold from some humans the volitional pressure characteristic of such a call. This could be a case in which, to use Paul's language, God "gave them up," or "delivered them," to their own self-destructive ways for corrective judgment (Rom. 1:24, 26, 28). This vital trait of the God of Abraham, Isaac, Jacob, and Jesus entails a living God who is intentionally active in purportedly corrective love, including judgment, toward humans. Unlike static evidence, this purposive activity can include the withdrawal of God's presence from a human, including the withdrawal of occurrent evidence of divine reality. In particular, such activity can be sensitive to the direction of a human will relative to God's character and purposes.

In keeping with the option of divine withdrawal, Isaiah 45:15 announces: "Truly, you are a God who hides himself, O God of Israel, the Savior." Unlike static idols, God is purposive, and evidence of divine reality follows suit, as Isaiah 46:11 suggests: "I have spoken, and I will bring it to pass; I have purposed, and I will do it" (NRSV). The message of purposeful divine hiding and seeking is reiterated in many of the New Testament writings, including in the teaching of Jesus and of Paul (see, for instance, Matt. 11:25–7//Luke 10:21–2, 1 Cor. 2:7–10). This message implies that the presence and the corresponding occurrent evidence of God's call to humans are divinely retractable given, for instance, willful human resistance to God. As a result, such evidence is experientially and thus personally variable in ways that allow for divine elusiveness and even hiddenness at times regarding divine purposes and divine existence. Natural theology, we shall see, fails to accommodate such distinctive personally interactive evidence of God's existence. Our talk of divine hiddenness, as suggested in Chapter 2, will signify a case in which God's existence is not beyond reasonable doubt for a reasonable person.

2. WHITHER NATURAL THEOLOGY?

The arguments of natural theology for God's existence, in *a priori* and *a posteriori* forms, have been highly, if surprisingly, influential in many quarters and eras. They include various ontological, contingency, cosmological, teleological, moral, and psychological arguments, among others, and the accompanying detail and sophistication can be Ptolemaic in spirit as well as breathtaking. Characterized generally, these arguments seek to establish, or at least confirm, God's existence on the basis of *natural* sources of human knowledge, without an appeal to any special revelation from God. Lacking that exclusion of special revelation, they arguably would qualify as arguments of *supernatural* theology rather than natural theology. In any case, to establish the existence of *God*, properly speaking, the arguments need to establish the existence of a *personal agent who is worthy of worship* and is thus morally perfect and hence perfectly loving toward all persons. This, of course, is a tall order, and none of the arguments of natural theology enjoys widespread support as having actually filled this particular order. In effect, the history of natural theology has been the history of attempting to secure knowledge of God's reality without acknowledging evidence of God's authoritative call to humans. We should address the reasons why this misleading but widely influential attempt has failed, does fail, and will fail.

In general, the familiar *a posteriori* arguments confirm *at most* the existence of causes *just adequate* (and not beyond just adequate) to yield their favored properties: perceived order or fine-tuning in nature, observed causal chains of contingent events, moral duties binding on humans, human self-reflective consciousness, and so on. The inferred just-adequate causes, however, clearly fall short of establishing or confirming the real moral character of a personal agent worthy of worship, who has perfect love toward enemies. Some natural theologians candidly have admitted as much, but they have then retreated, for various reasons, to arguments for something inferior to God as a personal agent worthy of worship. Even so, if the demanded conclusion is to yield a personal God worthy of worship, who seeks fellowship with humans on divine terms, then the familiar *a posteriori* arguments fail to deliver, either individually or collectively.

Consider, by way of example, Aquinas's cosmological argument (in the *Summa Theologica,* I, q.2, a.3) that first identifies an order of efficient causation in the sensory world, then observes that nothing is either the efficient cause of itself or part of an infinite causal chain, and finally concludes that it is necessary to acknowledge "a first efficient cause, *which everyone gives the name of God."* Just for the sake of argument, we now can grant Aquinas's inference that there is a *first* efficient cause, despite the endless flurry of philosophical controversy raised by this inference. A decisive problem is this: the inference gives us, at most, a first cause *just adequate* (and not beyond just adequate) for the observed causal chains in the sensory world. Clearly, however, *this* first cause falls far short of a living personal God worthy of worship who seeks fellowship with receptive humans. We have no good reason, for instance, to ascribe *moral perfection* to the inferred first cause. In addition, it is doubtful that we have good grounds to ascribe fellowship-seeking *personal agency* to this just-adequate first cause. At least it is not obvious that such personal agency is required to accommodate the pertinent sensory data regarding causal chains. Those data offer no definite indication at all, *de re* or otherwise, of a personal agent, let alone a personal agent worthy of worship.

It is just special pleading for Aquinas to refer to "a first efficient cause, *which everyone gives the name of God."* (A similarly dubious reference to God occurs in the corresponding argument in Aquinas's earlier *Summa Contra Gentiles.*) Certainly, skeptics will balk at that reference to God, and we should too, given the exalted demands of morally perfect personal agency for satisfying the title "God." If the conclusion of an argument does not include the existence of a morally perfect intentional agent, then that argument does not establish or even confirm that *God* exists, whatever else it establishes or confirms. Much natural theology runs afoul of

this simple fact, even when inductive inference is acknowledged as justifiable.

We should acknowledge an equally serious, but typically
overlooked, problem for natural theology that stems from
the elusiveness of the Jewish and Christian God. Consider
Aquinas's evidence consisting of efficient causation in the
sensory world. That empirical evidence is static in a way
that occurrent evidence of the presence and the reality of
the Jewish and Christian God is not. In particular, Aquinas's
evidence involving efficient causation is not variable relative to the volitional tendencies of human agents toward
God and God's will. As a result, Aquinas's evidence in
question fails to accommodate the personally interactive
character of God's self-revelation that emerges from God's
intermittent hiding and seeking relative to humans and their
volitional tendencies. In other words, God's self-revelation,
given its transformative redemptive aim for humans, should
be expected to be personally interactive, variable, and intermittent in ways that mere efficient causation in the sensory
world is not. As a result, Aquinas's proposed evidence in the
cosmological argument is not suited to the cognitively nimble and personally dynamic God of Jewish and Christian
theism.

Similar problems confront other familiar natural theological arguments that rely on sensory observation, including
Aquinas's teleological arguments in the *Summa Theologica*
(I, q.2, a.3) and in the *Summa Contra Gentiles* (I, Chapter 13,
Section 35). Again, the just-adequate cause in question (say,
of certain complex structures in nature) does not deliver
the morally perfect Jewish and Christian God who is a personal agent worthy of worship. As a result, Aquinas had no
adequate ground in *natural* theology for ascribing the title
"God" to his alleged designer. Likewise, more recent variations on Aquinas's teleological argument, however elaborate, cannot escape this problem while remaining within
natural theology and stopping short of special supernatural
revelation. Grounded ascription of the exalted title "God"

to an agent requires evidence of a morally perfect personal agent who calls receptive humans to fellowship with himself. In addition, any attempt to extend natural theology to include a humanly experienced divine call (perhaps in a robust argument from moral obligation) will move beyond natural theology proper to *supernatural* theology.

Teleological arguments cannot avoid the aforementioned problem of divine elusiveness that challenges Aquinas's cosmological argument. Aquinas's evidence, consisting of certain complex structures in nature, is static in a way that occurrent evidence of the presence and the reality of the Jewish and Christian God is not. Specifically, Aquinas's evidence from complex structures in nature is not personally variable relative to the wills of human agents toward God's will. As a result, Aquinas's evidence does not fit with God's personally interactive hiding and seeking relative to humans for the sake of their transformation. God's self-revelation, aiming at transforming humans morally, would be personally variable and interactive in ways that mere complex structures in nature are not. This means that the evidence offered in Aquinas's teleological argument does not line up with the personally and cognitively dynamic Jewish and Christian God who seeks human transformation toward God's moral character.

Ontological arguments may appear, at first blush, to offer the needed hope for natural theology. They move *a priori* from a *concept* of a perfect being to the *actual existence* of such a being, on the ground that without the actual existence of its represented object such a concept would not genuinely be that of a truly perfect being. The lack of existence in the represented object allegedly robs the concept of genuinely being a concept of a perfect object. As a result, an ontological argument may seem to fill the tall order at hand. Perhaps, in particular, such an argument underwrites the existence of a being worthy of worship rather than a being just adequate to yield some empirical, moral, or psychological feature of the world. Some doubts, however, arise immediately.

We need to distinguish between (a) an *existence-affirming* concept of a perfect being and (b) an *existence-guaranteeing* concept of a perfect being. An existence-affirming concept of a perfect being includes (if only by implication) either *correct or incorrect* affirmation of the existence of that being; the concept does not, by itself, guarantee the existence of that being. One could have the concept even though the conceptualized perfect being does not exist; analogously, a conceptualized perfect unicorn need not exist. In contrast, an existence-guaranteeing concept of a perfect being would logically exclude *incorrect* affirmation of the existence of that being (at least in any world where the concept exists), in virtue of guaranteeing the existence of that being. A concept of a perfect being can, and typically does, affirm (if only by implication) the existence of that being, but this affirming may be erroneous and, in that case, the concept is misleading in what it affirms (if only by implication).

Suppose, as is typically the case, that an ontological argument includes an existence-affirming concept of a perfect being. We then must ask whether its (implied) affirmation of the existence of the perfect being is correct rather than incorrect. More specifically, we must ask whether reality is such that it actually includes the perfect being in question. Perhaps reality does not include a perfect being, despite the concept's (implied) affirmation to the contrary. In other words, an existence-affirming concept of a perfect being will not, by itself, settle the issue of whether God actually exists. We cannot find here, then, a logically conclusive move from a concept of a perfect object to its existence, even if the existence of a perfect object is affirmed.

An existence-guaranteeing concept may seem able to save the day, but we should have some real doubts on reflection. Suppose, as is usually the case, that an ontological argument includes an alleged existence-guaranteeing concept of a perfect being, on the ground that if the concept's represented object fails to exist, then the concept is not genuinely that of a *perfect* object. We then need to ask whether we actually have a genuine concept of a perfect being that guarantees the existence of a perfect being. More specifically, we must inquire whether, necessarily, given the concept, reality is such that it includes a perfect being. We need to ask, in this connection, whether the concept in question is actually existence-*affirming* but *not* existence-*guaranteeing* regarding a perfect being. We readily can grant that the concept is existence-affirming, but this, of course, leaves open the question of whether a perfect being actually exists.

Clearly, it would be question begging simply to assume that the concept's affirmation of the existence of a perfect being is correct just by virtue of the affirmation. We may have a concept that is incorrect in its affirmation of the existence of a perfect being, even if that affirmation is essential to the concept. In that case, one might say, we have a concept of a perfect being without a corresponding real object. A similar concept–object disconnect threatens any alleged existence-guaranteeing concept of a perfect being. We therefore may not have the alleged existence-guaranteeing concept after all. It is not automatic that we actually have a *concept* of a perfect divine being that guarantees, beyond simply affirming, the existence of that being. It now would be question begging, furthermore, to construe the use of the word "of" in the phrase "concept of a perfect being" as *de re*, as though it actually denotes a perfect being. (Perhaps Anselm fell prey to that serious mistake, given a certain Platonic view of meaning as naming; for relevant discussion, see McGill 1967.) In any case, an alleged existence-guaranteeing concept of a perfect being, by itself, therefore will not settle the issue of whether God exists. Reality, including the reality of a perfect divine being, is not guaranteed by a concept in the manner suggested.

Ontological arguments do not fare well against the aforementioned problem arising from divine elusiveness that challenges Aquinas's cosmological and teleological arguments. The evidence consisting of the content of a concept of God, as offered in ontological arguments, is static in a way that the personally interactive occurrent evidence of the presence and the reality of the Jewish and Christian God is not. In particular, the evidence consisting of the content of a concept of God is not personally variable relative to the wills of humans toward God and God's will. As a result, the evidence offered in ontological arguments fails to fit with the personally interactive divine self-revelation that involves God's intermittent hiding and seeking relative to humans. God's self-revelation would aim at the transformation of humans toward God's moral character, and therefore would be personally variable and interactive in ways that the content of a concept of God is not. This means that the evidence offered in ontological arguments is at odds with the personally and cognitively dynamic God of Jewish and Christian theism. In the end, then, ontological arguments do not save the day for natural theology.

The aforementioned arguments of natural theology share a debilitating flaw. They offer no evidence whatever of a divine call to humans that includes human *de re* confrontation (via volitional pressure) with a living perfect will, and, accordingly, they offer no evidence of human *de re* confrontation with a living personal God who is worthy of worship and seeks fellowship with humans. Even ontological arguments fail on this score, and this would be so even if (contrary to what is the case) there were a nonquestion-begging inference from a concept of a perfect agent to a perfect agent worthy of worship. The relevant divine–human volitional confrontation involves an authoritative divine call for a human to commit to undergo moral transformation by way of response to a divine offer of fellowship. The arguments of natural theology, in contrast, lack evidence of an authoritative divine call for a human to commit to undergo such a transformation toward God's perfect will. As a result, whatever the arguments of natural theology actually confirm, they do not yield conclusive evidence of a volitionally interactive personal God who is worthy of worship and seeks fellowship with humans.

Omitting evidence of a volitionally interactive personal God, the arguments of natural theology instead offer volitionally static evidence that, with regard to its content, is independent of authoritative evidence of a divine personal call to a human. The arguments therefore offer, at best, evidence for mere spectators. In particular, the volitionally static evidence of natural theology is insensitive to the direction of a human will relative to God and God's will. More specifically, such evidence does not increase or decrease relative to the orientation of a human will toward God's perfect will. As a result, the evidence of natural theology does not provide for the kind of personally dynamic evidential variability, noted previously, that is central to some divine hiding from some humans. In particular, it neglects the personally variable but characteristic divine activity in which God intentionally hides and seeks in interaction with humans for the sake of divine redemptive purposes. Such hiding and seeking intend to challenge and transform humans toward God's perfect will and thereby to lead humans in fellowship and new life with God as Lord. The evidence offered by natural theology, in contrast, is volitionally casual and ineffectual relative to God's morally perfect authoritative will.

The decisive failure of natural theology is just this: conclusive evidence for a personal God who, in virtue of being worthy of worship and thus perfectly loving, calls and hides from people at different times must involve an evident divine call in its content. Otherwise, an undermining defeater will emerge from the absence of such a call, given this true (and, I submit, justified) conditional: if there is a perfectly loving God, then this God would call receptive people at opportune times into divine–human fellowship and new life with God for their own good. Natural theology, being devoid of such evidence of a divine call, thus falls short of conclusive evidence of God's existence. If, however, one has conclusive evidence of a divine call to humans, then the arguments of natural theology will be epistemically unnecessary, even if some people find those arguments to be helpful in various nonepistemic ways, such as psychological or aesthetic ways. As a result, the kind of philosophy-to-theology sequence familiar from Aquinas and other natural theologians ultimately fails. A perfectly loving God would have no cognitive need of this sequence, because such a God would seek to be, himself, the (objective) cognitive ground of human belief in God's reality, thus unifying the object and the (objective) cognitive ground of human faith in God.

We should expect a perfectly loving God, as suggested previously, to call willing humans to become personifying evidence of God's reality for the sake of bringing God's presence near for others. Natural theology offers no evidence to accommodate such a call that would be characteristic of God, and it therefore is irrelevant at best and misleading at worst. A divine call to us to become, ourselves, revelatory evidence of God is morally loaded in its demand, but the arguments of natural theology are not morally loaded at all in this respect. As a result, they fail to point to a personal God worthy of worship.

According to the Christian message, God's moral character is imaged perfectly in the evidence representing who Jesus Christ is as an intentional agent with definite demands and goals from God himself. In this message, God did not send humans just additional information or more laws or arguments. Instead, God sent revelatory personifying evidence in Jesus, and in the followers of Jesus who are being conformed to his self-giving moral image. John's Gospel therefore portrays Jesus as saying that people will know *his* disciples by the intentional *agape* they manifest in themselves for one another, after the pattern of Jesus's *agape* (13:35). (A related cognitive role for *agape* is found in 1 John 4:7–16 and in Paul's undisputed letters, for instance in Romans 5:3–8 and 1 Corinthians 2:1–13; cf. Gorman 2001, Chapter 8, 2009, Chapter 2, Moser 2008, Chapter 3.)

Some philosophers and theologians seek to recruit the apostle Paul as an advocate of natural theology, given his remarks in Romans 1:19–20. Attention to the details of his remarks, however, discloses that he does not propose that nature *alone* reveals divine reality. Rather, he explicitly claims that "God has manifested" divine reality to people (see Rom. 1:19), even if through nature (which is not to be confused with a claim about "through nature alone"). Paul could have claimed that nature *by itself* manifests God's reality, but he definitely does not. We also can benefit from a simple distinction between God's being revealed "through nature" and God's being revealed "in nature by itself." As Hendrikus Berkhof observes, "Nature in itself does not reveal God. He reveals Himself in history through his words and deeds" (1968, p. 52). A simple analogy illustrates the point: when I call my mother on the phone, the phone is not evidence of my existence for my mother; my voice, however, could supply such evidence for her. In other words, my existence is not revealed in the phone by itself, but it can be revealed through the phone as I speak to her.

Given an intention to redeem us, a perfectly loving God would have a definite purpose different from our casually knowing, via spectator evidence, that God exists – namely, the purpose of bringing humans into lasting reconciliation with God, in loving and obedient fellowship with God. We therefore should expect God to offer purposively available evidence of God's reality that advances this redemptive purpose. It is doubtful that the spectator evidence of natural theology serves such a purpose, because such evidence does not engage us with a challenge to our wayward tendencies that need redemption.

What about people altogether unreceptive to God's call? Might the arguments of natural theology serve such people? The answer depends, of course, on what it is to *serve* such people. We have seen good reasons to doubt that the arguments of natural theology deliver adequate evidence of a personal God worthy of worship, even if they deliver evidence of the reality of some lesser causal powers. Such evidence of lesser causal powers can figure, of course, in combinations with other kinds of evidence, and even benefit a person in that relatively modest connection. Even so, we should not lose sight of the kind of evidence needed for conclusive belief in a personal God worthy of worship. Such evidence would include a divine call to receptive persons, and would be sensitive, in terms of its depth and salience, to one's willingness to obey God's call toward human moral transformation in a Gethsemane struggle. Natural theology leaves us altogether empty-handed on this life-or-death front. Accordingly, it is cognitively beside the point, if the point is (the redemptive purpose of) a personal God worthy of worship.

Some philosophers will seek refuge in the claim that some arguments of natural theology are at least "confirmatory" of theism even if they fail to supply conclusive evidence of God's existence. The general idea is that some of the arguments in question raise the probability of theism to some extent even if they do not settle the question of whether theism is true. Two obstacles merit comment. First, the arguments of natural theology will not be confirmatory of theism if they do not confirm to some extent that a personal agent worthy of worship exists. We have seen some reason to doubt that the relevant confirmation concerns a personal agent worthy of worship, even if there is some confirmation that a lesser being exists. Second, the proposed standard for evidence being "confirmatory" must avoid being question begging regarding the alleged significant role of a personal agent worthy of worship, but this, as suggested, is no small task. (For elaboration on a version of the latter problem, in connection with fine-tuning arguments, see Colyvan, Garfield, and Priest 2005.)

My case against natural theology relies on an understanding of the title "God" in terms of a personal agent worthy of worship. Someone might wonder whether this case itself is a variation on natural theology. Actually, it is not because it does not offer, on the basis of natural sources of knowledge, an inference to the existence of a supernatural being. My case relies on a notion of God, as a personal agent worthy of worship, but this notion does not figure in an argument for God's existence from natural sources of information. As a result, we do not need to rely on natural theology to challenge natural theology.

3. NATURAL THEOLOGY AFTER DARWIN

We should ask how natural theology, particularly its teleological argument, fares in the wake of Charles Darwin. In 1872, Darwin turned the discipline of biology upside down, with the publication of *The Origin of Species*. The disciplines of philosophy and theology, among many others, likewise have not been quite the same since. Darwin combined random variation (or mutation) and natural selection (or, more accurately, natural destruction) to explain how biological life, including human biological life, has developed since its origin. The origin of species, he contended, can be explained in terms of the twofold mechanism of mutation and natural selection. This mechanism is *natural* in that it belongs to the domain of physical space–time and physical causal relations.

As suggested in Chapter 1, the fallout of Darwinism for philosophy and theology is far-reaching by any standard if it includes Fodor's "true scientific vision" of reality. What happens in Darwin's aftermath to the supposed role of *purpose* in human life? What happens, in other words, to the assumed *distinctiveness* of intentional human life? What happens, in addition, to the presumed role of *God* in purposefully originating and sustaining human life? The general answer on all fronts is: very much happens. Any move toward a more specific answer, however, attracts controversy on various fronts.

Two reactions to Darwin are noteworthy. The first reaction proposes that Darwin demolished human purpose, human distinctiveness, and God's place in creation, at least as many people have thought of these phenomena. Richard Dawkins

(1987) and Daniel Dennett (1995) suggest this reaction, with considerable rhetorical and polemical flourish. The second reaction, supported by various proponents of "intelligent design," aims to restore an intelligent nonnatural designer to biology on the basis of an argument from apparent design in nature. The latter reaction, in its contemporary form, looks for scientific support mainly to the kind of evidence presented in Michael Behe's *Darwin's Black Box* (1996), but it falls within the broad tradition of Aquinas's aforementioned teleological argument for an intelligent designer. The contemporary case for an intelligent designer, however, aims to come from the demands of adequate empirical scientific explanation, and not from a special philosophy or an antecedent theology. Proponents of this approach insist that their case for an intelligent designer is empirical and scientific. Accordingly, they aim to challenge naturalism (on which, see Chapter 1) on empirical scientific grounds.

Behe suggests that cells contain "irreducibly complex" systems that "cannot be explained by Darwinian evolution" (1998, p. 252). By "irreducible complexity," he means a "single system which is composed of several interacting parts that contribute to the basic function [of the system], and where the removal of any one of the parts causes the system to effectively cease functioning" (1998, p. 247). Proponents of intelligent design often cite the mammalian eye as an example of an irreducibly complex organ that requires an intelligent designer and that therefore cannot be explained just by a series of natural causes. If Darwinian natural selection must operate on a specifiable biological function, then, according to Behe, an irreducibly complex organ would have to arise and to be selected *as a unit* rather than piecemeal, because the parts individually lack the key function.

Behe invokes blood clotting, protein transport, and photosynthesis, among other biochemical phenomena, to contend that Darwinism is bad science when its twofold mechanism of natural selection and mutation is offered to account for all of the diversity of biological life. Good biological science, according to Behe, must acknowledge an intelligent designer that is irreducible to the world of natural phenomena. He adds: "The conclusion of intelligent design flows naturally from the data itself – not from sacred books or sectarian beliefs. Inferring that biochemical systems were designed by an intelligent agent is a humdrum process that requires no new principles of logic or science" (1998, p. 254). This, of course, appears to be a rhetorical strategy on Behe's part, because an inference to an intelligent designer is anything but humdrum. It is actually highly controversial and subject to serious objections.

Behe, to his credit, does not share Aquinas's aforementioned special pleading by referring to the cause of apparent design in nature as that "which everyone gives the name of God." In particular, regarding the moral character or the theological status of an allegedly needed designer, according to Behe, any such nonscientific topic is beyond the scope of the purportedly scientific program called "intelligent design." Accordingly, Behe may choose to disregard one of the aforementioned criticisms of Aquinas's natural theological arguments: that is, they fail to confirm the existence of a personal God worthy of worship. Even so, the charge is true, and perhaps even admittedly true, of Behe's design inference that it fails to confirm the existence of a personal God worthy of worship. In particular, we find no basis in cells for inferring the existence of a morally perfect intentional agent. This consideration will reduce, if not eliminate, the significance of Behe's design inference for natural theology regarding a God worthy of worship.

We must wonder how, if at all, Behe can substantiate his claim that irreducible complexity in cells "requires" an explanation via an intelligent designer. His case assumes that an object featuring irreducible complexity will not be so simple that it can be explained by chance combinations in nature, even over a vast amount of time. The substantive debate will focus, of course, on whether any biological pattern, however complex, actually *requires* acknowledgment of an intelligent designer beyond a natural cause. We have noted Behe's talk of irreducibly complex systems that "*cannot* be explained by Darwinian evolution" (1998, p. 252, italics added). This, of course, is strong modal language for someone claiming to do probabilistic, empirical science. Surprisingly, it is rather common language for Behe and other contemporary proponents of intelligent design. In similar language, Behe alleges that " . . . the fundamental mechanisms of life *cannot* be ascribed to natural selection, and *therefore* were designed" (1998, p. 256, italics added). We should note well the absence of the qualifier "probably," and therefore wonder whether Behe has moved beyond empirical science proper.

The basis of the strong language in question is the questionable assumption that irreducible complexity somehow eliminates chance and demands an intelligent designer. The troublesome issue, however, concerns *how strongly* chance is eliminated, if it is actually eliminated at all. Is it eliminated *at most* to a certain degree of probability less than (empirical) certainty? If so, Behe's strong modal language is misleading at best. Darwinian biologists, in any case, need not (and rarely do) appeal to pure chance alone in biological explanation; they readily can make use of a wide range of scientific laws in such explanations. Even so, Behe goes well beyond our scientific and empirical evidence in assuming that chance and natural, unintelligent causes *cannot* yield or account for the biological complexity in question. This modal assumption outstrips our scientific and empirical evidence in a manner that makes it *non*scientific. Its modal language takes us beyond the empirical domain to the domain of modal philosophy independent of science.

As suggested, Behe offers intelligent design as part of an empirical scientific research program. Accordingly, we should expect him to offer intelligent causes not as *required* or *necessary* explainers, but just as the *best available* explainers of certain biological phenomena. His strong modal talk suggests that a Darwinian biologist who does not countenance intelligent design in, for instance, the function of human cells is necessarily *irrational*. The only way to assess such a bold suggestion is to consider the actual explanatory resources of Darwinian biology.

Kenneth Miller has offered a serious challenge to Behe's hypothesis of irreducible complexity in biology. He explains:

The crux of [Behe's] design theory is the idea that by themselves, the individual parts or structures of a complex organ are useless. The evolutionist says no, that's not true. Those individual parts can indeed be useful, and it's by working on those "imperfect and simple" structures that natural selection eventually produces complex organs. In the case of the eye, biologists have realized that any ability, no matter how slight, to sense light would have had adaptive value. Bacteria and algae, after all, manage to swim to and from the light with nothing more than an eyespot – a lensless, nerveless cluster of pigments and proteins. . . . The existence of so many working "pseudo-eyes" and "semi-eyes" in nature convinced natural scientists that Darwin's imagined intermediates between primitive light-sensing systems and complex eyes were feasible and real (1999, pp. 135–6).

Accordingly, Behe underestimates the biological significance of less advanced functions antecedent to the function of a developed system deemed "irreducibly complex."

Miller draws from recent cell biology, including recently published experimental studies, to disarm Behe's contention that Darwinian evolution *cannot* account for biochemical systems called "irreducibly complex." Miller's case is straightforward and compelling, given that it is anchored in salient evidence from biochemistry and biology. Darwinism, in Miller's hands, is much more resilient than certain proponents of intelligent design would have us believe. At a minimum, the aforementioned strong modal language of Behe is now definitely out of place. In addition, it is doubtful that biology calls for Behe's design inference after all. As a result, natural theology will not find a straightforward foothold in this quarter.

Miller has not settled for deflating the anti-Darwinian cases of scientific creationists and intelligent-design theorists, but has offered a compatibility thesis that can be used to redirect natural theology. In this connection, he has opposed an "absolute materialism" that implies that full predictability and ultimate explanation are, or at least will be, available for the material world. Physics leads the way here, and evolutionary biology follows suit. Miller explains:

Quantum physics tells us that absolute knowledge, complete understanding, a total grasp of universal reality, will *never* be ours. Not only have our hopes been dashed for ultimate theoretical knowledge of the behavior of a single subatomic particle, but it turns out that in many respects life is organized in such a way that its behavior is inherently unpredictable, too. It's not just a pair of colliding electrons that defy prediction. The mutations and genetic interactions that drive evolution are also unpredictable, even in principle. . . . Life surely is explicable in terms of the laws of physics and chemistry, . . . but the catch is that those laws themselves deny us an ultimate knowledge of what causes what, and what will happen next (1999, pp. 208–9).

Because we are unable to link causes and effects for something as fundamental as electron emission, we lack the kind of knowledge needed for absolute materialism. Cognitive modesty, therefore, is recommended by the sciences themselves, contrary to absolute materialism.

Miller has found theoretical room to explain why there is no incompatibility between Darwinism and the monotheism of Judaism, Christianity, and Islam. His case rests on the following observation: "the breaks in causality at the atomic level make it fundamentally *impossible* to exclude the idea that what we have really caught a glimpse of might indeed reflect the mind of God" (1999, p. 214). This is not natural theology in any traditional garb, but it is the suggestion that the uncertainty featured by quantum reality blocks our having the kind of complete understanding of nature that would preclude God's involvement therein. As Miller notes, "the indeterminate nature of quantum events would allow a clever and subtle God to influence events in ways that are profound, but scientifically undetectable to us" (1999, p. 241). Miller is not looking for the basis of an argument for God's existence, but he does claim to have identified an important component of science that precludes the conclusive rejection of theism on scientific grounds. His case aims to underwrite not God's existence, but rather the *logical compatibility* of theism and contemporary science. This suggests a modest brand of compatibilist natural theology, free of an empirical argument for God's existence. (For a similarly modest approach to natural theology, see Allen 1989.)

Miller proposes that God may have used quantum physics and Darwinian evolution as the tools to enable human freedom. He remarks:

> ... if there is a God, consider what a master stroke quantum indeterminacy was. To create an orderly material world that didn't require constant intervention, the Creator *had* to make things obey defined laws. But if those laws were to run all the way down to the building blocks of matter, they would also have denied free will (1999, p. 251).

Free will is thus a live option, given our best science. In addition, the indeterminism of physical reality would allow God to influence the development of physical events in ways unknown to us. Miller therefore agrees with Ian Barbour: "Natural laws and chance may equally be instruments of God's intentions. There can be purpose without an exact predetermined plan" (1999, p. 238).

Miller's compatibility thesis is attractive, if only as a result of its modesty, but a problem arises with his unqualified talk of evolution as blind, random, and undirected and of nature as a self-sufficient system (see Miller 1999, pp. 137, 196, 244, 266). If quantum events do, indeed, "allow a clever and subtle God to influence events in ways that are profound but scientifically undetectable to us," and we acknowledge the reality of such a God, then we should refrain from claiming that the natural world is blind, random, or undirected. It may be unpredictable to us, but (so far as we know) it may be directed as well, at least at some points. Given a scientifically undetectable, elusive God allowed by quantum physics, Miller should back off his recurring portrayal of nature and evolution as blind and undirected. As far as our best science goes, nature and evolution may be influenced by a scientifically undetectable, elusive God. That is, God may very well influence the complexity-increasing march of evolution, but nonetheless be highly elusive and even hidden at times. Evolution may be unguided at some points but divinely guided at other, key points. Our best science allows as much, even on Miller's general account of physics and evolution.

Given Miller's compatibility thesis, one might offer a modest but constructive approach to natural theology. This approach would seek to illuminate the *logical compatibility* between empirical science and theology, but would refrain from arguments for God's existence on the basis of empirical science (and other natural sources of information). A key motivation for this compatibilist approach would be that we should not expect God to be an object of empirical science or expect the evidence for God's existence to fall within empirical science. Instead, we should expect the evidence for God's existence to be much more elusive than the evidence within empirical science, given what would be God's elusive redemptive purposes for humans. (Chapter 4 returns to the purposes of an elusive God.) Compatibilist natural theology, then, is no threat to the methods or the conclusions of the empirical sciences. In addition, it resists any use of the empirical sciences to underwrite theology or philosophical metaphysics. In the light of the very troubled history of natural theology, these are important virtues indeed.

4. FROM CALL TO KERYGMA

Given this chapter's argument against natural theology, we are well-advised to look outside natural science for any evidence of God's existence. In particular, given what would be God's redemptive purposes for humans, we should be attentive to experiences that convey a divine call to fellowship and new life with God. Philosophy can and should help with this life-giving project. It can make such contributions as (a) a phenomenology regarding human experiences of a divine call, (b) an elucidation of the human conditions for noticing and receiving a divine call, and (c) an account of how evidence of a divine call can be conclusive and thus resistant to skeptical challenges. It is, however, very rare to find such contributions in the philosophy of religion or even in philosophical theology.

In neglecting the potential divine call to humans, philosophy of religion has neglected the vital cognitive role of the Good News that God has reached out in Jesus to confront humans directly and personally in their distressed and dying condition, for the sake of divine–human fellowship and new human life. The cognitive foundations of this Christian Good News lie in human experience of God's intervening personal Spirit (as explained in Moser 2008). This fits with the apostle Paul's following epistemological observations:

... hope [in God] does not disappoint us, because God's love (*agape*) has been poured into our hearts through the Holy Spirit that has been given to us (Rom. 5:5, NRSV).

Now we have received, not the spirit of the world, but the Spirit who is from God, so that we may know the things freely given to us by God (1 Cor. 2:12, NASB).

Paul's epistemology is thus pneumatic (or Spirit-oriented), owing to its crucial role for a personal divine Spirit who cannot be reduced to any psychological faculty or process or even to Calvin's *sensus divinitatis*. Paul's epistemology therefore is foreign to secular epistemology and to much philosophy of religion and philosophical theology. It is also an *incarnational epistemology*, given its vital cognitive role for God's Spirit dwelling in humans, in such a way that they become a temple of God's Spirit (see 1 Cor. 6:19) and thereby become personifying evidence of God's reality. We may think of incarnational epistemology as requiring that human inquirers *themselves* become evidence of God's reality in virtue of volitional acquaintance with God that enables humans to become agents who receive and reflect God's moral character and God's presence for others. In this approach, characteristic evidence of God's reality is increasingly available and salient to me as I, myself, am increasingly willing to become such evidence – that is, evidence of God's reality. Indeed, according to Paul, it is part of the Good News that followers of Jesus are privileged to reflect the very glory (and thus the reality) of God as perfectly imaged in Jesus (see 2 Cor. 3:18, 4:6; cf. Ridderbos 1975, pp. 68–78, 223–30, Gorman 2009, Chapter 3).

The epistemology on offer is grace-based, in that first-hand knowledge of God's reality is a *direct powerful gift* of God's grace that cannot be separated from the gift-giver. The cognitive grace in question supplies a powerful cognitive gift and a personal ground that replace any demand for intellectual earning, controlling, or dominating with a freely given powerful presence of God's inviting and transforming Spirit, who seeks cooperative fellowship with humans. This cognitive, irreducibly personal gift and ground must be appropriated by humans in Gethsemane struggles, given the human condition of selfishness and pride, but it is not shrouded in philosophical sophistication of the sort accompanying natural theology. Accordingly, we are not dealing with the God of the philosophers or of natural theology. The cognitive grace in question does not depend on philosophical sophistication.

In offering unselfish fellowship and new life with God, the gift under consideration is *directly* challenging toward selfish and prideful human ways that resist God, including toward human cognitive idolatry, but it does not get bogged down in its own intellectual complications. It can be an object of careful philosophical assessment, of course, but it carries a simple assurance from God's personal Spirit in search of divine–human fellowship and new human life. The gift therefore acknowledges God himself as the (objective) cognitive ground of justified belief that God is real as well as the object of human faith in God. The underlying divine aim is twofold: that human faith have its (objective) cognitive and motivational ground not in human wisdom but rather in the personal power of God himself (see 1 Cor. 2:4–5), and that this ground provide what humans desperately need: fellowship and new life in God's presence. The cognitive grace in question is therefore intended to be redemptive, or salvific, for humans.

The apostle Paul announces: "When we cry, 'Abba! Father!,' it is the Spirit himself bearing witness with our spirit that we are children of God" (Rom. 8:15–16, RSV; cf. 2 Cor. 1:22, Eph. 1:13–14). We see here the often-overlooked role of simple filial prayer in receiving needed divine assurance, including evidence of God, directly from God himself. As a result, even young children can enter God's kingdom with *well-grounded* conviction, courtesy of the cognitive grace of God's intervening Spirit. For this, even sophisticated philosophers should be grateful, because we cannot supply evidence on our own that silences skeptics before God; only God can do that, and he does deliver at the opportune time for willing people. God's call to humans therefore should be kept front and center in philosophy of religion, however unpopular the results.

Unlike the incarnational epistemology under development, natural theology obscures the desperate human need for (a) the cognitive grace of God's personal redemptive call to humans and (b) human turning, in repentance, to receive and obey that life-giving transformative call to fellowship and new life. This obscuring arises from the focus of natural theology on merely *de dicto* arguments rather than on an experienced divine call *de re* to humans. When philosophy of religion moves from a focus on such arguments to attend to the divine personal call for fellowship and new life, we will see attention to a distinctive kind of evidence for God's reality. We then will attend to a distinctive kind of intervening volitional pressure that indicates God's reality and presence.

Traditional natural theology suffers from exclusive attention to what the Introduction called *spectator evidence* – that is, the kind of volitionally neutral evidence that does not offer a powerful volitional challenge to inquirers to yield to God and thereby to become personifying evidence of God's reality. It neglects *authoritative evidence* of God's reality that invites a human to cooperate with God's will and thereby to become personifying evidence of God's reality, including evidence of God as an intentional agent of perfect love. Given the prospect of such authoritative evidence, we should acknowledge that one's resolute commitment to remain volitionally neutral toward God's existence can block one from appropriating available evidence of God's existence.

As the Introduction noted, traditional natural theology seeks rationally to identify divine reality indirectly, inferentially, and discursively, and it uses distinctive premises to infer a conclusion in a natural-theological argument of one kind or another. It does not offer, however, evidence as inherently purposive, in the way that direct telic discerning does (as characterized in the Introduction). In connection with the Introduction's wilderness parable, we might think of traditional natural theology as overlooking the directness of a rescuer's intentional call to us in the ham radio transmission. In any case, natural theology does devote its focus to inference in an argument, and not to human acquaintance with a divine call, or divine volitional pressure.

Given a central role for a divine personal call to humans, philosophy of religion, itself, will become existence- and life-involving for humans, and even kerygmatic. It will then stand in sharp contrast to traditional natural theology. The news of a personal redemptive call to humans from a perfectly loving God is always Good News worthy of a kerygma (a Good News proclamation), even if the news is difficult and reorienting at times. Part of the Good News for philosophy of religion, including natural theology, is this: we have no end run around God's challenging personal call to us, as though (with shades of Jonah, the wayward prophet) we could approach God's reality without being morally challenged by God's perfect will. This would be in keeping with God's perfect redemptive love for us, and it would promise to make us new, in who we are and in how we live and think. We do well to consider conducting our philosophy accordingly, and thereby to bring philosophy and ourselves to the life of the living personal God. We philosophers would then be in our proper place relative to God, as faithful and indebted recipients, servants, and ambassadors of the Good News of the God who personally and authoritatively calls us to fellowship and new life with himself. If we have ears to hear this call, we can become revelatory personifying evidence of God in virtue of our receiving and reflecting God's moral character for others. (Chapter 4 develops the cognitive side of this story of Good News, and shows that it has distinctive but genuine foundations.)

5. VALUING THEISTIC BELIEF

We have seen that divine elusiveness and hiddenness do not sit well with the main arguments of natural theology. In invoking such elusiveness and hiddenness, however, we must face the charge that these phenomena indicate that theistic belief is not actually significant in the end. In other words, God, being elusive and even hidden at times, would appear not to be seriously interested in having humans believe that God exists. As the following discussion indicates, some theorists will offer this consideration as importantly true regarding God's purposes, and others will offer it instead as a dubious implication that challenges this chapter's line of objection to natural theology. This means that we need to clarify this matter. (Chapter 5 returns to the general topic in connection with a potential defeater for theism in general.)

According to Robert McKim, the fundamental feature of divine hiddenness is "the fact that God's existence and nature are not obvious" (2001, p. 5; page numbers in this section refer to this book). Perhaps, however, the key feature is that God's existence is *not beyond reasonable doubt* for at least some humans. In any case, McKim adds that " . . . God's existence and nature would be clearer if there were in the world clear and obvious signs of God's presence, as would be the case if virtue were always rewarded, vice always punished, and if various signs and wonders were constantly available" (p. 6). He imagines the following possible "signs and wonders" that allegedly would make God's existence clear or at least clearer: the morning sky overhead would always be lit up with a verse from the Psalms; a person's prayers to God would always be followed with help of a clear sort; and future astronomical discoveries would be announced to us in advance. It is unclear, however, that such signs would be clear indicators of God's reality for all people; at least some people would not regard them as obvious signs of God's existence. The latter people would consider, and perhaps embrace, alternative explanations free of theology, and this suggests that what is "clear" in perceived indicators of reality varies significantly among people.

McKim proposes that "if God exists, God is hidden to a considerable degree from all human beings at all times" (p. 10). He offers a number of supporting arguments but then weakens his thesis as follows: " . . . we have reason to conclude that, if God exists, God is hidden to a considerable extent from almost all human beings at almost all times" (p. 12). The thesis concerning "almost all human beings at almost all times" looks like a statistical empirical claim, the support of which would require salient statistical empirical evidence, but McKim has not supplied such evidence. In addition, it is unclear how he readily might gather such evidence. One obvious problem is that he would need statistical empirical evidence that bears on "almost all times," and this would not be easily forthcoming.

One of McKim's arguments for the thesis that "God is hidden to a considerable degree from all human beings at all times" runs as follows.

> ... it may be that the explanation of why some people find that God is hidden is that those people have the wrong attitudes or the wrong beliefs or have gone wrong in some other way. This ... might be thought of as a matter of failing to seek the truth with enough of their energies, being proud instead of humble, refusing to countenance the possibility that God might exist, being utterly unwilling to think or live or respond in ways in which one thinks one ought to think or live or respond if God were to exist, or something else. Insofar as the explanation [of divine hiddenness] is to be found in an area such as this, one has reason to concede that God is always hidden from everyone to some extent (p. 11).

As indicated, McKim began with talk of God's being simply "hidden," and he suggests that this is to be understood in terms of "the fact that God's existence and nature are not obvious." Such talk has shifted, however, to talk of God's being "hidden to a considerable degree" and "hidden to some extent" (pp. 10, 11).

We, of course, have an absolute use of the term "obvious," wherein something either is obvious or is not. A direct analogue to this is our absolute use of "unique": something either is unique or is not. Evidently, McKim initially uses "hidden" in an absolute manner on the basis of an absolute use of "obvious," but then shifts to a nonabsolute use that allows for degrees of hiddenness. His nonabsolute use evidently rests on a notion of degrees of obviousness that has not been clarified. Discussion becomes murky here owing to lack of clarity in a standard for measuring degrees of obviousness and thus of hiddenness. We sometimes talk rather casually of something's being *somewhat* obvious, just as we sometimes talk very loosely of something's being *rather* unique. This offends some linguistic purists, but the real concern is that such talk, in the present context, calls for a standard of measuring (at least in principle) degrees of obviousness. In the absence of such a standard, our nonabsolute use of "obvious" will be unclear, and McKim's use is, in fact, left unclear.

What exactly does McKim mean in saying that "God is always hidden from everyone to some extent" (p. 11)? If we use McKim's talk of what is "obvious" to supply clarification, we might have the claim that:

(1) God's reality is always not obvious to some extent for everyone.

In McKim's language, (1) seems to be synonymous with:

(2) God's reality is always not clear to some extent for everyone.

One might understand (2) as the innocuous claim that God's reality is never fully revealed to any human. McKim, however, does not understand (2) in that innocent manner; nor does he settle for a solely psychological lesson from (2). He aims to get cognitive, or epistemic, mileage from (2).

McKim proposes that "to say that God is hidden...is to say that religious ambiguity extends to the existence of God" (p. 21). He clarifies his talk of religious ambiguity as follows: "our lives are ambiguous in that they may reasonably be interpreted in entirely secular terms or in religious terms, but also in that they may reasonably be interpreted using the concepts of various religious traditions" (p. 22). Given the use of "reasonably" here, McKim has moved beyond any psychological notion of hiddenness or clarity to an epistemically or cognitively loaded notion. The notion of divine hiddenness now carries a notion of *reasonableness*. We may presume that *epistemic*, or *cognitive*, reasonableness of some sort is relevant, because the concern is with the *truth* of theistic claims, and not the practical utility of holding theistic beliefs. (Chapter 2 introduced the latter distinction in its challenge to fideism.)

McKim does not use divine hiddenness to recommend against any particular religious belief, but instead seems to grant the reasonableness, at least for some people, of the positions of the main world religions. He explains:

I do not feel that I am in a position to judge what it is like to be a member of a tradition, or to possess a viewpoint, of which I have no personal experience, or to consider all of the relevant evidence at once, or even seriatim. As far as I know, there are numerous positions that may reasonably be held on religious matters, including the positions that go with being a member of any of the main world religions (p. 203).

Even so, McKim adds: "An implication of my position is that most martyrs who have died for their faith have been misled, [for] ... they have died in the name of *certainty* about their beliefs" (p. 204). He therefore has a recommendation, on the basis of divine hiddenness, for *how* religious beliefs should be held: he proposes that they should be held tentatively, without subjective certainty.

It seems incorrect to say that most martyrs have died "in the name of certainty about their beliefs." Instead, they evidently have died in the name of the supposed God regarding whom they held subjectively firm, nontentative beliefs. There is, of course, a significant difference here. What a martyr dies *for*, relative to the martyr's intentions, is the supposed God being served, *not* the psychological or cognitive status of the martyr's beliefs. Even when subjectively certain beliefs are in place, they and their psychological or cognitive status are not the intended object of one's commitment. Accordingly, the latter factors, taken individually or as a pair, are not what martyrs die "in the name of." In fact, it is a category mistake (that is, a confusion of categories) to suggest otherwise.

It is altogether unclear how McKim could substantiate his claim that most martyrs who have died for their faith *should not* have held their religious beliefs with subjective certainty. As noted, he has already conceded the following: "I do not feel that I am in a position to judge what it is like to be a member of a tradition, or to possess a viewpoint, of which I have no personal experience, or to consider all of the relevant evidence at once, or even seriatim." If, as he admits, he cannot consider all of the relevant evidence at once, or even seriatim, then he is in no position to recommend that most martyrs who have died for their faith *should not* have held their religious beliefs with subjective certainty. By his own acknowledgment, McKim does not have an adequate vantage point on their evidence. By his own admission, *for all he knows*, their relevant evidence called for subjectively firm belief that resulted in martyrdom for the supposed God they followed. Divine hiddenness does not challenge this consideration at all, given that such hiddenness does not preclude salient evidence of God at some times for some people.

We must make judgments of epistemic, or cognitive, reasonableness carefully, given the different specific standards of reasonableness in circulation. Obviously, competent people of integrity disagree about such reasonableness. In suggesting that most martyrs have been misled owing to the cognitive mistake of subjective certainty, or nontentativeness, in their beliefs, McKim proposes that most martyrs have been unreasonable. This proposal, as suggested, has not been substantiated by McKim; nor can it be, given his own aforementioned standard for reasonableness. As suggested, many relevantly competent people of considerable integrity disagree about the specific conditions for reasonableness. McKim's position regarding reasonableness, which recommends tentativeness in religious belief, relies on such disagreement as a basis for recommending tolerance toward the reasonableness of alternative religious beliefs. For the sake of consistency, his tolerance should be extended to the case of martyrs and the reasonableness of their beliefs.

Martyrdom aside, McKim uses divine hiddenness to try to minimize the importance of theistic belief in general. He claims: "If theistic belief... were very important, each person, surely, would have an equal shot at it.... There is the fact of religious ambiguity, [which] suggests that theistic belief is not important" (p. 122). McKim therefore suggests that, given divine hiddenness, God regards theistic belief as "not important." This suggestion, however, is doubtful at best. A perfectly loving God could regard theistic belief as genuinely important but value other things as more important. For example, God could value letting human selfish opposition to God's unselfish ways mature into its destructive futility, so that its futility could be readily seen by all honest observers, even if this entails some obscurity about God's reality, at least at times. (This, in fact, is what the apostle Paul suggests in Romans 8:20–21, as Chapter 4 explains in undermining potential challenges to theistic belief from evil and divine elusiveness and hiddenness.) This prospect for divine purposes challenges any suggestion from divine hiddenness that theistic belief is "not important."

God could work for good, redemptive purposes in people who lack theistic belief – even for the good of the people who lack such belief (as Chapter 5 explains). It does not follow, however, that theistic belief is not important. Theistic belief can still be important to God's redemptive work, particularly to bringing into focus for humans the source of God's redemptive work in humans: that is, God. Accordingly, even if theistic belief is not a necessary condition of God's redemptive work, it still can function as an important contribution to this work among humans.

This chapter has invoked divine elusiveness and hiddenness to challenge traditional natural theology, but it has not offered any support for the suggestion that theistic belief is not important. On the contrary, it supports the view that theistic belief can be very important in one's becoming personifying evidence of God's reality by one's intentionally receiving and reflecting God's moral character for others. The basis of this chapter's challenge for the arguments of natural theology has come from the inadequacy of static or impersonal evidence for a God worthy of worship. The following chapter elaborates on the key idea of personifying evidence of God's reality, and explains how such evidence fits with a God worthy of worship.

6. SUMMARY ARGUMENT

In sum, this chapter has offered the following straightforward argument against traditional natural theology, in order to highlight the kind of evidence we should expect of a perfectly loving God.

1. By definition, a being who merits the maximally honorific title "God" would be *worthy of worship*, and thus would be *morally perfect* and hence *perfectly loving* toward all humans, even toward all human enemies of God, in such a way that God would seek *the best, all things considered*, for all humans.

2. By definition, it would be best, all things considered, for morally imperfect humans if they would agreeably receive a noncoercive *self-revealing call* from God that (a) directly and authoritatively invites them to enter into worship of God, including fellowship with God and volitional cooperation with God's perfect will, but (b) could be elusive and even hidden at times for divine purposes of a moral challenge to humans.

3. Hence, if some morally imperfect humans would agreeably receive the divine self-revealing call, noted in 2, then God would noncoercively extend such a call to them, at least at some times.

4. By definition, a *direct authoritative call* from God to a human requires a *de re agent-to-agent acquaintance* of the human with God's call that is irreducible to *de*

dicto truths (and, furthermore, need not coerce any particular *de dicto* interpretation of this acquaintance experience).

5. Hence, if God extends a self-revealing call to some humans at some times, God would offer those humans at those times agent-to-agent acquaintance with God's call that is irreducible to *de dicto* truths.

6. By definition, the humanly experienced acquaintance with God's call, noted in 4, is not an argument, but in the absence of defeaters can nonetheless be *conclusive evidence* of God's existence for a person.

7. By its nature, the conclusive evidence noted in 6, regarding God's call, is not volitionally static, but is, *as divinely retractable given human volitional resistance*, experientially and thus personally interactive and variable in a manner that allows for divine elusiveness and even hiddenness at times regarding divine existence (in keeping with what some of the Hebrew prophets, including Jesus, require of conclusive divine evidence).

8. The arguments of traditional purely *de dicto* natural theology, whether *a priori* or *a posteriori* (for instance, ontological, first cause, design, and moral arguments), offer volitionally static evidence that (a) is not only independent of a divine call in its content (nature, for instance, offers no call of its own) but also insensitive to the direction of a human will relative to God's will, and, thus, (b) does not allow for the kind of variability, noted in 7, that is central to elusiveness and hiddenness regarding divine existence.

9. By definition, any conclusive evidence suitable to a God who calls and hides from people at different times (see the God of Jewish and Christian theism) must not be volitionally static, but must allow for the kind of variability, noted in 7, that is central to elusiveness and hiddenness regarding divine existence, and must involve an evident divine call in its content; otherwise,

a defeater will emerge from the absence of such a call, given that a perfectly loving God would call receptive people at some times.

10. Hence, the evidence offered by the arguments of traditional purely *de dicto* natural theology does not qualify as conclusive evidence of the God of Jewish and Christian theism, who calls humans but is elusive and even hidden at times.

4

∾

Personifying Evidence of God

"... the ultimate decisions are not made in the sphere of language, where they are at most expressed; they are made at the point where we fall into arrogance or despair; or where we hear the call to obedience and true humanity – at the point, that is, where we make decisions of will."

– Ernst Käsemann 1967, p. 35.

The wilderness parable of this book's Introduction offered a specific predicament as a context for our inquiry about God's existence. Our predicament in the parable highlights our need to find a way out of a dangerous wilderness setting in Hells Canyon. It raises the question of whether an intentional rescuer for us is at hand. It also gives us an opportunity to reflect on our own resources or the lack thereof in the dangerous, life-threatening setting. We should do the same, of course, for our real-life setting. Some people doubt that anyone among us gets out alive in the end, whereas others propose that a rescuer for us is, in fact, available. If God is a real rescuer, how does one come to know that this rescuer is real? In particular, what kind of evidence is available to us?

We have not found much tenable encouragement about the reality of an intentional rescuer in the previous chapters. On the contrary, fideism and natural theology have generated some difficult problems that call into question their being commendably trustworthy avenues to knowledge of God's reality. In that regard, they have failed to deliver the needed rescuer in a trustworthy manner. The same holds for nontheistic naturalism, because this position seeks to free humans from commitment to a supernatural rescuer. We have found this position to be lacking at best, however, because it undermines itself by its own ontological and cognitive standard. As a result, we are not yet out of the wilderness, and the question of an intentional rescuer remains open. This chapter aims to show the way out, with the aid of a needed but widely neglected notion of personifying evidence of God's reality.

1. SKEPTICAL DOUBTS

Human inquirers have long been vulnerable to skeptical questions about their cognitive fitness, especially regarding the prospect of human knowledge of God. Skeptics persistently have raised general questions about the trustworthiness of human beliefs and of such human cognitive, belief-producing sources as perception, memory, and introspection. Do these sources yield true rather than false beliefs, at least characteristically or (more modestly) in some cases? Skeptics have considerable skill in generating doubts with such a question.

We naturally seek trustworthy *evidence* that our cognitive sources (characteristically) yield true rather than false beliefs. In doing so, we aim to avoid circular reasoning in which a source under question regarding its being trustworthy is treated as if it were not thus under question. We ask, accordingly, what *noncircular or nonquestion-begging reason* we have to regard our cognitive sources as trustworthy for acquiring truth and avoiding error. As a result, we might seek to confirm the trustworthiness of one cognitive source (say, auditory perception) *without* relying on another cognitive source (say, visual perception), because we have raised the same question concerning trustworthiness about the latter source as about the former. Ideally, we aim to avoid circularity in answering our question about the trustworthiness of our cognitive sources. Permitted circularity would make the task *too* easy because it would make it arbitrary.

In asking about *all* of our cognitive sources, regarding their trustworthiness, we cannot rely on those sources themselves to deliver nonquestion-begging or noncircular evidence of their trustworthiness. Otherwise, an arbitrary circularity would threaten. In addition, we evidently cannot assume a position independent of all of our own cognitive sources to obtain a noncircular test of their trustworthiness. It seems that we do not have a vantage point outside our cognitive sources from which we can assess their trustworthiness. This appears to be the human cognitive predicament, and no one has yet shown how we can escape it. This, too, is a straightforward consideration favoring the conclusion that we should take skepticism quite seriously, if only to clarify the nature of our actual cognitive sources.

Famously, in his *Meditations,* Descartes suggested that the existence of a trustworthy God can underwrite the trustworthiness of some of our cognitive sources. The suggestion is that if God is trustworthy, then God would not allow for widespread untrustworthiness in our cognitive sources. Such a suggestion calls for considerable argument, but an immediate problem arises. It seems that our reasonable acknowledgment of a trustworthy God, who insures trustworthiness in our cognitive sources, will rely on (the trustworthiness of) a cognitive source in question. That is, such a cognitive source as perception, memory, or introspection evidently will play a role (as trustworthy) in our coming to know that a trustworthy God exists. In that case, a kind of circularity will threaten and arguably undermine Descartes's suggestion. This is at least a potential problem that demands attention, and we do not have an easy answer.

Questions under dispute in a philosophical context cannot attract nonquestion-begging answers from the mere *presumption* of the correctness of a disputed answer. If we allow such question begging in general, we can support *any* disputed position we prefer. We then may simply beg the key question in any dispute regarding the preferred position. Given that strategy, argument becomes superfluous in the way circular argument is typically pointless. Question-begging strategies promote an undesirable arbitrariness in philosophical debate, and are rationally inconclusive relative to the questions under dispute. Hence, we have good reason to steer clear of question-begging strategies.

Of course, questions about the trustworthiness of our cognitive sources should be coherent. For instance, we should not demand nonquestion-begging evidence indicating the trustworthiness of vision while we call into question and therefore refuse, in principle, *any available evidence* indicating the trustworthiness of cognitive sources. That would be to demand that we stand somewhere to assess trustworthiness while we are not allowed to stand anywhere. Such a demand would undermine itself owing to a kind of incoherence – that is, what we may call *demand incoherence*. One *can* coherently question the trustworthiness of all evidence available to us, and some skeptics do just this. In that case, however, one *cannot* coherently demand that we supply nonquestion-begging evidence indicating the trustworthiness of our cognitive sources or even of a single cognitive source. If *all* available evidence (including that from our cognitive sources) is under question by skeptics, then *no* evidence will be nonquestion-begging (relative to the skeptics). As a result, a demand for nonquestion-begging evidence cannot coherently include *unrestricted* questioning of all available evidence. Any demand, then, that we establish the trustworthiness of our cognitive sources must allow that some evidence not be under question regarding trustworthiness. Otherwise, a kind of incoherence threatens: demand incoherence.

Arguably, we actually have a firm place to stand in answering skeptical questions about evidence and reasonable belief. That is, we may stand on our semantic, concept-forming intentions that give meaning to our terms.

Consider the term "epistemic reason," which signifies the kind of reason appropriate to cognitively grounded belief and to knowledge. Many philosophers of different outlooks share the general notion of an epistemic reason as a *(possibly fallible) truth indicator* for a proposition. An epistemic reason for a belief indicates, perhaps fallibly and with only a degree of probability, that the belief is true. Our meaning-forming intentions (to use terms in a certain way) give semantic content to our talk of an "epistemic reason for a belief." As intentional agents, we have an active semantic role in this connection, and we can benefit in epistemology from acknowledgment of this fact.

Suppose that we form the settled semantic intention to use "truth indicator" and "epistemic reason" as follows: a visual experience, for example, of an *apparent* book in a situation with no accessible opposing evidence is a (fallible) truth indicator and thus an epistemic reason for a visual belief that an actual book exists. This semantic intention, given its meaning-conferring role for us, could serve as a directly accessible semantic truth maker for our ascribing an epistemic reason, in such a case, to a visual belief that an actual book exists. It then would be *part of what we mean* by "epistemic reason" that such ascribing captures an epistemic reason for a visual belief that an actual book exists. Our semantic intentions concerning "epistemic reasons" therefore may serve as ultimate, even if revisable, truth makers for ascriptions of an epistemic reason.

What about skeptics who raise doubts about the trustworthiness and reasonableness of beliefs produced by our cognitive sources such as perception, memory, and introspection? They might object that our semantic intentions can be mistaken – say in virtue of failing to capture language-independent justification or evidence. We can sidestep such an objection, however, because reality (the objective world) does not settle how *in particular* we must seek truth. For better or worse, it does not settle which *specific* variant (or specific concept) of justification, evidence, or knowledge is binding on a truth seeker. Even so, a person seeking to acquire truth and to avoid error should accommodate any necessary conditions for truth acquisition (for instance, logical consistency in a belief) and for trustworthy, well-grounded belief.

In the end, skeptics cannot convincingly hold nonskeptics to a specific concept or strategy of truth acquisition and error avoidance that recommends skepticism. In particular, skeptics cannot cogently mandate an epistemic concept or strategy for us that undermines the aforementioned kind of epistemic reason (for instance, for visual beliefs) grounded in semantic intentions regarding "epistemic reason." One noteworthy problem for skeptics is that the aforementioned kind of epistemic reason is, so far as we can tell, at least as effective for trustworthy truth acquisition and error avoidance as anything skeptics, themselves, offer. In addition, skeptics have no stable foothold to propose that such a semantically grounded epistemic reason is untrustworthy as a fallible truth indicator.

Skeptics cannot plausibly charge us with question begging (or circular reasoning) here. It is *part of what we mean* by "epistemic reason" that the kind of ascription in question, in the kind of experiential context in question, captures an epistemic reason for a visual belief that an actual book exists. As a result, we now may shift the burden of argument to the skeptic, and we may call this "the skeptic's burden." We have produced, after all, a skeptic-resistant truth indicator grounded in cognitively significant semantic intentions. We also have challenged inquirers – particularly skeptics – to steer clear of demand incoherence.

The skeptic's burden is now *properly* the skeptic's. Until this burden is met, we may endorse with a clear conscience, under the specified conditions where there is no opposing truth indicator, the cognitive reasonableness of some of the beliefs delivered by our cognitive sources. We also may endorse, again under the specified conditions, the cognitive reasonableness of belief in the trustworthiness of some of our cognitive sources. It follows that an argument for the reasonableness of theism will not *automatically* be undermined by general skeptical worries about the trustworthiness of sense perception or of our cognitive sources. Of course, whether such an argument will be undermined in other ways remains to be seen. (For a more developed case against skepticism, see Moser 1989, 2008, Chapter 1 and Appendix; see also section 4 of this chapter.)

2. INQUIRERS UNDER SCRUTINY

In the Introduction's wilderness parable, although we canyon wanderers have a ham radio, it is unsettled whether we have a real intentional rescuer at hand. Some people will contend that the situation is likewise for our real-life setting. One point seems noncontroversial: to acquire evidence of intervening ham radios and their distinctive transmissions, we need to turn on a suitable radio scanner, raise its antenna, and then adjust the scanner to receive the appropriate frequency. In other words, we must *tune in* to the desired frequency, and this requires some decision making and focusing on our part.

People who fail to tune in will lack a certain kind of evidence that is *available* to them and is actually possessed by some other people who are suitably attuned. Obviously, radio waves can carry good news – even news of a needed rescue operation – but if we fail to tune in, we shall fail to receive or to appropriate such news. The transmitted good news can be readily available to us but not actually received, appropriated, or even acknowledged by us. In that case, the good news may seem absent and even hidden from us. Similarly, the source of the alleged good news may seem elusive at best and even nonexistent.

What, then, is the general condition of humans as inquirers about God's reality with regard to a needed intentional rescuer? Are humans cognitively or otherwise fit for the task of finding or receiving evidence of God's reality? The Introduction offered the term "God" as a maximally honorific title signifying worthiness of worship and thus moral perfection. We humans, of course, cannot plausibly lay claim to our having satisfied such an exalted title. On the contrary, humans arguably are experts at a kind of selfishness that is antithetical to God's moral character of unselfish love. We may call such selfishness and its accompanying pride "sin," for short, if only because there is no better word at hand. We should acknowledge that we can be experts at such sin even if we do not know that we have this expertise and even if we do not like to talk about it. In addition, it does not follow that we can immediately offer an adequate portrayal of the kind of sin in question. One can be an expert regarding deception, for instance, even if one cannot offer an adequate portrayal of deception.

The relevant distinction concerns an expert in the *realization* of sin in contrast with an expert in the *characterization* of sin. Realization expertise does not entail characterization expertise. One's *assessing* a claim to realization expertise in sin requires one's having a characterization of sin, but such assessing would go beyond mere realization expertise. Given our current interest in assessing, we need to begin with a characterization of sin. This will shed light on the condition, including the fitness, of human inquirers about the reality of God with regard to a needed rescuer. In particular, it will illuminate whether humans are cognitively or otherwise well suited to receive or to appropriate evidence of God's reality. Perhaps we humans possess some features that are resistant to or otherwise at odds with our receiving evidence of God's existence.

Famously, Reinhold Niebuhr (1965, p. 16; see also his 1941, 1949) suggests that the Christian view of sin is empirically verifiable. One relevant consideration, however, is that Christians have held many different views of sin, and therefore any talk of *the* Christian view of sin is questionable from the start. Augustine, for instance, suggested a view of "original sin" implying that one's being in a state of sin is somehow inherited from one's original ancestors, Adam and Eve. He writes:

Properly speaking, human nature means the blameless nature with which man was originally created. But we also use it in speaking of the nature with which we are born mortal, ignorant, and subject to the flesh, which is really the penalty of sin. In this sense the apostle says: "We also were by nature children of wrath even as others" (Eph. 2:3). As we are born from the first pair [namely, Adam and Eve] to a mortal life of ignorance and toil because they sinned and fell into a state of error, misery, and death, so it most justly pleased the most high God . . . to manifest from the beginning, from man's origin, his [God's] justice in exacting punishment, and in human history his mercy in remitting punishment (Augustine 395, Book III, xix, 54 – xx, 55).

Augustine thus regards human sin after the fall of Adam and Eve as, at least in part, an *inherited* defective state that is part of the divine penalty for the sin of Adam and Eve. According to Augustine, then, we human successors to Adam and Eve inherit our state of sin without initially choosing or willing it (for details see Mann 2001, Cherbonnier 1955, Chapters 8–9).

Niebuhr offers a view of original sin contrary to Augustine's. He holds, along with Augustine, that " . . . the corruption of evil is at the heart of the human personality," but he also holds, against Augustine, that original sin " . . . is a corruption which has a universal dominion over all men, though it is not by nature but in freedom that men sin . . . " (1949, p. 122). This view denies Augustine's position that original sin in the wake of Adam and Eve is an inherited defective state prior to one's free decisions. Niebuhr's view evidently finds support in the following statement of the apostle Paul: " . . . sin came into the world through one man and death through sin, and so death spread to all men *because all men sinned*" (Rom. 5:12, RSV, italics added). Paul does not say that sin and death spread *just because* Adam and Eve sinned; instead, he points to the significant fact that

"all men sinned." Paul's view is more attentive to individual human accountability than is Augustine's, and it thus
accommodates the moral truism that a child should not be
held accountable or punished (especially by a perfectly loving God) for the sins of his or her parents. One morally
important consideration is that the child lacks the ability
to prevent the parents from committing their sins or from
handing a corrupt nature down to their child.

Of course, we should avoid any simplistic view that characterizes sin as just morally wayward actions that violate
rules or regulations. This simplistic view depersonalizes the
objects of sin as rules or regulations. In contrast, according to
some important strands of Jewish and Christian theism, sin
is inherently *personal* in its subject and its object. For instance,
Emil Brunner proposes the following: "... sin is a change in
man's relation to God: it is the break in communion with
God, [owing] to distrust and defiance.... Man wants to be
on a level with God, and in so doing to become independent
of [God]" (1952, p. 92; cf. Brunner 1939, pp. 129–32). Abraham Heschel likewise offers an inherently personal characterization of sin: "To the [Jewish] prophets, sin is not an
ultimate, irreducible, or independent condition, but rather
a disturbance in the relationship between God and man; it
is ... a condition that can be surmounted by man's return
and God's forgiveness" (1962, p. 229). Similarly, the apostle
Paul identifies human sin with one's resisting the honoring
of God as God, including one's preferring to exclude God
from one's knowledge (see Rom. 1:21, 28). The irreducibly
personalist view of Paul, Brunner, and Heschel captures a
central theme of many of the Jewish and Christian biblical
writers: human sin is ultimately sin *against God*, even if it
is so in virtue of human sin against God's commands and
even if one denies that God exists.

According to the most plausible Jewish and Christian theology, human sin against God involves more than human
actions as external behavior against God. It includes human
psychological attitudes against God as well as habits against

God. In particular, according to such theology, human sin is anchored not in external behavior against rules, but rather in a morally responsible human *will* against God – specifically a human will against, or at least out of cooperation with, God's perfectly loving will. As a result, any genuine solution to human sin (as offered by a program of divine–human salvation) must be corrective somehow of not just external human behavior but human wills as well. More specifically, if human sin includes resistance to human volitional communion or fellowship with God, then divine–human salvation must somehow supply or empower human volitional fellowship with God.

Perhaps at its core divine–human salvation is divine–human fellowship, including human volitional cooperation with God. Such a view is suggested by the following remark attributed to Jesus in John 17:3: "This is everlasting life: that they know you, the only true God, and the one whom you sent, Jesus Christ." The relevant "knowing" of God is, of course, not mere propositional knowledge that God exists (which even resolute enemies of God can have). Instead, the knowing in question includes volitional agreement and even fellowship with God (as explained in what follows, and in detail in Moser 2008). We thus need to consider a kind of knowledge of God that is suitably salvific (that is, salvation oriented), or redemptive, for humans and can provide the needed powerful but noncoercive rescue from human selfishness and destruction. Let's turn to the nature of this robustly cognitive salvific solution to the human predicament.

3. FROM SCRUTINY TO RESCUE

As the Introduction suggested, an intentional rescuer who emerges in the wilderness parable may have a distinctive pedagogical aim toward the people to be rescued. Specifically, the relevant pedagogy could go beyond informational concerns to counter what the previous section would

have us call "human sin toward God." If such sin is volitional (even in part), the antidote will need to be similarly volitional in involving the human will, and not just
human beliefs and emotions. The corresponding salvific,
or redemptive, knowledge will follow suit, as this section
explains.

We can benefit now from clarification of what would be
human *appropriation* of the salvific gift on offer according
to Jewish and Christian theism. This clarification illuminates what would be the pedagogical expectations of a perfectly loving God toward wayward humans, and it saves us
from unhelpful abstractness in our talk of religious knowledge. At the heart of the Jewish and Christian Good News
of divine salvation of humans, we find an important (but
philosophically neglected) theme that exceeds divine forgiveness for human sin. It involves, in keeping with prophe-
cies in the Hebrew scriptures from Jeremiah, Ezekiel, and
Joel, *one's being made new in spirit by God's Spirit* as one dies to
one's selfish life and entrusts oneself to God's Christ-shaped
life of self-giving righteous love. God's Spirit, according
to this Good News, intervenes in a willing person's spirit
(or motivational center) to empower that person to love as
God loves, in volitional cooperation with God. The Jewish
and Christian salvation on offer is thus Spirit-oriented and
spirit-oriented. Accordingly, one must die to selfish ways,
including selfish autonomy, in order to live to God by the
power of God's Spirit. The power in question involves
the kind of noncoercive volitional pressure identified in
Chapter 2.

In Paul's distinctively Christian message, we humans
must be "crucified with Christ" (Gal. 2:19–20; cf. Col. 3:1–4),
in dying to the anti-God selfish ways of the world and of
ourselves, in order to live instead to God. Only then can we
be free to love as God loves, unselfishly and with forgiveness toward enemies. According to Paul's message, only
God's Spirit working powerfully within us can motivate
the sea change from human selfishness to unselfish love,

even toward enemies. This change resembles a heart transplant, but it occurs at the level of one's spirit or motivational center. It alters the core of the nagging human problem of sinful selfishness, even if some residue persists, and it offers an opportunity for a lasting life of divine–human fellowship and salvation in place of alienation and final death. Accordingly, as Chapter 2 suggested, we should expect a perfectly loving God to advance kardiatheology – that is, a theology aimed primarily at the human heart and not just human thoughts or feelings. (For discussion of the relevant notion of spirit, see Moser 1999 and Wiebe 2004; on the pertinent notion of heart, see Meadors 2006.)

According to Paul's Christian Good News, the gift of divine perfect love manifested in Jesus includes an offer of *dual* resurrection to humans. The duality includes willing humans being raised *spiritually* to new life *now* with God and their being raised *bodily* later, after the model of Jesus's bodily resurrection. Paul has spiritual, but not bodily, resurrection in mind when he writes: "We were buried therefore with [Christ] by baptism into death, so that as Christ was raised from the dead by the glory of the Father, we too might walk in newness of life.... So you also must consider yourselves dead to sin but alive to God in Christ Jesus.... [Y]ield yourselves to God as [people] who have been brought from death to life" (Rom. 6:4, 11, 13, RSV; cf. Col. 2:12). Accordingly, Paul supposes that followers of Jesus will "walk in newness of life" *now* toward God, "as Christ was raised from the dead" (cf. 2 Cor. 5:17). He assumes that they are already alive from the dead, as a literal translation of Romans 6:13 says. Paul holds that *bodily* resurrection for humans awaits a future time (1 Cor. 15:22–4); as a result, he must have *spiritual* resurrection in mind in the previous remarks (see also Gorman 2001, pp. 46–7, 2009, pp. 74–7, Byrnes 2003, pp. 214–18).

Paul credits the source of human spiritual resurrection to the divine Spirit of the crucified Jesus sent by God to receptive humans, "into [their] hearts, crying 'Abba!

Father!" (Gal. 4:6; cf. Rom. 8:9, 1 Cor. 15:45). Similarly, in John's Gospel, Jesus as God's atoning sacrifice is identified directly with the one who gives God's Spirit to receptive people *now* (John 1:29–33, 20:21–3; cf. Mark 1:8). The divine intended salvation of humans via Jesus therefore includes the divine *empowering means of realizing* this salvation in receptive humans: the sending of God's Spirit through Jesus to empower receptive people to live anew *now* in fellowship with God and with each other in lasting unselfish love. Accordingly, Paul announces: "If anyone is in Christ, [that person is a] new creation" (2 Cor. 5:17; cf. Gal. 6:15). Here we find, in such new creation, the divinely offered salvific antidote to human sin.

Paul's Good News "new creation" proclamation is Jewish as well as Christian. It echoes the remarkable prophecy of Ezekiel 36:26–7: "A new heart I will give you and a new spirit I will put within you; and I will take out of your flesh the heart of stone and give you a heart of flesh. And I will put my spirit within you and cause you to walk in my statutes and be careful to observe my ordinances" (RSV; cf. Ezek. 37:14, Jer. 32:39–40). In keeping with this promise, Paul proclaims the cross and the resurrection of Jesus as the salvific avenue for God to impart God's Spirit to all receptive people, including Gentiles as well as Jews (see Rom. 10:11–21). This fits with the aforementioned kardiatheology aimed primarily at the human heart, and not just thoughts or feelings. (Chapter 5 takes up the issue of how a perfectly loving God could work outside the beliefs of any particular religion, given the obvious fact of religious diversity among humans.)

A new human volitional center depends on the direct, firsthand reception and ongoing availability of God's empowering Spirit by a receptive human agent. Such a new volitional center is at the heart of spiritual resurrection as understood by Paul and John (cf. John 3:1–12). Such spiritual resurrection would have straightforward cognitive as well as salvific importance (as emphasized in Dickie 1954). In particular, it would yield experiential acquaintance with powerful evidence of God's intervening Spirit at work in one's motivational center, leading one away from selfishness and toward unselfish love, in volitional cooperation with God. Such experiential evidence indicates what Paul calls a "new creation" in a person and what John calls "a person's being born from above." (On the topic of new creation and conversion in Paul, Luke, and John, see Gaventa 1986, Segal 1990, Chapters 4–5, Hubbard 2002, and Thompson 2001, Chapter 4.)

As noted previously, Paul states: "... hope [in God] does not disappoint, because the love of God has been poured out in our hearts through the Holy Spirit given to us" (Rom. 5:5; cf. 2 Cor. 1:22, 5:5). Through God's Spirit given to us, as we willingly yield to God's authoritative call in conscience to volitional cooperation, our innermost personal center (that is, our heart) would welcome God's powerful self-revelation of perfect love and thereby begin to be changed from being selfish to manifesting God's imparted unselfish love, even if imperfectly. This would be an agent-to-agent salvific power transaction that moves willing humans noncoercively from human selfish fear (the root of sin) to shared divine unselfish love (the root of salvation), and from spiritual death to new spiritual life. It would occur at the innermost personal center of a human life, where the problem of sinful selfishness and pride arises and endures, but it would not automatically remove all human selfishness and pride at once. This personal power transaction would yield, nonetheless, a new default motivational center in a manner that no merely intellectual or emotional process could.

Paul's Spirit-focused approach to redemption bears directly on the reality and the relevance of *purposively available evidence* of divine reality. In this approach, human faith and hope in God (to fulfill divine promises, including the promise of salvation) can find a conclusive *cognitive* anchor in our evident experience of willingly receiving God's Spirit. In such receiving, God's love begins to change our hearts toward the distinctive character of divine unselfish love.

Paul expresses a related theme in referring to the God who "has put his seal upon us and given us his Spirit in our hearts as a guarantee" (2 Cor. 1:22, RSV; see also 2 Cor. 5:5; cf. Eph. 1:13). According to Paul, the Spirit given to receptive human hearts guarantees, as an evidential, cognitive down payment, that God will complete the salvific work of transformation begun in those hearts. Such human volitional transformation toward divine love can be salient evidence of God's reality and intervention in a receptive human life.

4. ARGUING FOR GOD

We can introduce a definition and an argument to elucidate the cognitive significance of divine merciful love. We begin with a definition of "the transformative gift" as:

one's being authoritatively convicted in conscience and forgiven by X of sin and thereby being authoritatively called into volitional fellowship with X in perfect love and into rightful worship toward X as worthy of worship and, on that basis, transformed by X from default tendencies to selfishness and despair to a new volitional center with a default position of unselfish love, including forgiveness, toward all people and of hope in the triumph of good over evil by X.

Given this definition, and refining an argument from Chapter 2, we can offer the following argument for the reality of an authoritative perfectly loving God:

1. Necessarily, if a human person is offered and receives the transformative gift, then this is the result of the authoritative power of a divine X of thoroughgoing forgiveness, fellowship in perfect love, worthiness of worship, and triumphant hope (namely, God).
2. I have been offered, and have willingly received, the transformative gift.
3. Therefore, God exists.

The transformative gift in question can be offered to a person but rejected or ignored by that person. Accordingly, this gift's being offered does not guarantee its being received for what it is intended to be: namely, a redemptive gift that seeks to trump human selfishness with divine love for the sake of human transformation by God.

If God inherently is perfectly loving, then God inherently is *personal* as an intentional agent with definite purposes. Accordingly, purposively available conclusive evidence and knowledge of God's reality *as God* would include evidence and knowledge of God *as personal and perfectly loving* as an intentional agent. (Chapter 3 explained how traditional natural theology has missed this important lesson, to its own demise.) We cannot separate God's reality from God's perfectly loving personal character that defines God's reality. Likewise, we cannot separate conclusive evidence and knowledge of God's reality from conclusive evidence and knowledge of God's perfectly loving personal character.

My direct, firsthand knowledge of God's reality and character would include my being acquainted with (at least) *God's personal and perfectly loving will.* This will would seek to lead me noncoercively, via volitional pressure, toward volitional cooperation with God in unselfish love while convicting me of any wrongful obstacle to such leading. In other words, my imperfect personal will would be challenged via my acquaintance with a perfect personal will that seeks to lead me from selfishness to unselfish love in divine–human fellowship. My conscience would be a focal place for receiving this person-to-person volitional challenge and pressure in such a way that I come to "know together" with God my actual moral status before God. It would include intended conviction of my moral waywardness and noncoercive nudging of my will toward divine–human cooperation in perfect love.

When we are acquainted with perfect unselfish love, we are acquainted with God's inherent personal character and thus with the reality of God. This is so even if we do not know *that* we are acquainted with divine reality in this case or in any other case. At least this view deserves serious consideration now. In knowing perfect unselfish love by acquaintance, we know God's reality by acquaintance, even if our understanding of *what* (or, better, *whom*) we then know is mistaken or otherwise deficient. In addition, when acquainted with such love, we face a person-defining and life-guiding choice: we can either welcome and support our transformation or turn away, directly or indirectly, in rejection or indifference. Faced with such a choice, we have a decisive cognitive opportunity, and we arguably are accountable before God for how we handle it.

Through acquaintance with perfect unselfish love, we experience what is being offered in the transformative gift. Perhaps we have experienced only vague glimmers of the gift, but these are enough to invite us to welcome and to support the gift rather than to turn away in either rejection or indifference. According to this approach, the unselfish love intruding via volitional pressure in our troubled lives is God's noncoercive attempt to rescue us by leading us from despair to hope and from spiritual death to new life. A person, however, could be offered such an invitation from God and not even know it, given obscuring confusions and corrupted motivational attitudes in that person. In any case, some cognitive and volitional pollution control may be needed among humans faced with divine intervention.

Three human impediments to acknowledging divine intervention from a perfectly loving God are noteworthy. First, we often look for God's reality in the wrong places, if we care to look at all. Philosophers typically look in areas involving abstruse, esoteric arguments that have nothing directly to do with God's inherent character of perfect authoritative love. For example, seemingly endless disputes about probabilities involving apparent design in biology or cosmology or about the need for an inaugural cause behind any parade of contingent causes and effects illustrate the point abundantly and decisively. One's antecedent commitments about God tend to color one's understanding of how the relevant probabilities or causal requirements go, and this consideration leaves the disputes marked by question begging and hence notoriously unresolved, at best. In any case, it is not clear that the empirical phenomena in question call for a personal agent worthy of worship. (See Chapter 3 for some serious shortcomings in natural theology on that front.) It therefore is unclear what, if anything, one actually gains from such disputes, beyond digging in deeper with one's antecedent commitments. Fortunately, we need not go there to get to God's reality. Instead, a perfectly loving God would come to willing humans in God's unique irreducibly authoritative and personal way.

Second, many people unreflectively think of perfect unselfish love as just another *natural* human capacity, akin to vision, speech, and taste. Accordingly, they uncritically think that humans have the power of perfect unselfish love on their own, without a morally superior power beyond themselves. The rough idea, then, is that many humans are naturally loving toward other people, and that therefore we have no basis here for introducing a God worthy of worship. This is presumptuous at best, and also implausible on any careful reflection that attends to actual human tendencies.

We obviously are hard put to come up with a human community that exemplifies perfect love on its own, and this is very telling of the actual human condition. Left to our own resources and motives, we evidently are too conflicted motivationally and too selfishly fearful of personal loss to generate and sustain perfect unselfish love in relationships. We therefore apparently need a morally superior power beyond us. In any case, we should not take self-credit in any situation in which self-credit is not due, including the situation of perfect unselfish love. If such unselfish love were under our own power via self-help or peer-help among humans, we would be much more effective and much less violent at conflict resolution, peace making, and community building. Our general record on these fronts obviously leaves a lot to be desired, to put the matter very charitably, and it suggests that perfect unselfish love is not ours to deliver.

The genuine offer and the human reception of the transformative gift, according to premise 1, require a divine source that has the power of thoroughgoing forgiveness and transformation of willing humans to a new volitional center of *default unselfish love and forgiveness toward all people*. Indeed, it is part of the concept of the transformative gift, as characterized, that the source of this gift (when this gift is real) is a powerful divine authority of thoroughgoing forgiveness who is worthy of worship. In the concept at hand, the transformation integral to this gift is the change of a person's motivational center to a default position of unselfish love and forgiveness for all people. This change involves a reported experienced reality that is prominent in Jewish and Christian theism, as outlined in the previous section: namely, the divine impartation of God's Spirit to humans whereby divine power is made available to them at their motivational center in a default manner. As a result, the change in question is not offered as just a product of human self-help or peer-help. Instead, it involves a distinctive power from beyond the domain of human power.

Third, many people think that conclusive evidence and knowledge of God's reality, if they are available at all, could be acquired by us without our receiving an authoritative challenge to participate in the kind of perfect unselfish love characteristic of God. We humans naturally prefer to keep God's authoritative perfectly loving reality at arm's length, in order to block this reality from challenging our own selfish plans. A perfectly loving God, however, would offer selfish humans an authoritative challenge to have divine unselfish love empower and guide their lives thoroughly, including in their interactions with dangerous enemies and morally perverse people. We therefore should consider the distinction from the Introduction between *spectator* evidence and knowledge of God's reality, which do not challenge a human will to yield to God, and *authoritative*, invitational evidence and knowledge of God's reality, which invite a human will to cooperate with God's will and thereby to become personifying evidence of God's reality. As inquirers about God's reality, we do well to be open to such authoritative evidence and knowledge, given the perfectly loving moral character of a God worthy of worship.

In keeping with authoritative direct, firsthand evidence of divine reality, as opposed to spectator evidence, premise 2 is irreducibly first-person and self-involving. It rests on undefeated authoritative evidence of divine reality that is inherently and directly firsthand and purposively available. Specifically, the evidence involves my evident willing reception of an authoritative call in conscience to volitional fellowship with an intentional agent worthy of worship. It also includes for me an evident new volitional center with a default position of unselfish love and forgiveness for all people. Of course, we should not confuse the direct, firsthand evidence in question with an argument of any kind. Arguments, as noted previously, do not have a monopoly on evidence, even if evidence can be characterized and relied upon in an argument.

Skeptics doubtless will question premise 2, if only because the first premise seems more secure. In the face of their challenge, however, I could plausibly argue for the cognitive well-groundedness, or trustworthiness, of premise 2 on the basis of its central role in an undefeated best-available explanation of the whole range of my experience and my other evidence. This role includes this premise's figuring in a best-available answer to the following explanation-seeking question: why is my experience regarding the supposed provisions of the transformative gift (including my evident change from default selfishness to a new volitional center with a default position of unselfish love toward all people) *as it actually is now*, rather than the opposite or at least very different? On the basis of my experiential evidence, the central role of premise 2 in answering such an explanation-seeking question can figure in its being well grounded for me and for anyone else who has similar evidence. If we failed to acknowledge the reality of causation, our explanatory resources would suffer considerably; an analogous point holds for the reality of God, although the crucial evidence is volitionally sensitive and beyond our control. (See Moser 1989 for details on explanation and its role in justification and knowledge.)

My experiential evidence will be conclusive if it is unaccompanied by defeaters, which can arise directly or indirectly. A *direct* defeater of initial evidence for a statement consists of additional evidence (not to be confused with mere beliefs) that significantly challenges *the support* of the initial evidence for the statement in question. Consider, for instance, my initial visual evidence indicating that there is a bent stick submerged halfway in a tub of water. The support that this evidence initially offers can be defeated by my additional visual evidence indicating, from a broader visual perspective, that my initial visual evidence fails, when supplemented with my broader evidence, to indicate that there is a bent stick in the tub of water. In contrast, an *indirect* defeater of evidence consists of evidence that significantly challenges *the truth (claim) indicated* by that evidence. For instance, my visual evidence indicating that there is a vase before me can be defeated by my broader visual and tactile evidence indicating that only a holographic image of a vase is before me. Such defeaters illustrate that evidence can be defeated, and is thus defeasible, in two ways by additional evidence (but not by mere beliefs, which can be altogether lacking in supporting evidence).

The kind of explanation-oriented well-groundedness, or trustworthiness, underlying premise 2 is rightly more demanding than a mere "consistency relation" with evidence (as proposed, for example, by Cottingham 2005, p. 24). It also avoids worries about a cognitively naïve realism that face a less demanding principle of credulity (as proposed, for example, by Swinburne 1979 and Davis 1989). In line with a so-called "commonsense" approach to evidence and knowledge, the latter principle of credulity assumes that reality is probably the way things appear to us to be, if there is no reason to question this. Our best science, however, can present subtle evidence independent of (some) commonsense beliefs (say, evidence in particle physics, regarding the constituents of physical objects) that challenges a commonsense belief resting on a principle of credulity. (See Wiebe 2004, pp. 142–4, for some confirmation.) In contrast, my proposed explanation-oriented approach makes well-groundedness more stringent, given its required role in a best-available explanation relative to the whole range of one's experience and evidence. As a result, skeptics cannot plausibly accuse me of just preaching to the choir or to people of "common sense," a practice that improperly would disregard skeptics.

Cognitive support for premise 2 could be *diachronic* rather than just synchronic, because God could manifest his worship-worthy personal reality *over time* in the transformative gift as a person willingly receives that gift increasingly deeply. To the extent that we are unwilling to undergo such reception of the transformative gift over time, we would block from ourselves significant evidence of God's existence as we obstruct evidence of God's desired intervention in our experience over time. Philosophers often look only for synchronic evidence of God's existence and thereby neglect the significant evidence of divine reality involved in *ongoing* human reception of the transformative gift. We, however, should look carefully for such diachronic evidence, given the ongoing purposes of noncoercive redemptive transformation that a perfectly loving God would have regarding willing humans (see Schweizer 1971, p. 50).

Of course, not all people share my evident experience underlying premise 2. That claim seems obviously true, but it yields no objection to premise 2, because that premise does not entail that all people have the experience in question. In addition, cognitive support for a claim, including for premise 2, can vary among people, owing to variation in experiences and corresponding evidence. Accordingly, some people know some things that are not known at all by others, and this should come as no surprise. Of course, a critic might allege that the explanation offered by premise 2 for my experience is not only false but ultimately ungrounded. In that case, the critic will owe us a falsifier of premise 2 and an undefeated defeater of my evidence for premise 2. So far as I can tell, it will not be easy for the critic to deliver either of these. At a minimum, the critic has some careful work to do.

Of course, I *could* have a defeater supplied by my experience (such as an indication of a hallucination or a dream), but the fact that I actually *do not* have one is cognitively significant and should not be disregarded. This chapter and the following chapter contend that the needed falsifier or defeater is not as readily available as many religious skeptics have supposed (see Wiebe 2004 for additional support in this area). In addition, given my appeal for antiskeptical purposes to an undefeated best-available explanation of the whole range of my experience and other evidence, the scope for potential defeaters is broad indeed and is not implausibly restricted to what fits with commonsense or naïve realism. Accordingly, I have not narrowly stacked the evidential deck against skeptics. Even so, we cannot plausibly excuse skeptics from their considerable evidential and explanatory burden now.

We should not offer the conclusion of the argument 1–3, that God exists, as a conceptually necessary truth – that is, as a truth the denial of which is not coherently imaginable. We coherently can imagine that God does not exist, but, as this section has argued, it is true that God exists and there is purposively available conclusive evidence that God exists. Clearly, the power of our imagination, with regard to what it can coherently present, outstrips what is real and what is conclusively supportable for us. As a result, we would risk implausible special pleading in suggesting that God's existence is conceptually necessary (unless, for some reason, we introduced a merely technical notion of conceptual necessity independent of what we can coherently imagine). In any case, it is enough for purposes of sound argument that the steps of argument 1–3 are true and their inference is valid. Given the previous considerations, I find no compelling reason to deny that the argument is sound or, for a suitably positioned person, rationally cogent.

Human reception of the divine transformative gift can come in varying levels or degrees, owing to varying depths of being led into noncoercive volitional cooperation or fellowship with God. At any level, however, one's undergoing the required transformation that brings a new default motivational center will entail one's becoming personifying evidence of divine reality, wherein one willingly receives and reflects God's moral character of unselfish love and thus God's distinctive kind of moral agency for others. In other words, one's receiving a new default motivational center supplies a basic, or foundational, threshold for one's becoming personifying evidence of God. Such life-giving, and self-giving, evidence, rather than that of natural theology, is characteristic of a God of perfect love. In accordance with its divine source, this personifying evidence is inherently for the sake of others. It is therefore inherently morally significant, in being motivated by divine unselfish love.

5. VOLITIONAL AND FILIAL KNOWLEDGE

The volitional change identified in the previous section may now be seen as crucial to a distinctive kind of *volitional* and *filial* knowledge of divine reality: that is, knowledge wherein one comes to know God as one's authoritative loving Father in virtue of the willingly received impartation of God's Spirit to one at one's motivational center. The relevant filial relation is, accordingly, a volitional and *spiritual* filial relation, owing to the central roles of a human's receptive will and God's empowering Spirit at work in new human life.

The present section characterizes the new volitional center and the impartation of God's Spirit for a person in terms of the direct, firsthand reception and continuing availability of the morally perfect power of God's Spirit by a willingly receptive person. This approach sidesteps metaphysical intricacies that are not essential to present explanatory purposes. It also enables us to avoid both a moralistic approach that characterizes a new motivational center just in terms of actual moral actions or episodes and a mystical approach that proposes that God's Spirit literally inhabits a human spirit. (For relevant discussion, see Brondos 2006, Chapter 6.)

We must distinguish two kinds of knowledge: (i) *propositional* knowledge that God exists, and (ii) *filial* knowledge of God's reality as one's humbly standing in a childlike, volitionally submissive relationship to God as perfectly authoritative and loving Lord and Father. (We should avoid confusion of one's being child*like* and one's being child*ish*.) Filial knowledge of God's reality requires propositional knowledge that God exists, but it exceeds such propositional knowledge. One could know, on the basis of conclusive evidence, that God exists, but fail altogether to submit volitionally to God as Lord. Filial knowledge of God's reality, in contrast, includes one's being reconciled to God, at least to some extent, through volitional submission to God as Lord and Father, on the basis of conclusive authoritative evidence that is purposively available. It requires our entrusting ourselves as obedient children to God in grateful love, thereby becoming transformed in *who we are* and in *how we exist and act*, not just in what we believe or feel. We may think of this as human *filial* attunement to God relative to God's morally perfect will. This, of course, goes significantly beyond merely historical knowledge of theologically interpreted events (on the latter kind of knowledge, see Bourke 1964, Perrin 1976, Chapter 5, and Allison 2009).

As perfectly loving, God would not be satisfied by our merely knowing that God exists. Such mere propositional knowledge falls far short of what God would value by way of the divine redemption of humans: namely, that all people, in response to purposively available authoritative evidence of divine reality, freely yield to God's call to receive transformation by God from selfishness to unselfish love toward all people. (For Jewish and Christian suggestions of this ideal, see, for example, Deuteronomy 6:5, 10:12–13, Leviticus 19:18, Mark 12:28–31; for some historical background, see Furnish 1972, Klassen 1984, and Meier 2009.) As perfectly loving, God would aim to have all people freely come, in volitional cooperation with God, to be morally perfect as God is morally perfect. Given this aim, God would have no reason to offer spectator evidence of divine reality to humans. In contrast, authoritative evidence that includes a divine call to human transformation would serve God's redemptive purpose for humans.

We can elucidate filial knowledge of God by attending more carefully to the kind of human transformation it demands, and, in this connection, we can benefit from some helpful suggestions in Paul's letters. According to Paul, the Spirit of God is also the Spirit of Jesus, who gave his life as God's Son in order to manifest and to offer his Father's powerful unselfish love for humans and thereby to offer divine–human reconciliation. Accordingly, the Spirit of God is the Spirit of *adoption* of humans into God's family of children who acknowledge God as "Abba, Father" (see Rom. 8:9, 15), and this adoption includes one's being led by the unselfish power of God's Spirit (see Rom. 8:14). This approach to God's Spirit, portrayed as leading humans to become God's unselfish children, fits well with the importance of filial knowledge of divine reality. By way of contrast, worldly powers of human selfishness go in the opposite direction of one's being led by the unselfish power of God's Spirit. In expecting evidence of God's reality to fit with worldly powers, including worldly religious powers incompatible with unselfish love, people blind themselves from apprehending God's reality.

According to Paul, God's intervening Spirit reveals God's reality and our relationship with God; thus: "... we have received ... the Spirit from God, *in order that* we may know the things freely given to us by God" (1 Cor. 2:12, italics added; cf. 1 Cor. 12:7–8, where Paul speaks of the "manifestation" of God's Spirit). The Spirit of God, as God's own divine agent of salvific intervention and communication, would automatically know the things of God, including divine intentions and other attitudes. As a result, the Spirit of God could authoritatively reveal God's reality and God's ways to humans. Paul therefore concludes that we are given the Spirit of God *in order that* we may know God's reality and God's ways of self-giving love. He arguably has a kind of *volitional* and *filial* knowledge in mind, because human reception of God's Spirit requires human willingness to be adopted into God's family of obedient children, in cooperative fellowship with God.

By giving God's own empowering Spirit to receptive humans, as a resident default but noncoercive guide and motivator, God extends volitional and filial knowledge of God's reality to humans. More specifically, God's intervening Spirit confirms to a receptive individual's spirit, via conscience, that he or she is a child of God, called into filial fellowship – including volitional cooperation – with God as perfectly authoritative and loving Father (see Rom. 8:15–16, Gal. 4:6–7, 1 Cor. 1:9; cf. 1 John 4:13). The role of conscience is crucial because it involves the spiritual heart of a person and, accordingly, is a place of profound conviction under certain conditions. Of course, God could use various means, including other people, to introduce noncoercive "volitional pressure" in one's conscience and thereby lead a person toward a certain attitude or action. Even so, one's conscience would have a crucial role in the divine leading.

Filial fellowship, including volitional cooperation, with God involves both noncoercive perfectly authoritative and loving *ownership* of a child on God's part and willingly *being owned* by God on the child's part. Accordingly, Paul states that followers of Jesus under God as Father are not their own but "have been bought with a price" and thus belong to God (1 Cor. 6:19–20; cf. Rom. 14:7–9). Paul would say that the urgent question for a human is not so much "Who am I?" as "*Whose* am I?" John's Gospel follows suit: "The one who is of [that is, belongs to] God hears the words of God; on account of this, you do not hear them, because you are not of [that is, do not belong to] God" (8:47). A key motivational question therefore arises, and takes on cognitive significance: *by whose power* am I living? Am I living by the lasting noncoercive power of God's Spirit of unselfish love, or instead by my own short-lived, largely selfish power? The presence of one's selfishness can be a litmus test for one's being motivated by dying human power antithetical to the lasting unselfish power of a perfectly loving God.

In Paul's message, obedient human reception of God's Spirit is no merely subjective matter. It yields one's becoming, by way of a default motive, unselfishly loving to some discernible degree as God is unselfishly loving, even toward enemies. It bears observable fruits of the intervening Spirit of a perfectly loving God, such as love, joy, peace, patience, kindness, goodness, faithfulness, humility, and self-control (see Gal. 5:22–3). These fruits are not merely subjective phenomena but are, instead, discernible by anyone suitably attentive to them. As the powerful overflow of divine love in a receptive human life, they emerge in human lives in ways that are identifiable and testable, even if one needs willing "eyes to see and ears to hear" them. The fruits of God's Spirit arise and function in a larger context of a willing life under transformation as a salvific gift from God to be received via experientially grounded self-entrustment to God (see Gal. 3:2, 14). Accordingly, they figure directly in one's becoming personifying evidence of God's reality in one's willingly receiving and reflecting God's powerful moral character for others.

Jesus himself announced the human need to test competing people and their positions: "Beware of false prophets, who come to you in sheep's clothing but inwardly are ravenous wolves. You will know them by their fruits.... Every sound tree bears good fruit, but the bad tree bears evil fruit. A sound tree cannot bear evil fruit, nor can a bad tree bear good fruit" (Matt. 7:15–18). Similarly, one can know the authenticity of God's intervening Spirit by means of the fruits demanded and yielded by the Spirit in one's own life. As noted previously, this Spirit noncoercively demands and empowers one, in fellowship with God, to become loving (at least to a certain degree) as God is unselfishly loving, even toward enemies. In keeping with God's perfectly loving character, this is the primary fruit of God's intervening Spirit in a receptive person (see 1 Cor. 13:1–13; cf. Eph. 3:17–19, Col. 2:2, 3:14). God's intervening Spirit, then, comes with salient evidence observable by any suitably attentive person, and such evidence enables one to exclude imposters and even to become personifying evidence of God. This consideration bears directly on a test for the reality of divine salvation from sin and the falsity of the many dangerous counterfeits in circulation.

We have suggested that the kind of human transformation sought by a perfectly loving God would bear on the kind of evidence of divine reality we should expect. Let's use the ancient Greek term *agape* to refer to the divine morally righteous unselfish love that noncoercively seeks what is good, even what is best all things considered, for all people involved. (Obviously, we should not confuse *agape* with much of what is ordinarily represented as "love," particularly the fluffy stuff of romance novels, popular love songs, and television soap operas.) Let's distinguish between (a) an *agape*-enhancing occasion in which a human is willingly *agape*-receiving and/or *agape*-advancing toward God and other agents, in virtue of the value of *agape*, and (b) an *agape*-resisting occasion in which a human is willingly *agape*-neglecting and/or *agape*-opposing toward God and other agents.

God's desired transformation of humans would include a change from *agape*-resisting occasions to *agape*-enhancing occasions for humans, in divine–human fellowship. In other words, God would want to empower humans, without coercion, to transform any occasion fully, including the involved human agents themselves, from *agape*-resisting to *agape*-enhancing. Such noncoercive empowering of what we may call "*agape* transformation" would aim for cooperative divine–human fellowship, and would include a manifestation, if temporary and incomplete, of God's morally perfect character, even in the willing recipients of God's *agape*. This divine manifestation, in keeping with God's perfectly loving character, would seek to offer divine love to a wider audience or to a particular audience more deeply. In doing so, God would seek to have humans themselves become personifying evidence of God's reality, in virtue of their willingly receiving and reflecting God's distinctive moral character for others.

Agape-enhancing occasions are *agape*-enlightening in that they bring *agape* regarding God and other agents into human attention (at least for the willing humans involved) as valuable – that is, at least as worthy of being received and/or advanced. In contrast, *agape*-resisting occasions are *agape*-dimming in that they obscure or reduce the value of *agape* regarding God and others for the relevant humans. If God's character is inherently a character of (morally righteous) *agape*, as some of the Hebrew prophets (including Jesus) and the New Testament writers suggest, then *agape*-resisting tendencies among humans could obscure the value of God's presence for those humans. In doing so, those tendencies also could obscure the reality of God's presence, because in neglecting the value of divine love, we easily could fail to look for it at all. How we treat *agape* toward people could be equivalent to how we treat God: with acceptance, indifference, or rejection. To the extent that we take self-credit for unselfish love toward people, we obscure its real source and the evidence for that source. We also then fail to give credit where credit is due: to God. As a result, our attitudinal treatment of *agape* in our lives can be cognitively significant in addition to being morally significant.

The question of evidence for God's existence should become for us humans the question of how we respond, at the volitional level of a decision, to the powerful gift of *agape* to us and others. In this connection, philosophy can remove obstacles and clear a path for something ultimately non-philosophical, because that "thing" is uncontrollable and more profound and powerfully transformative than any philosophy. It involves something irreducibly person-to-person – specifically, an I–Thou acquaintance of a person with the living God. At this sacred place, humans will be in the presence of the personal God of powerful holy love, and they will be called to a fitting, self-entrusting response. Accordingly, their role as intentional responsible agents will be as important as their role as knowers. In highlighting personifying evidence of God, this book's epistemology of religious knowledge aims to capture this important consideration.

6. GOOD NEWS GIFT AS POWER

The divine–human volitional fellowship central to human redemption would be lasting fellowship, and not just a temporary fix. This consideration agrees with the talk of everlasting life in John 17:3. However, some people doubt that divine perfect love, as a redemptive antidote to human sin, would actually yield everlasting life for willing recipients of such love. For instance, Timothy Jackson has raised such a doubt, on the ground that "to have love is not to have all good things [including everlasting life], but it is to have the *best* thing" (1999, p. 170). Evidently, Jackson assumes that having love, even if temporary, is "the best thing."

Let's consider the prospect that the "best thing" would be for willing humans to have divine love *everlastingly*, and not just for the short term. Accordingly, if God is perfectly loving and thus wants *the best* for humans, God would give them the opportunity to have divine love everlastingly. Failing to give this view due consideration, Jackson claims that "love can endure even without faith in one's own resurrection" (1999, p. 168). The immediate issue, however, is whether a perfectly loving God's wanting the best for humans would include God's giving them the opportunity to have a life of divine love everlastingly, rather than just for the short term. The answer is definitely *yes*. Indeed, Jackson himself unknowingly offers the needed support as follows: "Love is concerned with preserving and enhancing *all* good things, *to the greatest extent possible....* " (1999, p. 218, italics added). Accordingly, a perfectly loving God would offer willing humans the opportunity to receive a life of divine love everlastingly, in lasting fellowship with God. The divine–human fellowship central to human redemption would follow suit.

The divine redemption of humans from sin would rest on divine authority, anchored in divine perfect love, and not on morally questionable human preferences. We can find some indications of such authority in the earliest reports about Jesus, who stood in contrast with his Jewish contemporaries who dared to speak for God (Matt. 7:28–9). Such authority was very different from that of secular authorities who, according to Jesus, "lord it over" others (Mark 10:42–5). The apostle Paul referred to this authority from God and Jesus as "the authority in the gospel" (1 Cor. 9:18), and he understood "the gospel" as "*the power* of God for salvation" (Rom. 1:16, italics added). According to Paul, if the gospel of divine Good News is an authoritative gift, it is a power gift (as emphasized in Käsemann 1961). Let's clarify this power authority and see how it contributes to the divine redemption of humans. We shall see that the kind of redemption in question harks back to the need of an intentional (and thus personal) rescuer in the Introduction's wilderness parable.

Strikingly, Jesus manifested a kind of powerful authority that led to his being worshipped as the divine personal means of human salvation by his earliest followers, including even such an educated Jewish monotheist as the apostle Paul (see Phil. 2:5–11, 1 Cor. 1:2, Gal. 4:4–5, 1 Thess. 5:8, Rom. 3:24; cf. Hurtado 2003 and Bauckham 2008). Jesus began his ministry as the preacher of the Good News about *God's* arriving kingdom, under clear influence from the book of Isaiah (cf. Mark 1:1–15), but he became, very soon after his death, *an object of focus* in the preaching of the Good News by his earliest, Jewish disciples. In short, the *preacher* became part of the *preached*; the *proclaimer* became part of the *proclaimed*, as Bultmann (1955, Vol. 1, p. 33) and many other New Testament scholars have noted.

In the path of C.H. Dodd (1936), Eugene Lemcio has identified a common kerygma, or proclamation, regarding the Good News of redemption in nineteen of the twenty-seven books of the New Testament. He has isolated this kerygma in all of the main representatives and traditions of the New Testament, and he sums up the unifying kerygma as follows: "It declares the Good News of God's sending [Jesus] or raising Jesus from the dead. By responding obediently to God, one receives the benefits stemming from this salvific event" (1991, p. 127). We therefore may speak of *the* Good News kerygma of redemption, beyond any multiplicity of kerygmas (for further support for such unity of message, see Hunter 1943, Wenham 1993).

In one of the earliest statements of the Good News proclamation in the New Testament, Paul writes:

For I delivered to you of first importance what I have received: that Christ died for our sins according to the Scriptures, that he was buried, that he was raised on the third day according to the Scriptures, and that he appeared to Peter, and then to the twelve. After that, he appeared to more than five hundred brothers at the same time, most of whom remain until now, but some have fallen asleep. Then he appeared to James, then to all the apostles, and last of all he appeared also to me, as to one untimely born. . . . If Christ has not been raised, our preaching is futile and your faith is futile too. We are also then found to be false witnesses about God, because we have testified about God that he raised Christ from the dead.... If Christ has not been raised, your faith is futile; you are still in your sins.... If we have hope in Christ only for this life, we are to be pitied more than all men. But Christ has been raised from the dead, the firstfruits of those who have fallen asleep (1 Cor. 15:3–8, 14–15, 17, 19–20).

The Good News of redemption, according to Paul, includes the twofold fact that "Christ died for our sins" and was raised from the dead. Indeed, Paul regards the Good News as "false" and "futile" in the absence of the resurrection of Jesus, because he links the resurrection of Jesus to divine forgiveness of human sins in such a way that if there is no divine resurrection in vindication of Jesus, "you are still in your sins."

A central theme of the Pauline Good News of redemption is that human sins are forgiven, or pardoned, by God, and humans are thereby offered reconciliation with God, in connection with the life, death, and resurrection of Jesus. If *atonement* is divine–human reconciliation that effectively deals with human sin as resistance to divine unselfish love and fellowship, then the heart of the controversy about the life, death, and resurrection of Jesus, at least by Paul's lights, is a debate about atonement. Even so, some important questions remain. For instance, exactly how do the life, death, and resurrection of Jesus figure in (intended) divine–human atonement? In addition, how is such atonement to be appropriated by humans for redemption from sin?

According to Matthew's Gospel (26:28), Jesus announced at the Last Supper that he will die "for the forgiveness of sins." In Matthew's account, the atoning sacrifice of Jesus as God's sinless offering for sinful humans is at the center of God's effort for human redemption. John's Gospel (1:36) and Paul's undisputed letters (see 1 Cor. 5:7, 2 Cor. 5:21, Rom. 3:24–6) agree with this lesson about redemption. The unique role assigned to Jesus in divine–human redemption clearly sets him apart from every other known seminal religious leader, including Moses, Confucius, Krishna, Gautama the Buddha, and Muhammad. As portrayed by Matthew, John, and Paul, Jesus uniquely offered himself as God's atoning sacrifice to God for human redemption from sin. Jesus therefore emerges at the center of the Good News proclamation of God's intended redemption of humans. In other words, he becomes part of what is proclaimed in the Christian Good News, and thus he does not remain as just a proclaimer of the Good News.

The Roman crucifixion of Jesus may seem to leave him as ultimately a failure, even as one "cursed" before God (see Gal. 3:13, Deut. 21:23). Nonetheless, at least Paul, Matthew, and John proclaim the crucified and risen Jesus as the central mediating figure in God's atoning sacrifice and turnaround victory for the redemption of humans. Out of the apparent defeat of Jesus on the cross, according to the Good News, God brought a unique manifestation and offering of divine love and forgiveness toward humans, including God's enemies, while setting aside any human means of triumphant power (see 1 Cor. 1:23–9). The cross of Jesus therefore carries a word of divine judgment, as noted by Käsemann (1967, p. 40): "The cross shows that the true God alone is the creator who works from nothing, who continually draws creation out of chaos and who has hence constantly manifested himself since the beginning of the world as the raiser of the dead. The cross also shows us that from the aspect of the question of salvation, true man is always the sinner who is fundamentally unable to help himself, who cannot by his own action bridge the endless distance to God, and who is hence a member of the lost, chaotic, futile world, which at best waits for the resurrection of the dead." The crucifixion of Jesus, accordingly, is proclaimed as a central part of God's intended powerful reversal of the dark human tragedy of alienation from God for the sake of human redemption by God. It serves, in short, as a powerful divine invitation to humans bent on lesser, ultimately failing powers.

The intended divine reversal aims at divine–human reconciliation by means of a powerful manifestation of God's unselfishly loving moral character. This manifestation is exemplified in Jesus, God's innocent victim (of human sin) who offers forgiveness and fellowship instead of condemnation to guilty humans. We may call this *the divine manifest–offering* approach to atonement or redemption, in keeping with Romans 3:21–6 (which uses talk of "manifestation" repeatedly). What is being made *manifest* is God's powerful moral character of righteous and forgiving love, and what is being *offered*, in keeping with that character, is lasting divine–human fellowship as a powerful divine gift for the sake of human redemption. This divine gift for humans is anchored in both (a) the unique love offered and manifested via God's powerful atoning sacrifice in Jesus, the innocent victim of humans, and (b) God's powerful resurrection of Jesus as Lord and as Giver of God's Spirit. This gift, accordingly, is inextricably linked to its life-giving gift *Giver*. In an important sense, the gift of salvation is God himself.

The manifestation of God's self-giving character in Jesus reveals the kind of God who is thereby offering forgiveness and lasting fellowship to humans for the sake of their redemption. The death of Jesus does not bring about divine–human reconciliation by itself, but it aims to provide God's means of redemption of humans via divine manifestation and offering. To realize divine–human reconciliation, humans must *receive* the manifest offering of forgiveness and fellowship via grounded faith, or self-entrustment, toward the God who extends the manifest offering. Atonement will then become more than an offer to humans; it will become actual redemption of humans by God. (For some prominent alternatives to the manifest-offering approach to atonement, see Aulén 1961, Berkhof 1986, pp. 304–12; cf. O'Collins 1995, pp. 197–201.)

According to Paul's message (1 Thess. 5:10), Jesus as divinely appointed Lord and Giver of God's Spirit came from God to identify with us humans in our weakness and trouble, while he represented his divine Father in righteous and merciful love. Jesus therefore aims as God's salvific mediator to represent, and to serve as a personal bridge between, God and humans by seeking to reconcile humans to his Father. Accordingly, he manifests and offers the divine gift of fellowship anchored in merciful, forgiving love as the power of God's own intervening Spirit. Jesus's obedient death on the cross, commanded of him by God (see Rom. 3:25, 1 Cor. 5:7, Phil. 2:8; cf. Mark 14:23–4, John 18:11), aims to manifest how far he and his Father will go – even to gruesome death – to offer redemption, including divine forgiveness and fellowship, to humans. By divine assignment, then, Jesus gives humans all he has, from his Father's self-giving love, to manifest that God mercifully and righteously loves humans to the fullest extent and to offer humans redemption as the gracious gift of unearned forgiveness, fellowship, and membership in God's everlasting family via reception of God's own Spirit (see, for instance, Rom. 5:8, John 3:16–17). This is the heart of the Good News of redemption that emerges from Jesus and his immediate followers, and it differs strikingly from the various redemptive plans on offer elsewhere. (Chapter 5 returns to the latter consideration in connection with the topics of religious diversity and exclusivism.)

The Good News in question proclaims the cross of the obedient Jesus as the place where selfish human rebellion against God is mercifully judged and forgiven by God. This does *not* mean that God punished Jesus, a reportedly innocent man who obeyed God in willingly going from Gethsemane to Calvary. No New Testament writer teaches that God punished Jesus, although some later, less careful theologians have suggested a contrary view. According to the Good News, God sent Jesus into the rebellious world to identify with wayward humans in ways that manifest and offer divine love to them, even to the extent of undergoing, willingly and obediently, gruesome suffering and death at human hands. In this identification by Jesus with wayward humans, God would deem his obedient suffering and death as adequate for dealing justly, under *divine righteousness*, with selfish human rebellion against God and God's unselfish love. Accordingly, Jesus pays the price on behalf of humans for righteous divine reconciliation of sinners, and thereby, in manifesting and offering divine forgiveness, removes any need for selfish fear, condemnation, anxiety, shame, guilt, and punishment among humans in relation to God (see Rom. 8:1). God employs the cross of Jesus independently of characteristic human powers, and thereby manifests that salvation comes from *God's* power rather than human power.

A central lesson of Paul's Epistle to the Romans, in keeping with Jesus's parables in Matthew 20:1–15 and Luke 18: 9–14, is that divine righteous grace trumps "justice as ordinarily understood." It is therefore a serious (but common) mistake to treat God's salvific atonement of humans via Jesus as an episode where "justice as ordinarily understood" is satisfied. On this ordinary understanding of justice, Jesus would have to undergo punishment (by God) for every sin ever committed, because justice is retaliatory, requiring "an eye for an eye" (see Exod. 21:23–4, Lev. 24:19–20, Matt. 5:38–41). Divine righteous grace, according to Jesus and Paul, cannot be understood by the standard of such justice, despite the demands of some people to the contrary. Instead, God's righteousness, or justice, must be understood in terms of divine grace that manifests and offers mercy, even to enemies of God, including religiously devout enemies.

The Pauline Good News identifies the ultimate motive for the crucifixion of Jesus as (the manifestation of) his Father's *righteous love* for humans. Unlike many later theologians, Paul definitively links God's righteousness, or justice, with God's powerful self-giving love: "God manifests his own love (*agape*) for us in that while we were yet sinners, Christ died for us.... Since we have now been justified by his blood, how much more shall we be saved by him from the wrath [of God].... [W]hile we were enemies [of God], we were reconciled to God through the death of his Son. . . . " (Rom. 5:8–10). God, according to Paul, takes the initiative and the crucial means through Jesus in offering a powerful gracious gift of divine–human reconciliation for the sake of human redemption. This offer, as suggested, manifests God's forgiving love as well as God's righteousness. Accordingly, Paul takes the sacrificial death of Jesus to manifest divine forgiving love and righteousness. Indeed, he seems to think of divine gracious love as powerful *righteous love* (see Käsemann 1961, Way 1991, Chapter 4, Martyn 1997, Chapter 9).

Mere forgiveness of humans by God would fail to counter adequately the wrongdoing that called for divine forgiveness – namely, human neglect and dismissal of divine gracious authority (on the latter topic, see Rom. 1:21, 28; cf. Meadors 2006). In exposing and judging the basis of human wrongdoing, God upholds perfect moral integrity in the divine redemption of humans, without condoning evil. Through the loving self-sacrifice of Jesus, according to the Good News, *God* meets the standard of morally perfect love *for us* humans, when we could not, would not, and did not. God then offers this gracious powerful gift of divinely provided righteousness to us, as God's Passover lamb for us (see 1 Cor. 5:7), to be received by self-entrustment to Jesus and God as salvific gift givers. Otherwise, our prospects for meeting the standard of divine perfect love and thus for salvation would be bleak indeed. (On gift righteousness from God, in contrast to human righteousness via the law, as central to Paul's thought, see Philippians 3:9, Romans 3:21–6, 10:3–4, and Galatians 3:11–12; cf. Way 1991, Chapter 4, Westerholm 2004.)

Jesus's main motivation for undergoing the cross was his unselfishly loving obedience to his divine Father on our behalf for the sake of divine–human reconciliation. Jesus expresses the crucial role of obedience to his Father in Gethsemane: "Not what I will, but what You will" (Mark 14:35–6; cf. Mark 14:22–5, John 12:27–8). Likewise, Paul vividly identifies the central role of Jesus's obedience in this connection: "Christ Jesus, who, being in the form of God, did not consider equality with God something to be grasped, but he emptied himself, taking the form of a servant, being made in human likeness. Being found in appearance as a man, he humbled himself and became *obedient* to death, even death on a cross" (Phil. 2:6–8, italics added; cf. Rom. 5:18–19). The acknowledged obedience of Jesus in his death is obedience to the redemptive mission of his divine Father, who gave Jesus his salvific commission of suffering and death for the sake of reconciling humans to God (see Rom. 8:3–4; cf. John 18:11).

Jesus obeyed in Gethsemane in order to manifest and to offer divine merciful reconciliation to humans. As a result, Jesus emerges as God's salvific Passover lamb on our behalf (1 Cor. 5:7; cf. John 1:29), that is, as God's atoning sacrifice as manifest offering for us (Rom. 3:25), because he was perfectly obedient and thus fully righteous in the eyes of his divine Father. God's standard of righteousness is therefore met by God on our behalf, by way of a powerful personal gift for us. The gift, in other words, is in the divine gift giver, and humans have no basis for claiming to having earned this gift. It is, accordingly, a powerful gift that excludes boasting in human power or achievement. That is, it rightly deflates human pride as a source of human alienation from God. (On such pride, see Niebuhr 1941, Chapter 7.)

The Good News redemptive mission of Jesus included not only his death but also his resurrection by God. The aforementioned divine manifest-offering approach to redemption captures this fact by acknowledging the divine gracious offering of *lasting* divine–human fellowship under Jesus as Lord. Such divinely offered fellowship and redemption require that Jesus *be alive* to be Lord *lastingly* on behalf of humans. This illuminates Paul's comments that Jesus "was raised for our justification" and that "we shall be saved by his life" (Rom 4:25, 5:10), once we acknowledge that justification and salvation (from human alienation and final death) are, like forgiveness, divine powerful gifts for the sake of lasting divine–human fellowship under Jesus as Lord (see 1 Thess. 5:10).

The resurrection of Jesus from death is part of God's approval and even exaltation of God's obedient Son, the atoning sacrifice from God for humans (see Phil. 2:9–11). Accordingly, the resurrection of Jesus gets some of its significance from the cross, where Jesus gave full obedience to his Father in order to supply a manifest offering of divine–human reconciliation, including divine forgiveness, to humans. In his life-surrendering obedience, Jesus manifested his authoritative Father's worthiness of complete trust and obedience, even when death ensues. In other words, through his full obedience, Jesus confirmed the pre-eminent authority of his Father for the sake of forgiving and redeeming humans. His divine Father, in turn, vindicated and exalted Jesus, likewise for the sake of forgiving and redeeming humans. Both Jesus and his divine Father, then, play a crucial role in the divine manifest offering aimed at the atoning redemption of humans.

The cognitive basis for accepting the resurrection of Jesus is no mere empirical or historical matter, contrary to the suggestion of some Christian writers. As Emil Brunner has remarked:

[A] faith whose authority is merely history has no worth. The real Easter faith does not come from the fact that one believes the report of the apostle without doubting; rather, it comes from the fact that one is reconciled to God through Jesus Christ. This reconciliation is not a mere belief but a rebirth, a new life. Through this reconciliation, godlessness and anxiety are rooted out, and one becomes a new [person]. From this reconciliation through Jesus Christ, faith in his resurrection from the dead arises of itself. . . . [Y]ou believe in the resurrection . . . because the resurrected One himself encounters you in a living way as he who unites you with God, as the living Mediator (1961, pp. 92–3).

Accordingly, Brunner identifies a way to escape merely theoretical historical assessment regarding the resurrection of Jesus, even given this resurrection as occurring at a particular time.

The escape comes from God's evident authoritative intervention in the lives of willing people with a call to divine–human reconciliation. This intervention is not just a matter of imparting theoretical information, as if our problem were mainly the lack of information. Instead, when willingly received, the divine intervention makes the receptive person volitionally and spiritually new by the unique power of God's intervening Spirit, as suggested by Paul and John (see 2 Cor. 5:17, Gal. 6:15, John 3:5–8). Clearly, this transformative divine intervention cannot be reduced to a body-to-body encounter with the risen Jesus. The needed newness in life, as suggested previously, resides ultimately in one's new volitional center, empowered by God's Spirit. One thereby becomes free to participate in volitional fellowship with God (and God's reconciled people) and in God's self-giving and forgiving love, even toward enemies. (For further discussion of the cognitive basis for accepting the resurrection of Jesus, see Brunner 1952, pp. 363–78, Schweizer 1971, pp. 49–51, Moser 2008, Chapter 3.)

According to the Good News, we should think of Jesus, who died to sinful, disobedient options and was raised to life by God, as an *empowering life model*, including cognitive model, for us, and not a mere *substitute* for us. Clearly, Jesus offered himself as a life model (see, for example, Luke 9:23–4, 14:27–33), and Paul likewise offered Jesus as a life model, even for our ongoing suffering and dying (see Phil. 2:5–13, 3:7–11, 2 Cor. 4:7–15, Rom. 8:17; cf. Gorman 2001, 2009, Byrnes 2003). In obediently humbling himself, even to a place of suffering and death, Jesus aimed to manifest what a perfectly forgiving, self-giving God is really like and what *we*, too, should be like as children of such a God who willingly receive and reflect God's moral character for others. Jesus, accordingly, aimed to manifest and to offer what it is to be a human person fully in the image of God, that is, a human person under the power of God's Spirit, serving in the kingdom of God.

To the extent that Jesus is actually our empowering life model, we can be persons empowered to receive filial knowledge of God as our perfectly loving Father. In this capacity, we can become personifying evidence of God's reality and, accordingly, agents who willingly receive and reflect God's reality for others. We may regard human "dying and rising" with Christ, as God's obedient child, as the substance of our becoming personifying evidence of God's reality. It would be a mistake, therefore, to leave dying (to all anti-God ways) out of the new life, including the new means of evidence, characteristic of divine redemption.

The Good News calls humans to receive divine redemption as a powerfully re-creative gift, because humans are unable on their own to uphold fellowship with God, owing to their inability on their own to love as God loves. God's intervening Spirit is offered as the personal power enabling willing people to enter into the redemption and fellowship provided by God through Jesus. This is an integral, if widely neglected, part of the Good News, and it was anticipated in section 4 of this chapter by the idea of a new volitional center with a default position of unselfish love. We now can credit the new volitional center to the direct, firsthand reception and ongoing availability of God's empowering Spirit by a willingly receptive human agent. The cognitive relevance of such newness involving spiritual resurrection is straightforward. It yields experiential acquaintance with powerful evidence of God's intervening Spirit at work in one's motivational center, leading one away from selfishness and toward self-giving love, in fellowship with God. Such evidence indicates what Paul calls a "new creation" in a person (2 Cor. 5:17), and it amounts to the basis of what we have called *personifying evidence* of divine reality in a willing human. Such evidence is central to the new manner of knowing suggested by Paul in connection with the new creation in a redeemed person (see 2 Cor. 5:16; cf. Martyn 1997, pp. 89–110).

The "well-foundedness" of a receptive human response to the Good News of redemption is ultimately anchored in willing volitional acquaintance and fellowship with God's authoritative intervening Spirit. The ultimate anchor is not in theoretical hypotheses or arguments, and it would be a conceptual confusion to suggest otherwise. Each person, however, must himself or herself face the authoritative call of God's Spirit to forgiveness and reconciliation. One cannot have the volitional encounter by proxy, because responsible humans need, and have, direct accountability before the redemptive God worthy of worship.

Critics might wonder whether proponents of *every* religion could offer the kind of epistemological account at hand. The answer is clear: *only if* the religions in question offer a perfectly loving God who has intervened noncoercively to redeem people by divine grace rather than by human earning. Not all religions, of course, offer this kind of redemption; in fact, many explicitly reject it, as Chapter 5 illustrates. (That claim is, as it happens, a verifiable empirical point, and it undermines any naïve thesis of the redemptive unity of religions.) If some religions do offer the kind of perfectly loving God in question, then we may be talking about the same God *under different names*. Of course, we then would need to look carefully to see if that is actually the case. The theological epistemology of this book clearly (and properly) excludes an "anything goes" approach to theological evidence, but it allows (again, properly) for God's intervening in and redeeming the lives of people from various ethnic, racial, intellectual, and religious traditions. In fact, we readily should expect the latter from a perfectly loving God worthy of worship. (Chapter 5 elaborates on this important theme in connection with the vast diversity of actual religions.)

Finally, we all now face a life-or-death question that brings us more existential focus than any abstract argument would. Specifically, are we sincerely attending to the divine call via conscience and experienced *agape* in a way that welcomes the address from the God of Abraham, Isaac, Jacob, and

Jesus, where we can become part of God's new creation? The analogous question in the Introduction's wilderness parable is clear: are we willing to be led out of Hells Canyon by an intentional rescuer who seeks to transform us noncoercively from selfishness and pride to unselfish love? If we are willing, the crucial evidence for God can be clarified and deepened in such a way that we, ourselves, become personifying evidence of God as newly re-created children of the living God who willingly receive and reflect God's moral character. The best explanation of our new lives then will be that God has indeed visited us redemptively, and that is evidence enough. We turn now to the bearing of this lesson on the reality of devastating evil and vast religious diversity in the world.

5

❧

Diversity, Evil, and Defeat

"If we hold that living religion arises at the point where ultimate reality manifests itself to the human spirit, then obviously our understanding of religion will necessarily be determined by the view we take of that ultimate reality and of the relationship with the human spirit into which it enters."

– H.H. Farmer 1954, pp. 26–7.

The wilderness parable in the Introduction prompted a question about the availability of an intentional rescuer for the people lost in Hells Canyon. If the rescuer has a distinctive pedagogical aim for the lost people – specifically, for their being morally transformed in the rescue effort – then the rescue strategy on offer may be subtle and elusive rather than explicit and straightforward. In that case, the rescue process may be rather messy, given the need for the lost people to be challenged morally and changed in various ways. As a result, we should not expect a simple recipe for the rescue, as if the rescue process were akin to baking a simple cake.

The rescuer may allow parts of Hells Canyon to be overgrown with thickets of thorns to highlight both the lost people's need for a rescuer and the inadequacy of their own strategies for a rescue. In other words, the rescuer may allow the surrounding conditions to deteriorate, even toward futility, in order to reveal that the power of the lost people is not genuinely life giving, whereas the power of the rescuer is. This lesson is evidently hard-won – if won at all – by humans, given a deep-seated tendency to seek self-credit and self-sufficiency. As a result, an analogy of easily baking a cake will not serve at all. A complex rescue of stubbornly resistant lost people is more to the point, by way of analogy. Accordingly, a morally purposive rescuer may allow both for a diversity of rescue plans in circulation and for some suffering among the lost people. These complications may appear to challenge the reality of a rescuer, but the rescuer would want the lost people to look more closely and more seriously at their available options, for purposes of needed transformation in the rescue. We therefore do so in this concluding chapter. We shall see that neither the extensive religious diversity nor the extensive evil in this world undermines grounded belief in an intentional rescuer worthy of worship.

1. RELIGIOUS DIVERSITY AND LOGICAL EXCLUSION

It is no easy task to specify clearly when something is a religion (and when something is not), and when we have one religion rather than two or more religions. Familiar candidates for a religion include, of course, the following: Judaism, Christianity, Islam, Buddhism, Hinduism, Confucianism, Sikhism, Taoism, Shinto, and Bahaism. Some of these religions are theistic, in virtue of acknowledging the existence of a divine agent; others are not. Sometimes we call a system of *claims* of a particular kind a religion, and sometimes we call a human *commitment* of a particular kind a religious commitment. Accordingly, the term "religion" is slippery at best.

In general, we might say that a commitment is religious for a person if and only if the commitment is intrinsic (that is, not *merely* instrumental toward something else) and is intended to be life defining (that is, intended to be

constitutive of living) for that person. This is a broad, lati-
tudinarian approach to something's being a religious commitment. It may allow even some intrinsic commitments
of sports fans to their favorite sports to count as religious,
at least in a "fanatical" sense. This is no defect for current
purposes – specifically for our asking: can all religions get
along? This question is intolerably vague until we specify
what *getting along* consists in. Perhaps advocates of various
religions can "get along" even if religions themselves, in
being contrary, cannot.

We need to examine both (a) the sense in which religions
can be exclusive and excluded and (b) the sense in which
advocates of religions can also be exclusive and excluded.
We shall see that some versions of religious exclusivism are
undeniably true, and that at least one version is undeniably
false. As a result, "exclusivism" should not be regarded as a
dirty word in itself. It actually captures something important
about the way religions are distinctive.

Religions, even in their theistic forms, manifest remarkable diversity and even logical conflict in their religious
statements, at least across different religions. Some religions
affirm that God exists, but others deny that God exists. Some
religions affirm that only one God exists, but others affirm
that many gods exist, and still others claim that no God
exists. Even across versions of monotheism, diversity and
conflict in positions are obvious and enduring. For instance,
some versions of monotheism teach that God loves all people, including even resolute enemies of God; other versions
of monotheism firmly deny this. In addition, some versions
of monotheism teach that humans must earn or merit their
approval before God; other versions strongly deny this, and
affirm instead that God approves of people by way of a gracious (humanly unearned) divine gift. This is just a small
sample of the extensive diversity and conflict in positions
across religions.

Clearly, no complete thematic unity across religions is
available, however much some people might hope (and

incorrectly allege) otherwise. Taken together, the claims of the various religions are logically inconsistent: they *cannot* all be true. (It is almost incredible that anyone would suggest otherwise after even a quick review of the religions in question.) Any available unity of religions therefore will be, at best, partial – that is, incomplete.

Even if, for example, Judaism and Hinduism in their most prominent forms agree on some religious views, they disagree on monotheism. In particular, the exclusive monotheism of classical Judaism is denied, at least by implication, by the prominent versions of Hinduism. As a result, we should not expect both Judaism and Hinduism to be true; they are logically contrary religious positions, at least regarding some central religious claims. The same holds among many, if not all, other mainline religious positions. Accordingly, some mainline religious positions logically exclude some other mainline religious positions. This view is *logical religious exclusivism* regarding logically contrary religious positions, and its truth cannot be denied with any plausibility. In addition, it is puzzling why anyone should want to deny its truth. We shall see that some other kinds of theistic religious exclusivism also merit our acceptance.

The Introduction offered the term "God" as a most exalted *title* rather than as a name. The aim was to allow us to talk intelligibly about whether God exists, even if God does not actually exist and even if we disavow knowledge that God exists. The Introduction also proposed that the title "God" signifies *worthiness of worship*, and that a being is worthy of worship if and only if that being, having inherent moral perfection, merits worship as unqualified adoration, love, trust, and obedience. Given this exalted moral standard for worthiness of worship, we can exclude, as noted previously, most of the familiar candidates for the preeminent title "God" on the ground of moral deficiency. Moral defects bar a candidate from the status of being God, without an opportunity for appeal. For example, a failure to be perfectly loving toward other personal agents will exclude a candidate from worthiness of worship and thus from being God.

The Introduction offered an approach to inquiry about God that fits with the demand of worthiness of worship. A God worthy of worship would desire that all capable agents willingly receive divine love and then manifest it from their hearts toward all agents (including toward their enemies), thereby reflecting God's moral character for others. This consideration led the Introduction to propose *kardiatheology*, that is, theology aimed primarily at one's motivational heart – including one's will – and not just one's mind or emotions.

A self-revelation to humans from a God worthy of worship would accommodate kardiatheology by aiming non-coercively to realize divine perfect love in human hearts, and not just to expand human information or emotion. Accordingly, in self-revelation, God would aim to transform humans *motivationally* toward perfect love, and not just intellectually or emotionally. This consideration, as already noted, supports a distinctive account of the purposively available evidence of God's reality, and it bears on debates about religious inclusivism and exclusivism. The key point is that God would seek to have humans, as intentional agents, personify (and thus themselves become) evidence of divine reality in order to reflect God's moral character for others.

The Introduction raised the following widely ignored issue: are we humans in a position on our own to answer the question of whether God exists, without our being morally challenged by God, if God exists? We have no reason to suppose that we are. We therefore should be open to kardiatheology and its implications for needed human transformation by divine intervention. Religious inquiry, in that case, will be no merely intellectual matter for humans. Instead, it will involve us as intentional agents who are morally accountable as inquirers before a God who seeks volitional cooperation, and thus obedience, from humans.

2. REDEMPTIVE EXCLUSIVISM

For the sake of manageable focus, let's continue to limit our talk of religion to theistic religions – that is, religions that acknowledge the existence of a divine agent. Many advocates of the traditional monotheism of Judaism, Christianity, and Islam use the term "God" as a title connoting a unique agent worthy of worship. Other proponents of such monotheism claim that their use of the title "God" connotes a unique agent worthy of worship, but they set the standard for worthiness of worship too low for genuine moral perfection. For instance, some advocates of monotheism acknowledge a God who arguably lacks moral perfection (at least by the most compelling standard of such perfection) in virtue of God's hating evil people. Psalms 5:5 and 11:5, for example, claim that God "hates" wicked *people*, and not just wicked thoughts, desires, intentions, or actions.

The view of a God who hates some people conflicts explicitly with the portrait of God offered by Jesus's Sermon on the Mount, in Matthew 5:43–8 (cf. Luke 6:27–36, John 3:16–17). In fact, Jesus is arguably correcting a misguided view of God offered by some of the Hebrew scriptures, perhaps including Psalms 5 and 11. Consider, for instance, Matthew 5:43–5: "You have heard that it was said . . . 'hate your enemy', but I say to you, 'love your enemies . . . , in order that you may be children of your Father in Heaven'." We have no way to reconcile this clear and distinctive portrait of a perfectly loving God offered by Jesus with the hate-based image sketched in Psalms 5 and 11. They are, in fact, logically incompatible. As a result, we have to choose between the two, and carefully reflective theists will side with Jesus and his portrait. (For an attempted moral defense of hating evil people, see Hampton and Murphy 1988; for criticism, see Moser 2008, Chapter 3.)

Jesus identifies God's love of even enemies of God as central to divine moral perfection, and this approach to moral perfection is preeminently commendable in virtue of excluding divine hate of people. Such hate would be destructive and condemning of people in a way incompatible with perfect moral goodness and thus with worthiness of worship. We may plausibly hold, then, that there is significant religious diversity and even conflict within the teachings of the Jewish and Christian scriptures. In addition, we may conclude that a "God" who hates some people lacks moral perfection and therefore is not worthy of worship. Jewish and Christian monotheism, accordingly, comes in sharply conflicting variations relative to the moral characters those variations ascribe to God.

Given the morally preeminent standard of worthiness of worship, we are well advised to rank the competing variations on monotheism by means of the required standard of moral perfection. By that standard, of course, the perfectly loving God acknowledged by Jesus would, if real, morally trump the psalmist's God who hates some people. In any case, the God of Jesus is a viable candidate for the morally preeminent title "God" that signifies worthiness of worship, but the psalmist's God is definitely not. The psalmist's God is morally too much like us morally defective humans to be worthy of worship. Our hate toward other people, according to Jesus, conflicts with God's morally perfect character, and thus does not reflect God at all. At best, it reflects a false, counterfeit God.

Monotheism seems initially more credible than polytheism, because we are hard put to come up with even one case of an intentional agent who is morally perfect and worthy of worship. The various and sundry gods of the polytheist pantheon are too much like us morally imperfect beings regarding their moral failings. In particular, these gods share the fate of the hate-motivated God of Psalms 5:5 and 11:5 in falling short of moral perfection and, thus, worthiness of worship. Polytheists may find it convenient, if not self-supporting, to relax the standard for being divine, but they then risk divorcing being divine from being worthy of worship. In that case, the category of being divine would lose its moral preeminence. This is a serious problem for the prominent versions of polytheism in circulation, and, as just suggested, some variations on monotheism also suffer from this problem.

Logical religious exclusivism, as suggested previously, is compelling, given the actual logically contrary claims made by various religions. It yields the platitude that the claims of some religions logically exclude some claims of some other religions. That is, necessarily, if the claims of the former religions are true, then some claims of the latter religions are false. If this were the only species of religious exclusivism in circulation, we should all be avid religious exclusivists. Dissenters would be guilty of obvious logical confusions, and could be offered some straightforward logical corrections. Matters, however, are not so simple in the domain of religions and religious theorists.

Some people have proposed *redemptive religious exclusivism*: the view that some religions are redemptively exclusive, that is, exclusive regarding the redemption, or salvation, of humans by God. Redemptive religious exclusivism offers two central variations: *strategic* redemptive exclusivism and *personal* redemptive exclusivism. We need to clarify this distinction in order to clarify redemptive religious exclusivism. We shall see that some important truth resides in this area of exclusivism.

Strategic redemptive exclusivism states that some strategies or programs for religious redemption exclude some other such strategies or programs. Consider a Jewish–Christian strategy that characterizes redemption as originating solely from divine grace (that is, a humanly unearned divine free gift) through human faith. Such a strategy excludes any religious strategy that characterizes redemption as originating from the human earning, or meriting, of salvation from God via a righteousness of one's own – say, from one's obeying a law. Redemption originating solely from divine grace, at least in the Pauline Christian strategy (see Rom 4:4), logically excludes redemption originating from human earning or meriting, in terms of one's own righteousness. (See Philippians 3:5–9 and Romans 9:32 for Paul's clear suggestion that as a zealous Pharisee he had previously advocated the latter kind of redemption originating from human earning, but that he has renounced this position for the sake of divine grace; cf. Fee 1995, pp. 305–37.)

If the divine redemption offered to humans originates solely in a humanly unearned free gift from God (that is, in divine grace), then it does not originate in any human's own righteousness, including one's righteousness from obeying a law. Accordingly, the redemptive strategy promoted by the Christian religion of the apostle Paul excludes the earlier redemptive strategy offered by the Pharisaic religion of Saul of Tarsus. Of course, this does not suggest that all versions of Judaism agree with the Pharisaism of Saul of Tarsus; clearly, the Judaism of Jesus, for instance, did not agree with the Pharisaism of Saul. (On the relation between the two, see Furnish 1968, Bruce 1977, and Wenham 1995.)

Strategic redemptive exclusivism is a specification of logical religious exclusivism, regarding strategies for religious redemption. Such redemptive exclusivism is undeniably true, given the logical conflict between at least the Pharisaic redemptive strategy of Saul of Tarsus and the later Christian redemptive strategy of the apostle Paul. We could illustrate this kind of logical conflict across the redemptive strategies of various religions, but we need not do so here. Any sustainable philosophy (or history or sociology) of religion will embrace strategic redemptive exclusivism, given the conflicting programs of redemption across various religions.

Personal redemptive exclusivism states that given certain religions, some people are excluded from divine redemption or salvation. We need to distinguish between the following two positions:

Conditional personal exclusivism: If certain religions are correct in what they state or at least imply, then some people are excluded from divine redemption, and

Actual personal exclusivism: Religion *X* is correct in stating or at least implying that some people are excluded from divine redemption.

Conditional personal exclusivism is clearly true, because it is clear that some religions deny universalism about salvation. That is, they deny that all people will be redeemed by God. This is a straightforward empirical fact about some religions, quite aside from whether all people actually will be redeemed by God.

Consider the Reformed Protestant predestinarian view of either John Calvin's 1536 *Institutes of the Christian Religion* or the 1647 *Westminster Confession of Faith.* (We can bracket now any theological differences between the two.) Following the later Augustine, Calvin endorsed the following predestinarian exclusivist position:

By predestination we mean the eternal decree of God, by which he determined with himself whatever he wished to happen with regard to every man. All are not created on equal terms, but some are preordained to eternal life, others to eternal damnation; and, accordingly, as each has been created for one or other of these ends, we say that he has been predestinated to life or to death (1536, Book 3, Chapter 21, Section 5).

The *Westminster Confession of Faith,* influenced by some central themes of Calvin's theology, offers an equivalent predestinarian exclusivist view, at least regarding humans:

By the decree of God, for the manifestation of his glory, some men and angels are predestinated unto everlasting life, and others foreordained to everlasting death. These angels and men, thus predestinated and foreordained, are particularly and unchangeably designed; and their number is so certain and definite that it cannot be either increased or diminished. . . . The rest of mankind [beyond those foreordained to everlasting life], God was pleased, according to the unsearchable counsel of his own will, whereby he extendeth or withholdeth mercy as he pleaseth, for the glory of his sovereign power over his creatures, to pass by, and to ordain them to dishonor and wrath for their sin, to the praise of his glorious justice (Chapter 3; see Schaff 1919b).

A straightforward implication of the second sentence just quoted is that God's foreordaining activity makes some people "particularly and unchangeably designed" for "everlasting death." Calvin's corresponding idea is that God "determined with himself whatever he [that is, God] wished to happen" to each person, including each person excluded from salvation forever.

The Reformed exclusivist view implies that, in divine sovereignty, God foreordains, or predestines, some people to everlasting damnation (or condemnation) rather than redemption (or salvation). In particular, it implies that this divine decision to exclude some people is ultimately *God's* own will and is therefore not determined by human wills. In Calvin's influential approach to the matter, what God wishes to happen to people who are not redeemed *does, in fact,* happen to them. That is, they are excluded *by God* from redemption forever, and this is ultimately by *divine intent*. Bracketing the highly questionable moral character of a God who would proceed in this way toward people, we cannot plausibly deny that hypothetical personal exclusivism follows from some influential religious views. Such exclusivism, we shall see, also follows from some religious views that oppose predestinarian Calvinism and attribute the cause of redemptive exclusion to humans, themselves, who resist salvation.

3. EXCLUSIVISM TOWARD GOD

For any version of actual personal exclusivism (as characterized previously), we helpfully can raise the following crucial question: o*n what basis*, or *in virtue of what*, are some people (allegedly) excluded from divine redemption forever? One exclusivist Christian view, in keeping with the previous Reformed predestinarian view, implies that some people are excluded from divine redemption in virtue of God's own decisively condemning sovereign will, and that God's will in this connection is not determined at all by human wills. On this view, *God* is causally responsible for the permanent exclusion of some humans, given that God intentionally wills their permanent exclusion.

Another exclusivist Christian view avoids a predestinarian view. It implies that if an adult person of normal intelligence fails to believe a redemptive Christian *message* about what God has accomplished via Jesus Christ, then that person is thereby excluded from salvation. This view has been embraced by many Christians who hold that a person's lacking a specific belief about salvation (or at least about God) excludes that person from salvation. We shall see that both of the exclusivist views, the predestinarian and doxastic views, are actually implausible, because they exclude a God worthy of worship.

As suggested previously, we are using the term "God" as a preeminent title with definite semantic content, requiring worthiness of worship and thus moral perfection in God. We therefore should ask how our notion of God bears on actual personal exclusivism. The predestinarian variation implies that God chooses to exclude some people permanently from redemption on the basis of God's own sovereign condemning will, and that this divine choice is not determined at all by any human will, such as a human will opposing God or redemption. According to this predestinarian view, God foreordains some people to be condemned and not to be redeemed by God, and this sovereign divine action causes the actual permanent exclusion of these people from redemption.

Some predestinarians invoke a careless and dubious reading of Chapter 9 of Paul's Epistle to the Romans for support, but Chapter 11 of Romans explicitly states that the unredeemed people in question are excluded on the basis of their own distrust or unbelief toward God (see Rom. 11:20). Paul could have said that these people are excluded just by God's own sovereign will, but he does not, of course; instead, he invokes their distrust or unbelief toward God. Paul does not teach, then, that a sovereign divine choice causes some people to be excluded from salvation. On the contrary, Paul writes concerning God: "But of Israel he says, 'All day long I [God] have held out my hands to a disobedient and contrary people'" (Rom. 10:21, RSV, citing Isa. 65:1–2). The holding out of divine hands suggests a genuine divine invitation, rather than divine predestinarian exclusion or condemnation. Paul therefore contradicts any thesis of divine predestinarian exclusion. (See Meadors 2006, Chapters 8–10, on divine judgment in Paul's Epistle to the Romans, particularly on its nonpredestinarian role.)

As noted previously, a God worthy of worship must be morally perfect; in other words, worthiness of worship excludes moral deficiency. One who is morally defective in some way lacks the moral character needed for worthiness of adoration and complete trust. As a result, such a being lacks worthiness of worship. One who fails to be perfectly loving toward all people (when one could be so) is morally deficient, at least regarding one's failure to love others perfectly. In addition, if one condemns another person (even *one* other person) to destruction as the constitutive result of one's own will, then one fails to be perfectly loving toward the person condemned. Accordingly, one fails to be worthy of worship. The relevant talk of "the constitutive result of one's own will" is intended to suggest full intended causal responsibility (that is, an intended constitutive role) in one's own will, with regard to the permanent exclusion of certain people from divine redemption.

One's perfect love toward a person rules out, by definition, one's condemning that person to destruction as the constitutive result of one's own will. Accordingly, if one permanently excludes a person from redemption as the constitutive result of one's own will, then one fails to be perfectly loving and likewise fails to be worthy of worship. It would distort the idea of being "perfectly loving" beyond recognition to suggest that such excluding is actually perfectly loving. As a result, if one excludes a person from redemption as the constitutive result of one's own will, then one fails to be God. The "God" of the aforementioned predestinarian position is not the true God worthy of worship, because that position actually excludes the true God by excluding divine perfect love toward all human persons.

An influential representative of the aforementioned doxastic exclusivist view is the Christian Athanasian Creed (ca. 500). The relevant statements of the Athanasian Creed are these:

1. Whosoever will be saved, before all things it is necessary that he hold the catholic faith;
2. Which faith, except every one do keep whole and undefiled, without doubt he shall perish everlastingly.
3. And the catholic faith is this: that we worship one God in trinity, and trinity in unity; ...
4. This is the catholic faith which, except a man believe faithfully, he can not be saved (see Schaff 1919a).

The doxastic redemptive exclusivism of the Athanasian Creed is straightforward. If a person does not actually believe the Christian trinitarian faith, according to this Creed, that person "can not be saved." Specifically, the required belief in question is irreducibly propositional, because it is belief, or faith, "*that* we worship one God in trinity, and trinity in unity." It follows that pre-Christian Semitic, Jewish, and Muslim monotheists (including even Abraham, Isaac, Jacob, Moses, and David), and, for that matter, all others who are not Christian trinitarians, are excluded from salvation. They all lack the required trinitarian belief about God, specifically the belief or faith that "we worship one God in trinity, and trinity in unity." Augustine and Thomas Aquinas, among many other Christians, seem committed to such doxastic exclusivism, at least regarding people who have lived since the time of the inception of the trinitarian faith.

Clearly, the exclusivism of the Athanasian Creed conflicts with the character of a perfectly loving God. As Ernst Käsemann observes: "The choice of the patriarch [Abraham in Romans 4] as example and prototype would be absurd if we were meant to confine the possibility of experiencing the divine righteousness to the period *post Christum crucifixum*" (1971, p. 86). Consider, in addition, a simple case in which an adolescent child from an isolated island in the South Pacific has not heard of the trinitarian "catholic faith" and will not hear of it during her life on earth. The Athanasian Creed evidently implies that this child's mere failure to believe is sufficient for morally acceptable permanent exclusion by a perfectly loving God. This is definitely a mistaken position.

Suppose that the child fails to believe the "catholic faith" *only because* she has not heard of it. Suppose also that she eagerly would believe it if she heard of it (although, as it happens, she will not be presented with it in her life on Earth). In other words, the child is disposed to believe the "catholic faith" (because she eagerly would believe it if she heard of it), but she does not actually believe it, and will not actually believe it during her earthly life. Suppose also that the child's will is sincerely open to God's will, and that therefore she is willing to receive and even obey any well-grounded redemptive message from God.

God, of course, is not obligated to redeem the child (or any other morally defective person) *on the basis of what she (or any other mere human) has earned from God*. Even so, God's morally perfect character must uphold the highest moral standards, including the standard of unselfish merciful love (*agape*) in connection with human redemption. As a result, if God condemned the girl to everlasting death *solely* as a result of her failing to believe the "catholic faith," we rightly could question the moral perfection and thus the divinity of God's character. We would need to ask what "moral perfection" actually means under such circumstances, because it seems clear that a condemning God in this case could do much better from the standpoint of moral perfection.

Divine moral perfection, as suggested previously, entails morally perfect love, and such love seeks what is *morally best* for any person. It therefore includes an offer of forgiveness for the sake of reconciling estranged people to God. Of course, an offer of forgiveness and reconciliation need not actually be received or even seriously considered by a person. In addition, divine coercion of a person would not be a genuine option, because it would undermine the needed human agency in genuine divine–human reconciliation. If human agency is removed, there will be no human agent who responsibly can enter into reconciliation with God.

God's condemning the girl to everlasting death would not include seeking what is morally best for her, because God would have a morally better alternative at hand. That is, at some point God could remove the girl's doxastic deficiency (say, with suitable evidence for belief) and thereby enable her to enter into explicit fellowship with God. This alternative would obviously be morally better for the girl than for her to undergo condemnation to everlasting death solely for a doxastic deficiency. A God of perfect love would not allow such a morally insignificant deficiency to preclude the girl's ultimately entering into explicit fellowship and new life with God. The doxastic version of personal exclusivism fails to accommodate this point about God's perfectly loving character and therefore offers a morally deficient God. That version of exclusivism, accordingly, excludes the God worthy of worship.

Many exclusivists of a Calvinist or Reformed persuasion will reply that God is "sovereign" and therefore has a right to exclude whomever he wishes. That reply, however, neglects divine worthiness of worship as central to God's character. Specifically, God's will is not morally permitted to violate the moral perfection inherent to worthiness of worship. (God, of course, would not be able to make divine actions morally permissible *just* by an act of will; morality is more robust than that.) An agent's violating the moral perfection inherent to worthiness of worship would exclude that agent automatically from the category of being divine. Accordingly, given a perfectly loving God, one's being excluded from salvation is not the result of one's failure to pass a mere informational test. A perfectly loving God always would seek what is morally best for one, including the provision of needed information at the opportune time. Conversely, salvation (or redemption) is not anchored in one's passing a mere informational test. Various gnostic and intellectualist approaches to redemption imply otherwise, but they neglect the inherent morally perfect character and redemptive concerns of a God worthy of worship.

Morally perfect divine concerns would approach redemption (or salvation) relative to a person's will and moral character, and would steer clear of any mere informational test. That is, they would fit with the kardiatheology mentioned previously, and therefore would seek to have humans, themselves, become personifying evidence of God's reality in willingly receiving and reflecting God's moral character for others. A mere informational test is too demanding from the standpoint of divine moral perfection, because one can fail an informational test owing just to an easily correctable cognitive inadequacy (even while one's will is genuinely open to conformity to God's will and moral character). In such a case, one would not be a lost cause at all relative to divine redemption of humans. On the contrary, one would be an excellent candidate – that is, "good soil" for redemption, in the language of Mark 4:20. A mere informational test is also too weak, because one can pass the test by having the correct belief (say, belief that the "catholic faith," in the previous Athanasian sense, is true) but hold this belief solely out of selfishness and hate, even with one's will resolutely opposed to God's will and moral character. Doxastic versions of exclusivism run afoul of these considerations and therefore end up excluding a God worthy of worship. We have good reason, then, to set aside such versions of exclusivism.

4. INCLUSIVE CHRISTIAN EXCLUSIVISM

Doxastic Christian exclusivism fails to accommodate an inclusive Christian version of exclusivism regarding the unique redemptive role of Jesus as God's atoning Son. The relevant inclusive Christian version of exclusivism affirms that Jesus is God's unique mediator for human redemption and that, therefore, the divine redemption of humans depends uniquely on Jesus. The key question concerns what the language "depends uniquely on" means in this context. It would be a serious mistake, given divine moral perfection, to affirm that a person must believe or trust in this earthly life that Jesus is Lord to be a candidate for redemption by God. The previous discussion of the isolated girl illustrates this point adequately. Accordingly, the relevant sense of "depends uniquely on Jesus" must not require that one believe in this earthly life that Jesus is Lord. Nonetheless, one could consistently hold that a candidate for divine redemption must *ultimately* believe that Jesus is Lord, even if after death, upon one's acquiring adequate evidence regarding God's plan of redemption. (The apostle Paul may have had the latter view in mind in Philippians 2:9–11; at least, the present view is compatible with his position.)

According to the inclusive Christian exclusivism under development, divine salvation of humans is inherently christological, being mediated uniquely by Jesus Christ. (See Chapter 4 on the relevant idea of mediation, or atonement). Even so, such salvation can be christological *de re* without being *de dicto* in a human's earthly life. Given this inclusive Christian exclusivism, the ultimate offer of divine–human reconciliation includes Jesus as atoning mediator, *in reality*, but it does not follow that ultimate recipients of the offer must assent to or even conceive of such christological mediation in this earthly life. As a result, we should contrast the inclusive Christian exclusivism under development with the aforementioned doxastic exclusivism represented in the Athanasian Creed. Like traditional Christian belief, this inclusive Christian exclusivism excludes as false any account or doctrine of redemption that omits Jesus as the unique divinely appointed mediator for human redemption. Unlike doxastic Christian exclusivism, however, it allows for (that is, in principle includes) human candidates for redemption who do not and will not acknowledge Jesus as Lord in their earthly lives. We briefly shall consider both of these features, the exclusive feature and the inclusive feature.

The exclusive side of the present view fits with the traditional Christian view, suggested by various writers of the New Testament documents, that Jesus is God's unique revealer and mediator for redemption. For instance, Matthew's Gospel states:

At that time Jesus declared, 'I thank you, Father, Lord of heaven and earth, because you have hidden these things from the wise and understanding, and revealed them to babes. Yes, Father, for this was your gracious will. All things have been delivered to me by my Father; and no one knows the Son except the Father, and no one knows the Father except the Son and any one to whom the Son chooses to reveal him' (Matt. 11:25–7, RSV; see also Luke 10:21–2, John 5:22–3, 17:25–6; cf. O'Collins 1995, pp. 123–4, 133–4).

Accordingly, Jesus refers to himself as "the Son" of God, and identifies himself as the *only* one who can reveal God (perfectly?) to humans.

Going beyond talk of knowledge of God, some writings in the New Testament characterize Jesus as the unique atoning mediator between God and humans. For instance: " . . . there is one God, and there is one mediator between God and men, the man Christ Jesus, who gave himself as a ransom for all. . . . " (1 Tim. 2:5–6, RSV). In addition: " . . . by the name of Jesus Christ of Nazareth, whom you crucified, [but] whom God raised from the dead, by him this man is standing before you well. . . . [T]here is salvation in no one else, for there is no other name under heaven given among men by which we must be saved" (Acts 4:10,12, RSV). The New Testament, then, includes claims implying that Jesus is *exclusively* the (perfect?) revealer and mediator for God. We cannot establish the independent correctness of this demanding exclusivist position here, but we can identify how this position can be inclusive in an important manner.

The inclusive side of the Christian exclusivism under development finds support in the following story of judgment told by Jesus:

When the Son of man comes in his glory, and all the angels with him, then he will sit on his glorious throne. Before him will be gathered all the nations, and he will separate them one from another as a shepherd separates the sheep from the goats, and he will place the sheep at his right hand, but the goats at the left. Then the King will say to those at his right hand, 'Come, O blessed of my Father, inherit the kingdom prepared for you from the foundation of the world; for I was hungry and you gave me food, I was thirsty and you gave me drink, I was a stranger and you welcomed me, I was naked and you clothed me, I was sick and you visited me, I was in prison and you came to me.' Then the righteous will answer him, 'Lord, when did we see thee hungry and feed thee, or thirsty and give thee drink? And when did we see thee a stranger and welcome thee, or naked and clothe thee? And when did we see thee sick or in prison and visit thee?' And the King will answer them, 'Truly, I say to you, as you did it to one of the least of these my brethren, you did it to me.' Then he will say to those at his left hand, 'Depart from me, you cursed, into the eternal fire prepared for the devil and his angels; for I was hungry and you gave me no food, I was thirsty and you gave me no drink, I was a stranger and you did not welcome me, naked and you did not clothe me, sick and in prison and you did not visit me.' Then they also will answer, 'Lord, when did we see thee hungry or thirsty or a stranger or naked or sick or in prison, and did not minister to thee?' Then he will answer them, 'Truly, I say to you, as you did it not to one of the least of these, you did it not to me.' And they will go away into eternal punishment, but the righteous into eternal life (Matt. 25:31–45, RSV).

The surprise experienced by "the righteous," coupled with the King's focus on their caring behavior toward others, suggests something other than a doxastic standard for approval by God. This fits with the remark of Jesus in Matthew 7:21: "Not everyone who says to me, 'Lord, Lord', will enter the kingdom of heaven, but only the one who does the will of my Father who is in heaven." As Jesus illustrated in the previous story of judgment, one can do the will of God without explicit doxastic commitment to God. This consideration speaks against excluding the isolated girl, in the aforementioned hypothetical case, from redemption by God. It therefore speaks against doxastic exclusivism.

There is an exclusivist *nondoxastic* criterion at work in Matthew's judgment story from Jesus: namely, the human manifestation of divine unselfish love toward others. Such a manifestation arguably requires one's yielding, and being conformed, to the divine unselfish love manifested in one's own life, but it does *not* follow that one must believe during this earthly life that God exists. One could yield volitionally to God's unselfish love and thereby to God *de re*, without any corresponding acknowledgment *de dicto* and thus without one's knowing (or believing) that one is yielding to God or even knowing (or believing) that God exists. This consideration accounts for the element of surprise in Matthew's previous judgment story from Jesus.

We should acknowledge a corresponding *de re* approach to rejection of God, in keeping with Matthew's judgment story from Jesus. One can resist or otherwise neglect conformity to the unselfish love presented to one and thereby resist or otherwise neglect *de re* the purported redemptive activity of God in one's life. This would amount to resisting or neglecting *God*, especially on the Christian view that "love (*agape*) is from God" (1 John 4:7) or that "God is love" (1 John 4:16). In fact, one's resisting or neglecting unselfish love could have dire cognitive results regarding one's knowing divine reality. As one New Testament writer states: "The one who does not love does not know God, because God is love" (1 John 4:8). (For an attempt to make good cognitive sense of this distinctive position, see Moser 2008.)

If "Hell" (not to be confused with Hells Canyon) is simply final exclusion from a life of fellowship with the God who graciously gives life, then Hell should be understood as ultimately *self*-exclusion from such a life with God (see Kvanvig 1993). Such self-exclusion can be *de re* in the sense just indicated, and it need not be *de dicto* in terms of a belief that one is rejecting God or even belief that God exists (or does not exist). As a result, one can be living in Hell or moving toward Hell without even knowing this *de dicto*. Accordingly, how one responds to unselfish love can be important indeed relative to one's ultimate destiny. How one responds to such love can amount to how one responds to God, if only *de re*.

Variation in beliefs among humans regarding divine redemptive activity raises various difficult questions about evidence and knowledge of God's reality. For instance, why do some people (avowedly) have evidence regarding God's redemptive activity and believe (or trust) in God on that basis, whereas others (avowedly) lack the needed evidence and thus refrain from trust in God? Perhaps some people are not ready to receive the needed evidence aright, on God's terms of unselfish love. In that case, God could have a good reason for withholding pertinent evidence of divine reality from some people. If anything is clear, however, it is clear that we have no simple answer to the previous question. That is, we have no theodicy or comprehensive explanation of God's ways regarding the elusiveness of divine evidence. In addition, given the limited place of humans, cognitively and otherwise, in the grand scheme of things, we should not expect ourselves to have one.

It is arguable (following Moser 2008) that divine redemptive purposes account for the ways divine evidence is given and not given among humans. It does not follow, however, that we can always specify the exact divine purposes at work among humans. Just as we have no comprehensive exact theodicy regarding evil (and should not expect to have one in our cognitively limited situation), so also we have no comprehensive exact account of divine elusiveness and variation in divine self-revelation. Even so, our lacking any such comprehensive account does not undermine our having conclusive evidence of divine reality. One still can have evidence of divine reality based on experience of divine intervention in the absence of undefeated defeaters (as outlined in Chapter 4). Such evidence does not require a theodicy of us, given our limited cognitive resources regarding God's particular purposes.

Even in the absence of *de dicto* human acknowledgment that there is divine intervention and evidence, God effectively can advance judgment and redemption of humans (where God's judgment is characteristically aimed at redemption). As a result, in connection with divine judgment and redemption of humans, we are well advised to consider human attitudes more profound than mere belief and then to understand redemptively relevant faith toward God accordingly. This would be in keeping with the redemptive purposes of a God truly worthy of worship. In addition, this would fit with the kardiatheology introduced previously, according to which God primarily would seek transformation of a human's motivational center and not just intellectual or emotional improvement. In doing so, God would seek to have humans themselves become personifying evidence of divine reality wherein they willingly receive and reflect God's moral character for others.

According to kardiatheology, human belief that God exists is not a litmus test (or necessary condition) for God's redemptive work in humans. Inclusive Christian exclusivism accommodates this lesson, and points us to an elusive but profound God of perfect love and of kardiatheology, who can work *de re* in humans despite the absence of human belief that God exists. In keeping with this lesson, the diversity of religious positions in circulation is no defeater of the

evidence for this book's version of volitional theism. Neither the evidence nor the reality of God's redemptive work
de re is undermined by the world's striking diversity of religious views. On the contrary, God can use such diversity
to challenge and transform misplaced human attitudes for
the sake of human redemption. Beliefs can and do matter,
of course, but they are ill-suited to challenge the reality or
the evidence of the redemptive power of a perfectly loving God. We see this power distinctively in humans who,
themselves, are becoming personifying evidence for God in
willingly receiving and reflecting God's moral character for
others.

5. EVIL AS DEFEATER

Many people will object that, even given the experiential
evidence for God in question, the world's unexplained evil
provides an undefeated defeater of any such evidence. This
objection travels far and wide, and it has taken in many confident advocates. Careful reflection, however, suggests that
the matter is actually more complicated. One's *having conclusive (undefeated) purposively available evidence of God's reality*
is not the same as one's *having a comprehensive explanation of
God's purposes* (say, in allowing evil).

We need to distinguish between:

(a) When I seek God with due volitional openness to
    authoritative divine reality, I will find, at the oppor-
    tune time, God's self-revelation on the basis of con-
    clusive purposively available evidence,

and

(b) When I seek God with due volitional openness to
    authoritative divine reality, I will find a comprehen-
    sive explanation of why God acts as God does, includ-
    ing in permitting evil.

Many people wrongly assume that option (b) would automatically come with option (a). The matter is actually more complex than that false assumption suggests.

The promise of (a) regarding God's self-revelation at the opportune time does not depend for its correctness or justification on one's understanding all of God's purposes, even regarding the permitting of evil. As a result, it does not yield a theodicy that fully explains and justifies God's purposes in allowing evil. Accordingly, (a) does not entail (b). The promise of (a) regarding God's self-revelation, if satisfied, entails one's acquiring conclusive evidence of God's reality at the opportune time, *not* one's acquiring a comprehensive explanation of God's purposes, including God's purposes in allowing evil.

It would be logically invalid to infer that, given the kind of theism at hand and our cognitive limitations, " . . . we simply are *in the dark* about the goods that God will know, and the conditions of their realization" (Rowe 2006, p. 90; cf. Schellenberg 2007, pp. 300–3). Such an inference aims to underwrite skepticism about God's existence on the basis of unexplained evil in the world. Given the clear and definite ingredients of (the notion of) divine perfect love, however, our limited explanatory darkness regarding some divine purposes in allowing evil cannot plausibly be generalized in that skeptical manner. On that dubious kind of generalization, one could not *ever* know that an agent is truly morally good when one lacked a comprehensive understanding of the agent's purposes, including the agent's purposes in allowing evil. That implication is obviously excessive, and it seriously challenges the skeptical inference in question.

In demanding that humans seek God, God aims to uphold the supreme value and authority of divine self-revelation, thereby saving it from devaluation by naturally selfish humans. Accordingly, God aims to have humans *supremely and wholeheartedly value* divine perfect love, and to be *personally transformed* by it, in fellowship with God, not just to think about it or to formulate arguments about it. Even so, human seeking of God, even when accompanied by one's finding God with conclusive evidence, would not yield a theodicy, because it would fall short of the cognitive resources for a comprehensive explanation and justification of God's purposes in allowing evil.

We have no reason to look for a skeptical defeater in the fact that a person who has experienced God can lack understanding of the specific intentions motivating God's actions at times, including in permitting evil. This should be no surprise, given the significant differences – cognitive and otherwise – that exist between God and humans. The closing chapters of the book of Job illustrate that one's lacking a comprehensive explanation and justification of God's purposes in allowing evil does not challenge one's having conclusive evidence of God's perfectly loving reality (cf. Ford 2007, Chapters 3–4, Schneider 2004). Humans should not be cognitively timid, then, about lacking a theodicy regarding God's permitting evil. In addition, people who hope to find God should not delay their search on the ground that they lack a theodicy that fully explains and justifies God's intentions in allowing evil. As suggested, one's finding *God*, with conclusive evidence of divine reality, is not necessarily finding a *theodicy*; nor is this necessarily finding a full explanation and justification of God's purposes in occasional hiding from some people.

The plausible view that humans lack a theodicy must not be conjoined with the implausible view that God is beyond having moral obligations to humans. Marilyn McCord Adams has offered the latter view in connection with "the problem of horrendous evils" – that is, the problem of "evils the participation in (the doing or suffering of) which constitutes *prima facie* reason to doubt whether the participant's life could (given their inclusion in it) have positive meaning for him/her on the whole" (2006, p. 32). Rape and torture are paradigm cases, and Adams claims that "traditional free-will approaches – with their move to shift responsibility and/or blame for evil away from God and onto personal creatures – are stalemated by horrendous evil." Her ground for this claim is this: "Human radical vulnerability to horrors cannot have *its origin* in misused created freedom, because – even if one accepted the story of Adam's fall as historical (which I do not) – the way it is told, humans were radically vulnerable to horrors from the beginning, even in Eden" (p. 36).

Two considerations challenge Adams's portrait of the problem of evil at the start. First, "traditional free-will approaches," including the version in Plantinga 1977 (which is the most rigorously developed free-will approach to date), are *not* offered as a theodicy intended to explain or justify divine permission of evil, including horrendous evil. They are offered instead as a consistency argument against the charge of J.L. Mackie (1955) and others that theism is inconsistent with acknowledgement of the world's evil. Second, if vulnerability is susceptibility, then a modal confusion threatens the portrait, given the distinction between human vulnerability to horrors and actual human (experienced) horrors.

It is, of course, logically possible that humans are vulnerable to horrors but do not actually experience those horrors (say, because the horrors are not actualized in their lives). As a result, the main problem of horrendous evil is not in human vulnerability to horrors, but is rather in *human experience of actual horrors*. If one insists that human vulnerability to horrors itself is evil, then, despite Adams's suggestion to the contrary (2006, p. 49), it is unclear that one can consistently say that the creation of this world was good before the human fall (since, by hypothesis, Adam was vulnerable to evil before the fall). In any case, we have no reason to suppose that human vulnerability as susceptibility to evil is, itself, evil.

According to many theologians and philosophers of religion, divine perfect love must allow for the real possibility of human rebellion against God if it is to allow for

genuine human agency in relation to divine reality. Otherwise, human wills would be restricted in a way that blocks
a kind of free agency needed for robust love in genuinely
interactive relationship with God. Even so, God's allowing for human rebellion and for horrifying human suffering
does not underwrite Adams's talk (which sounds explicitly
Calvinist) of "the horrors that God has perpetrated on us"
or of Jesus as "a perpetrator of horrors" (2006, pp. 41, 71; cf.
p. 274).

God's *allowing for human susceptibility* to horrors is one
thing, and it is arguably required by robust freely given
love in divine–human genuinely interactive relationships.
God's perpetrating horrors on humans would definitely be
something else, and it would at least suggest that God causes
evil and thus falls short of moral perfection and worthiness
of worship. In that case, we would have a counterfeit God
who fails to satisfy the preeminent title "God." Horrors, we
should recall, are genuine evils, and moral perfection does
not allow one (even God) to do evil that good may come.
We do well, in this connection, not to risk lowering the
bar for being God in a manner that removes worthiness of
worship.

Adams offers Jesus Christ as the God-man who can defeat
horrendous evils. More specifically, Jesus participates in horrendous evils in such a way that he turns horrors into "occasions of personal intimacy with God" for humans. Adams
denies that human powers are adequate to defeat horrors
and restore a person after participation in horrors. Divine
power, she contends, is needed. One big question, of course,
is this: how does the process of defeat go? Part of the answer
offered is:

Christ is the One in Whom God's friendliness towards the
human race is integrated. Christ is the One Who shares our
human nature. . . . It is within the framework of His human personality that God especially befriends the whole human race,
not least by sharing both our vulnerability to and our actual
participation in horrors. Christ befriends us in a more intimate

way through His Divine nature, through psychological-sense personal omnipresence and functional collaboration: I-not-I-but Christ. "What a friend we have in Jesus!" (2006, pp. 167–8).

The key assumption is that the participation of Jesus as the God-Man in human horrors can defeat the power of those horrors to rob a life of positive meaning. The corresponding proposal is that the offered friendship with God (and all this eventually involves, including bodily resurrection) can make human life worthwhile, horrors notwithstanding.

Adams does not offer a theodicy, "because God has no obligations to creatures and hence no need to *justify* Divine actions to us." The ultimate ground offered for this striking claim is this: "Personal though God is, the metaphysical size gap is too big for God to be drawn down into the network of rights and obligations that bind together merely human beings" (2006, p. 43). Adams's God emerges, then, as a God beyond moral obligation toward humans, even though it is altogether unclear why we should think that "the *metaphysical* size gap" (is that a power gap?) between God and human entails a relevant difference concerning *moral* obligations.

At this point, we lose any moral grip on what Adams means by the preeminent title "God." The best way to understand the idea of the God and Father of Jesus is, in keeping with the Sermon on the Mount, as the one God worthy of worship in virtue of moral perfection, the same perfection required of followers of Jesus in virtue of required enemy-love (see Matt. 5:43–8; cf. Luke 6:27–36). If God is not morally obligated to love his enemies (as the followers of Jesus are commanded in the Sermon on the Mount), then this God is not the God and Father of Jesus. In addition, this proposed God is not morally perfect and thus is not worthy of worship. In short, this God is not the worship-worthy God characterized by Jesus in the Sermon on the Mount. In offering a God beyond moral obligation toward humans, Adams offers a God unworthy of the title "God," which, properly understood, connotes worthiness of worship and thus moral perfection.

If "God" is beyond moral obligation toward humans, then it is unclear why one should bother with a treatment of evil that proposes the defeat of horrors by the "God-Man." We then may acknowledge that God (if God exists) is beyond moral obligation toward us and be done with the whole matter. At least, the whole effort loses its moral relevance given the dubious assumption in question. Consider how this result bears on Adams's universalist thesis regarding salvation of humans: "For God to succeed, God has to defeat horrors for everyone.... To be good to us, God will have to establish and fit us all for wholesome society...." (2006, p. 230). A natural reading of this thesis finds a moral duty of God toward humans lurking in the background, particularly if the thesis concerns the *moral* success or the *moral* goodness of God toward humans. Even so, the thesis is misguided. Part of God's being "good to us" includes God's not depersonalizing us by robbing us of our volitional agency. Predestinarian theology does not wear well at all in this connection.

Some people, including Thomas Nagel (1997), do not want to live in a universe governed by God, and they have this striking want resolutely, even after very careful consideration. God would not be good at all in suppressing their personal agency in this regard; in fact, God would then be a depersonalizing tyrant. If we hold, however, that God has no moral obligations toward humans, then we will be open to holding that God need not respect either human agency or robust, freedom-based love among and toward humans. We then risk obscuring the vast difference between a morally perfect God worthy of worship and a depersonalizing tyrant (a difference obscured, dangerously, by various predestinarian theologians). That would be a horror indeed. We all need a straightforward concept of God (such as that outlined in the Introduction) that clearly defeats that horror. Otherwise, an account of horror defeat will seem to be a parlor game at best or, at worst, our alleged horror defeater will be the worst horror of all. "God" as such horror is definitely horror without defeat or end.

The apostle Paul plausibly suggests that this world has been subjected to frustration and futility by God, in divine hope that people will enter into "the glorious freedom of the children of God" (Rom. 8:20–1). This is an affirmation of God's using life's troubles – without causing evil – for a deeper good. Even so, this God, in honoring "glorious freedom," does not rob people of their volitional agency. Otherwise, there would be no genuine agents to enjoy the "glorious freedom" uniting the children of God. There would be only God's dominating will, to the exclusion of all other wills. In that case, the Jewish and Christian stories of the divine redemption of humans would be a charade at best.

Of course, we still lack an account of why God's subjecting creation to futility or defeating horrors is, at times and places, so humanly painful – even crushing from an earthly point of view. If the closing chapters of the book of Job are on the right track, we should not hold our collective breath while waiting for the illuminating account. We may not be up to adequately comprehending such an account, given our considerable cognitive limitations, or at least God may have no good purpose served by offering an account to us now. Even so, we can take some comfort in the fact that our having conclusive evidence of God's existence does not require our having any such account, and, in this horror-drenched world, we should take all the good, well-grounded comfort we can get.

We must acknowledge that God does not always draw near as a comforting "friend" in our times of trouble. In fact, God often seems hidden from some people at such times (in that God's existence is not beyond reasonable doubt for them), and this fact of hiddenness emerges as a cognitive variation on the problem of evil. Even so, it would be question begging to portray such hiddenness as falsifying or undermining widespread religious experience of God's reality. Divine hiding facing some people at some times, or even some people at all past and present times, does not entail divine hiding relative to *all* people at *all* times. More specifically, there is no defensible way to generalize from actual cases of divine hiddenness for some people to encompass *all* people with regard to the alleged lack of adequate evidence of divine reality. A generalized argument for atheism or agnosticism, then, does not emerge from divine hiddenness (for details, see Moser 2008, Chapter 1). Any such argument would require specific premises independent of divine hiddenness, but it is altogether unclear what such premises would be in a cogent argument. In sum, then, it is doubtful that divine hiddenness in particular or evil in general will yield a successful defeater to this book's volitional theism.

6. CONCLUSION

Having begun with the wilderness parable involving people in need of a rescuer, we find ourselves now similarly in need of a rescuer. Even so, we cannot point to an obvious rescuer or to a rescuer we can control. Our rescuer is elusive and even hidden at times, but, on reflection, this should come as no surprise. If our rescuer is worthy of worship and thus seeks what is morally best for us, we should expect challenges from divine elusiveness and hiddenness aimed at our transformation toward God's moral character. More specifically, we should expect God to encourage our becoming, ourselves, personifying evidence of God, in our willingly receiving and reflecting God's moral character for others. In particular, we should expect to be under challenge by God for our own good, to learn to love as God loves. As a result, our having evidence of God would be no spectator sport. Instead, it would be akin to a purportedly transformative rescue operation, in which we are the (sometimes resistant) people being rescued, or at least intended to be rescued, largely from our own destructively selfish ways.

The world around and within us actually looks, at times, as if it is the kind of place where we humans are to learn humbly to love unselfishly as God loves, in volitional cooperation with God. It certainly is not the kind of place where we are to receive maximal pleasure, maximal pain, or maximal understanding of our surroundings or even ourselves. Given this book's volitional theism, if we become properly attuned to purposively available evidence of God's reality, including God's authoritative self-giving love, then God's reality will become, at the opportune time, adequately indicated for us by undefeated authoritative evidence. We would do well, then, to seek and to appropriate the purposively available evidence of God's reality, however morally challenging the process.

Given volitional theism, the extent to which we know God, including God's reality, depends on the extent to which we are sincerely willing to cooperate with God in a program of divine redemption of humans. As a result, it becomes obvious why we humans (whether theists, atheists, or agnostics) have difficulty in knowing God. The difficulty stems from our resisting cooperation in God's redemptive program of reconciliation. Accordingly, it is naïve, if not arrogant, for us humans to approach the question of whether God exists as if we were naturally in an appropriate moral and cognitive position to handle it aright. Careful reflection on the redemptive purposes inherent to a perfectly loving God recommends an approach less presumptuous. We are, after all, inquiring about a very special kind of agent with distinctive redemptive purposes in virtue of being perfectly loving, and not a household object or a laboratory specimen. Perhaps we humans have deep-seated difficulty with a gracious God who evades our own sophisticated cognitive nets in order to demonstrate that our own powers are not life giving apart from God. Stubbornly, we seem to insist on our own inferior terms for redemption, and we thereby end up with cheap counterfeits of the genuine life-giving article.

We should expect God to care about how we handle evidence of God's existence. In particular, God's aim is for humans to become, in the image of God's moral character, more loving in handling this elusive and humanly uncontrollable evidence. In other words, humans are, themselves, to become personifying evidence of God in willingly receiving and reflecting God's moral character for others. Indeed, as we increasingly become personifying evidence of God, our evidence of God becomes more salient, if only because we ourselves are more salient evidence of God. In our inquiry about God, then, we are put under challenge by God to become the evidence of God we claim to seek.

Contrary to a typical philosophical attitude, knowledge of God is not spectator entertainment, casual speculation, or an opportunity for self-credit, but is instead part of a process of God's thorough make-over of a person. It is, from our side of the process, an *active self-commitment* to a morally transforming personal relationship of volitional cooperation rather than to a mere subjective state or disposition. We come to know God only as God becomes *our God*, the Lord of our lives, rather than just an object of our entertainment, speculation, or manipulation. God refuses, for our own good, to become an idol of human proportions. Instead, God seeks to remove all of our idols, ideally by our cooperating in removing them.

The God worthy of worship is anything but cognitively "safe" or controllable. We cannot control either God or God's hiding on occasion, and we should formulate our understanding of knowledge of God accordingly. The God worthy of worship leaves us empty-handed when we insist on seeking with our self-made tools, including familiar philosophical arguments or religious spiritualities. We are, after all, neither God nor God's advisers, but we can become, at our best, God's obedient children. As a result, we should not be surprised at all that we lack our own devices to explain all of God's occasional hiding or God's permitting evil.

Given our considerable cognitive limitations, we should expect God not to be fully comprehensible to us. Accordingly, Karl Rahner suggests that humans may (and should) willingly "fall into the abyss of God's incomprehensibility" (1983, p. 161). We should not confuse this abyss, however, with an empty abyss, a chaotic abyss, or an abyss lacking evidence of divine reality. Instead, the abyss is the mystery of perfect divine love that outstrips human understanding, even when the giver of such love offers purposively available evidence of divine reality to humans. As Rahner comments, the mystery is "encompassed by the reality of God who is for us" (1983, p. 161). Contrary to fideism, we should add the following: encompassed, too, *by purposively available authoritative evidence* of the divine agent who is for us, in redemptive love. The suggested "falling into the abyss" is *volitionally active* in that it includes one's willingly yielding, on the basis of purposively available evidence, to the divine power of self-giving love that is available even beyond the limits of human power, including the power of human comprehension. Accordingly, this falling includes a *willing, volitional and obedient surrender* to the authoritative God who can show up, with an authoritative call to divine–human fellowship, even in the midst of human puzzlement, darkness, suffering, and death.

Even given divine mysteries, our habitual refusal to love unselfishly as God loves prevents us from seeing the humanly available things of God. As 1 John 4:3 states: "Whoever does not love does not know God, because God is love." Still, many people will ask: why does God not become more obvious to us? The question, we now can see, suffers from a misplaced emphasis and therefore should be redirected, as follows: why do *we* fail to apprehend God's perfectly loving reality? Instead of uncritically embracing Russell's charge, "God, you gave us insufficient evidence," we should question ourselves, including our moral and cognitive standing before God.

God's turnaround question to us includes this query: why do you humans refuse to receive God's love and thereby learn to love as God loves? In addition: why do you humans refuse to become, yourselves, personifying evidence of divine reality, in willing reception of and conformation to God's moral character of unselfish love? Challenged thus, we are invited to undertake a cognitive and moral adventure of learning to love as God loves, in volitional fellowship with God, even through personal suffering, frustration, perplexity, and physical death. Our wilderness parable then will give way to the reality of a genuine rescue operation for us in our weakness, from death to new life with God, come what may.

The ever-present question, for better or worse, is just this: are we sincerely willing to yield in cooperation with the needed self-giving Rescuer? Each of us is called to answer, now and in the future. Diversions aside, this life-giving challenge is at the very heart of the evidence for God, and it invites us, even in our weakness, to become the evidence for God. At this point, philosophy gives way to personal decision regarding not only the evidence one seeks but also the chosen direction of one's life. We all do well, then, to give careful attention to the profound demands of our becoming the evidence for God.

References

Adams, Marilyn McCord. 2006. *Christ and Horrors*. Cambridge: Cambridge University Press.

Allen, Diogenes. 1989. *Christian Belief in a Postmodern World*. Louisville, KY: Westminster Press.

Allison, Dale. 2009. *The Historical Christ and the Theological Jesus*. Grand Rapids, MI: Eerdmans.

Alston, William P. 1997. *A Realist Conception of Truth*. Ithaca, NY: Cornell University Press.

Augustine. 395. *On Free Will (De Libero Arbitrio)*. In *Augustine: Earlier Writings*, ed. and trans. J.H.S. Burleigh, 102–217. Philadelphia, PA: Westminster Press, 1953.

Aulén, Gustaf. 1961. *Christus Victor*, trans. A.G. Hebert. New York: Macmillan.

Barth, Karl. 1933. *The Epistle to the Romans*, 6th ed., trans. E.C. Hoskyns. Oxford: Oxford University Press.

Bauckham, Richard. 2008. *Jesus and the God of Israel*. Grand Rapids, MI: Eerdmans.

Behe, Michael. 1996. *Darwin's Black Box*. New York: Free Press.

———. 1998. "Molecular Machines: Experimental Support for the Design Inference." In *Intelligent Design Creationism and its Critics*, ed. R.T. Pennock, 241–56. Cambridge, MA.: MIT Press, 2001.

Berkhof, Hendrikus. 1968. "Science and the Biblical World-View." In *Science and Religion*, ed. Ian G. Barbour, 43–53. New York: Harper and Row.

———. 1986. *Christian Faith*, 2d ed., trans. S. Woudstra. Grand Rapids, MI: Eerdmans.

Bishop, John. 2007. *Believing by Faith*. Oxford: Clarendon Press.

Bourke, Myles. 1964. "The Gospels and Theologically Interpreted History." In *Studies in Salvation History*, ed. C.L. Salm, 160–78. Englewoods Cliffs, NJ: Prentice Hall.

Brondos, David A. 2006. *Paul on the Cross: Reconstructing the Apostle's Story of Redemption*. Minneapolis, MN: Fortress Press.

Bruce, F.F. 1977. *Paul: Apostle of the Heart Set Free*. Grand Rapids, MI: Eerdmans.

Brunner, Emil. 1939. *Man in Revolt*, trans. Olive Wyon. London: Lutterworth Press.

_____. 1952. *The Christian Doctrine of Creation and Redemption*, trans. Olive Wyon. London: Lutterworth Press.

_____. 1961. "Easter Certainty." In Brunner, *I Believe in the Living God*, trans. John Holden, 86–97. Philadelphia, PA: Westminster Press.

_____. 1964. *Truth as Encounter*, trans. A.W. Loos. Philadelphia, PA: Westminster Press.

Buber, Martin. 1951. *Two Types of Faith*, trans. N.P. Goldhawk. New York: Macmillan.

_____. 1958 [1923]. *I and Thou*, 2d ed., trans. R.G. Smith. New York: Charles Scribner's Sons.

Bultmann, Rudolf. 1955. *Theology of the New Testament*, vol. 2, trans. Kendrick Grobel. New York: Charles Scribner's Sons.

_____. 1966. "Reply to John Macquarrie." In *The Theology of Rudolf Bultmann*, ed. C.W. Kegley, 273–5. New York: Harper and Row.

_____. 1969. "The Concept of the Word of God in the New Testament." In Bultmann, *Faith and Understanding*, vol. 1, trans. L.P. Smith. London: SCM Press.

Byrnes, Michael. 2003. *Conformation to the Death of Christ and the Hope of Resurrection*. Rome: Gregorian University Press.

Calvin, John. 1536. *Institutes of the Christian Religion*, trans. Henry Beveridge. Grand Rapids, MI: Eerdmans, 1989.

Cherbonnier, Edmond La B. 1955. *Hardness of Heart*. Garden City, NY: Doubleday.

Churchland, Paul. 1979. *Scientific Realism and the Plasticity of Mind*. Cambridge: Cambridge University Press.

Colyvan, Mark, Jay Garfield, and Graham Priest. 2005. "Problems with the Argument from Fine Tuning." *Synthese* 145: 325–38.

Cottingham, John. 2005. *The Spiritual Dimension: Religion, Philosophy, and Human Value*. Cambridge: Cambridge University Press.

Crane, Tim, and D.H. Mellor. 1990. "There is No Question of Physicalism." *Mind* 99: 185–206. Reprinted, with a postscript, in *Contemporary Materialism*, eds. Paul Moser and J.D. Trout, 65–89. London: Routledge, 1995.

Davidson, Donald. 1963. "Actions, Reasons, and Causes." In Davidson, *Essays on Actions and Events*, 3–19. Oxford: Clarendon Press, 1980.

_____. 1970. "Mental Events." In *Experience and Theory*, eds. L. Foster and J. Swenson, 79–101. Amherst, MA: University of Massachusetts Press.

Davis, Caroline Franks. 1989. *The Evidential Force of Religious Experience*. Oxford: Clarendon Press.

Dawkins, Richard. 1987. *The Blind Watchmaker*. New York: Norton.

———. 2006. *The God Delusion*. New York: Houghton Mifflin.

Dennett, Daniel. 1987. *The Intentional Stance*. Cambridge, MA: MIT Press.

———. 1995. *Darwin's Dangerous Idea*. New York: Simon and Schuster.

———. 2006. *Breaking the Spell: Religion as a Natural Phenomenon*. New York: Penguin.

Dickie, Edgar P. 1954. *God is Light*. New York: Charles Scribner's Sons.

Dodd, C.H. 1936. *The Apostolic Preaching and its Developments*. London: Hodder and Stoughton.

Farmer, Herbert H. 1942. *The Servant of the Word*. New York: Charles Scribner's Sons.

———. *Revelation and Religion*. London: Nisbet.

Fee, Gordon. 1995. *Paul's Letter to the Philippians*. Grand Rapids, MI: Eerdmans.

Fodor, Jerry. 1974. "Special Sciences," *Synthese* 28: 77–115.

———. 1998. *In Critical Condition*. Cambridge, MA: MIT Press.

Ford, David F. 2007. *Christian Wisdom: Desiring God and Learning in Love*. Cambridge: Cambridge University Press.

Forsyth, P.T. 1913. *The Principle of Authority*. London: Hodder and Stoughton.

Friedman, Michael. 1974. "Explanation and Scientific Understanding." *The Journal of Philosophy* 71: 5–19.

Furnish, Victor Paul. 1968. *Theology and Ethics in Paul*. Nashville, TN: Abingdon Press.

———. 1972. *The Love Command in the New Testament*. Nashville, TN: Abingdon Press.

Gaventa, Beverly. 1986. *From Darkness to Light*. Philadelphia, PA: Fortress Press.

Gorman, Michael J. 2001. *Cruciformity: Paul's Narrative Spirituality of the Cross*. Grand Rapids, MI: Eerdmans.

———. 2009. *Inhabiting the Cruciform God: Kenosis, Justification, and Theosis in Paul's Narrative Soteriology*. Grand Rapids, MI: Eerdmans.

Gould, Stephen Jay. 1999. *Rocks of Ages: Science and Religion in the Fullness of Life*. New York: Ballantine.

Hampton, Jeanne, and Jeffrie Murphy. 1988. *Forgiveness and Mercy*. Cambridge: Cambridge University Press.

Hanson, N.R. 1971. *What I Do not Believe and Other Essays*. Dordrecht: Reidel.

Heschel, Abraham. 1962. *The Prophets*. New York: Jewish Publication Society.

Horgan, Terence, and James Woodward. 1985. "Folk Psychology is Here to Stay." *The Philosophical Review* 94: 197–226. Reprinted in Lycan 1999, pp. 271–86.

Hubbard, Moyer. 2002. *New Creation in Paul's Letters and Thought*. Cambridge: Cambridge University Press.

Hunter, A.M. 1943. *The Unity of the New Testament*. London: SCM Press.

Hurtado, Larry. 2003. *Lord Jesus Christ: Devotion to Jesus in Earliest Christianity*. Grand Rapids, MI: Eerdmans.

Jackson, Timothy. 1999. *Love Disconsoled*. Cambridge: Cambridge University Press.

Juergensmeyer, Mark. 2003. *Terror in the Mind of God: The Global Rise of Religious Violence*, 3d ed. Berkeley: University of California Press.

Käsemann, Ernst. 1961. "'The Righteousness of God' in Paul." In Käsemann, *New Testament Questions of Today*, trans. W.J. Montague, 168–93. Philadelphia, PA: Fortress Press.

———. 1967. "The Saving Significance of the Death of Jesus in Paul." In Käsemann, *Perspectives on Paul*, trans. Margaret Kohl, 32–59. Philadelphia, PA: Fortress Press, 1971.

———. 1971. *Perspectives on Paul*, trans. Margaret Kohl. Philadelphia, PA: Fortress Press.

Kierkegaard, Søren. 1991 [1848]. *Practice in Christianity*, trans. H.V. Hong and E.H. Hong. Princeton, NJ: Princeton University Press.

———. 1992 [1846]. *Concluding Unscientific Postscript*, trans. H.V. Hong and E.H. Hong. Princeton, NJ: Princeton University Press.

Kim, Jaegwon. 1989. "Mechanism, Purpose, and Explanatory Exclusion." In *Philosophical Perspectives*, vol. 3: *Philosophy of Mind and Action Theory*, ed. James Tomberlin, 77–108. Atascadero, CA: Ridgeview.

Kitcher, Philip. 1981. "Explanatory Unification." *Philosophy of Science* 48: 507–31.

———. 1989. "Explanatory Unification and the Causal Structure of the World." In *Minnesota Studies in the Philosophy of Science*, vol. 13: *Scientific Explanation*, eds. Philip Kitcher and W.C. Salmon, 410–505. Minneapolis: University of Minnesota Press.

Klassen, William. 1984. *Love of Enemies*. Philadelphia, PA: Fortress Press.

Kvanvig, Jonathan L. 1993. *The Problem of Hell*. New York: Oxford University Press.

Lemcio, Eugene. 1991. "The Unifying Kerygma of the New Testament." In Lemcio, *The Past of Jesus in the Gospels*, 115–31. Cambridge: Cambridge University Press.

Lycan, William G., ed. 1999. *Mind and Cognition*, 2d ed. Oxford: Blackwell.

Mackie, J.L. 1955. "Evil and Omnipotence." *Mind* 64: 200–12.

Mann, William E. 2001. "Augustine on Evil and Original Sin." In *The Cambridge Companion to Augustine*, eds. Eleonore Stump and Norman Kretzmann, 40–48. Cambridge: Cambridge University Press.

Marras, Ausonio. 1998. "Kim's Principle of Explanatory Exclusion." *Australasian Journal of Philosophy* 76: 439–51.

Martyn, J. Louis. 1997. *Theological Issues in the Letters of Paul*. Nashville, TN: Abingdon Press.

McGill, Arthur C. 1967. "Recent Discussions of Anselm's Argument." In *The Many-Faced Argument*, eds. John Hick and Arthur McGill, 33–110. New York: Macmillan.

McKim, Robert. 2001. *Religious Ambiguity and Religious Diversity*. New York: Oxford University Press.

Meadors, Edward. 2006. *Idolatry and the Hardening of the Heart*. London: T&T Clark.

Meier, John P. 2009. *A Marginal Jew: Rethinking the Historical Jesus, vol. 4: Law and Love*. New Haven, CT: Yale University Press.

Mele, Alfred R. and Paul K. Moser. 1994. "Intentional Action." *Noûs* 28: 39–68. Reprinted in *The Philosophy of Action*, ed. Alfred R. Mele, 223–55. Oxford: Oxford University Press, 1997.

Miller, Kenneth R. 1999. *Finding Darwin's God*. New York: Harper Collins.

Moser, Paul K. 1989. *Knowledge and Evidence*. Cambridge: Cambridge University Press.

———. 1993. *Philosophy after Objectivity*. New York: Oxford University Press.

———. 1999. "Jesus on Knowledge of God." *Christian Scholars Review* 28: 586–604.

———. 2008. *The Elusive God: Reorienting Religious Epistemology*. Cambridge: Cambridge University Press.

Moser, Paul K. and J.D. Trout, eds. 1995. *Contemporary Materialism*. London: Routledge.

Nagel, Thomas. 1997. *The Last Word*. New York: Oxford University Press.

Niebuhr, Reinhold. 1941. *The Nature and Destiny of Man*, vol. 1: *Human Nature*. New York: Charles Scribner's Sons.

———. 1949. *Faith and History*. New York: Charles Scribner's Sons.

———. 1965. *Man's Nature and his Communities*. New York: Charles Scribner's Sons.

O'Collins, Gerald. 1995. *Christology*. Oxford: Oxford University Press.

Oman, John. 1928. *Vision and Authority*, 2d ed. London: Hodder and Stoughton.

Papineau, David. 1993. *Philosophical Naturalism*. Oxford: Blackwell.

Perrin, Norman. 1976. *Rediscovering the Teaching of Jesus*. New York: Harper and Row.

Plantinga, Alvin. 1977. *God, Freedom, and Evil*. Grand Rapids, MI: Eerdmans.

———. 1983. "Reason and Belief in God." In *Faith and Rationality*, eds. Alvin Plantinga and Nicholas Wolterstorff, 16–93. Notre Dame, IN: University of Notre Dame Press.

———. 1993. *Warrant and Proper Function*. New York: Oxford University Press.

_____. 2000. *Warranted Christian Belief*. New York: Oxford University Press.

Quine, W.V. 1957. "The Scope and Language of Science." In Quine, *The Ways of Paradox*, 215–32. New York: Random House, 1966.

_____. 1990. *Pursuit of Truth*. Cambridge, MA: Harvard University Press.

Rahner, Karl. 1983. "Christian Pessimism." In Rahner, *Theological Investigations*, vol. 22, trans. Joseph Donceel, 155–62. New York: Crossroad.

Ridderbos, Herman. 1975. *Paul: An Outline of His Theology*, trans. J.R. De Witt. Grand Rapids, MI: Eerdmans.

Rowe, William L. 2006. "Friendly Atheism, Skeptical Theism, and the Problem of Evil." *International Journal for Philosophy of Religion* 59: 79–92.

Russell, Bertrand. 1903. "A Free Man's Worship." In Russell, *Mysticism and Logic*, 44–54. New York: Doubleday, 1957.

_____. 1970. "The Talk of the Town." *The New Yorker* (February 21, 1970): 29.

Savellos, E.E. and Ü.D. Yalçin, eds. 1995. *Supervenience: New Essays*. Cambridge: Cambridge University Press.

Schaff, Philip, ed. 1919a. *The Creeds of Christendom*, vol. 2: *The Greek and Latin Creeds*. New York: Harper and Row. [Includes the Athanasian Creed].

Schaff, Philip, ed. 1919b. *The Creeds of Christendom*, vol. 3: *Evangelical Protestant Creeds*. New York: Harper and Row. [Includes the Westminster Confession of Faith].

Schellenberg, J.L. 2007. *The Wisdom to Doubt: A Justification of Religious Skepticism*. Ithaca, NY: Cornell University Press.

Schneider, John R. 2004. "Seeing God Where the Wild Things Are: An Essay on the Defeat of Horrendous Evil." In *Christian Faith and the Problem of Evil*, ed. Peter Van Inwagen, 226–62. Grand Rapids, MI: Eerdmans.

Schweizer, Eduard 1971. *Jesus*, trans. D.E. Green. London: SCM Press.

Segal, Alan F. 1990. *Paul the Convert*. New Haven, CT: Yale University Press.

Sidgwick, Henry. 1902. *Outlines of the History of Ethics*, 5th ed. London: Macmillan.

Smart, J.J.C. 1963. "Materialism." *The Journal of Philosophy* 60: 651–62.

Swinburne, Richard. 1979. *The Existence of God*. Oxford: Clarendon Press.

Thielicke, Helmut. 1990. *Modern Faith and Thought*, trans. G.W. Bromiley. Grand Rapids, MI: Eerdmans.

Thompson, Marianne Meye. 2001. *The God of the Gospel of John*. Grand Rapids, MI: Eerdmans.

Wainwright, William. 2005. *Religion and Morality*. Aldershot, England: Ashgate.

Way, David. 1991. *The Lordship of Christ: Ernst Käsemann's Interpretation of Paul's Theology*. Oxford: Clarendon Press.

Wenham, David. 1993. "Unity and Diversity in the New Testament."
In George Ladd, *A Theology of the New Testament*, 2d ed., 684–720.
Grand Rapids, MI: Eerdmans.

———. 1995. *Paul: Follower of Jesus or Founder of Christianity?* Grand
Rapids, MI: Eerdmans.

Westerholm, Stephen. 2004. *Perspectives Old and New on Paul.* Grand
Rapids, MI: Eerdmans.

Wiebe, Phillip. 2004. *God and Other Spirits.* New York: Oxford University Press.

Wilson, E.O. 1987. *Consilience: The Unity of Knowledge.* New York:
Knopf.

Index